W9-BMQ-617

Advertising by Design

Robin Landa

Advertising by Design

Creating Visual Communications with Graphic Impact

John Wiley & Sons, Inc.

This book is printed on acid-free paper. ⊗

Copyright © 2004 by Robin Landa. All rights reserved

Published by John Wiley & Sons, Inc., Hoboken, New Jersey
Published simultaneously in Canada

No part of this publication may be reproduced, stored in a retrieval system, or transmitted in any form or by any means, electronic, mechanical, photocopying, recording, scanning, or otherwise, except as permitted under Section 107 or 108 of the 1976 United States Copyright Act, without either the prior written permission of the Publisher, or authorization through payment of the appropriate per-copy fee to the Copyright Clearance Center, Inc., 222 Rosewood Drive, Danvers, MA 01923, (978) 750-8400, fax (978) 750-4470, or on the web at www.copyright.com. Requests to the Publisher for permission should be addressed to the Permissions Department, John Wiley & Sons, Inc., 111 River Street, Hoboken, NJ 07030, (201) 748-6011, fax (201) 748-6008, e-mail: permcoordinator@wiley.com.

Limit of Liability/Disclaimer of Warranty: While the publisher and author have used their best efforts in preparing this book, they make no representations or warranties with respect to the accuracy or completeness of the contents of this book and specifically disclaim any implied warranties of merchantability or fitness for a particular purpose. No warranty may be created or extended by sales representatives or written sales materials. The advice and strategies contained herein may not be suitable for your situation. You should consult with a professional where appropriate. Neither the publisher nor author shall be liable for any loss of profit or any other commercial damages, including but not limited to special, incidental, consequential, or other damages.

For general information on our other products and services or for technical support, please contact our Customer Care Department within the United States at (800) 762-2974, outside the United States at (317) 572-3993 or fax (317) 572-4002.

Wiley also publishes its books in a variety of electronic formats. Some content that appears in print may not be available in electronic books.

Library of Congress Cataloging-in-Publication Data:
Landa, Robin.
  Advertising by design : creating visual communications with graphic impact /Robin Landa.
      p. cm.
  Includes index.
  ISBN 0-471-42897-3 (cloth)
  1. Advertising. 2. Creative ability in business. I. Title.
  HF5823.L23 2004
  659.1—dc22
                        2004009412

Printed in the United States of America

10 9 8 7 6 5 4 3 2 1

Contents

Foreword

Advertising is a mirror. It reflects its audience. Advertising reflects what's going on in our world, what is happening in music, movies, and art. And (uh-oh) it reflects what's happening in your kitchen, in your living room, and on your commute—it even reflects your uncool parent's uncool habits.

In this book, Robin Landa will ask you to get to know your audience before you sit down to concept. Who are these people reflected in advertising's mirror? What are these people into? Which human truth can you bring to the audience's attention? What motivates them? (Heck, you are a person who hangs out with these people; you may be your own target audience.) These are some of the questions that can help direct your search for the big idea.

As my professor at Kean University, Robin Landa was an inspirational figure. She encouraged looking at things differently and taught me to weed out the most expected thought and find the bigger idea. She encouraged finding inspiration through art history, architecture, and even mundane life occurrences. These are the things I still fall back on almost every day in my career as an art director. I could see that Robin was a fan of advertising from the first day I walked into her classroom. Robin's passion for and love of advertising will be evident in the pages to follow. It has certainly rubbed off on me.

Many things have changed in my life since I first stepped into Robin's advertising class. But one thing hasn't—the creative process. It's a wonderful, horrible, frightful process! Just think: you make a blank page come to life. Your work sticks its head into people's living rooms (a little scary, I know). Your ad might be seen from one end of the country to the other. An ad idea can emerge from anything. Anything! And the beauty of it all is that creating a great ad starts with you. Sure, there is a real client. A creative brief. A creative director (or two). And lots of prying eyes. But the original idea comes from you. And that is the rush that keeps me coming back for more.

I have been an art director for over ten years now, and I am still amazed when I show up at a shoot and there are about forty people there all working on my idea. That amazement is always followed by fear: "I hope this actually works." What I do know is that the little stick figure that lived on the once blank page of my notebook now is in front of a camera driving a Volkswagen Jetta GLS; he has spiked hair and goes by the name of Nick. That is pretty cool.

I am constantly reminded of how lucky I am that I didn't stick with my accounting major—no offense to all the accountants out there. (And if you are an accountant reading this book, welcome to the other side.) I mean, look, 75 percent of your day is spent at work. You may as well like what you do.

Try this—read the next lines really fast three times:

> Does he like it? Does she like it? Does my creative director like it? Does the client like it? Does my mom like it? Does my wife like it? Does her mom like it? Does my dog like it?

And before you get to that type of madness, stop and ask yourself this: "Do I like it?"

Well, do you? You should. You'd better. One of the biggest lies out there is that people go to the bathroom when the commercials are on. People will see what you have created. So be proud of what you do.

After all, you searched for this idea.

You lost sleep over this idea.

You gave up home life for this idea.

You looked for this idea on your drive into work.

You looked for it as you watched a double feature over the weekend.

You tried to find this idea when you were trying on jeans at the mall.

You sat in a room for hours at a clip, with a ton of books and magazines and blank stares, just to find this ever-elusive idea. Not a little idea. The big one. And whom were you kidding when you thought you had it when you were in line at the market? And then again at the gym, only to realize later that idea wasn't it? Therefore, love this thing that you finally create. And when you think you've found that big idea, tackle it, tie it up, and don't let it go. Because, believe it or not, it can get away.

Then hold it up to the mirror. If the idea is done right, the product you are selling will sell (which means you get to keep your job). You may win a few industry awards. Make a good living. And someone may even hang up your ad in her cubicle at work. How's that for changing the world?

There are a ton of things swimming around in the head of a student. Multiply that by ten if you are a visual communication student. I encourage you to read this book front to back. Keep absorbing information and visuals. Seek out the people who are doing the type of work that you'd like to do. Find out which agency and which creative team created your favorite ads (some of which may be on the pages that follow). Call the creatives. Ask if they will take a look at your book. You may not always like their feedback. But that's okay. The creatives just might like your work. The sooner your skin gets thicker, the better. Robin taught me that as well.

When you read the following pages that Robin prepared for you, remember: Picasso had to learn to draw before he mesmerized and confused us. Some of the fundamentals of design and the history of advertising are right here in this book. Use them as your tools. They will be the rock from which you will jump every time you create an ad.

Enjoy.

—PAUL RENNER
Associate Creative Director
on ESPN / Wieden + Kennedy / New York
Kean University Alumnus 1992

Acknowledgments

To all the gracious creative and marketing professionals whose work and wisdom appears in this book, my grateful acknowledgment is extended. A special acknowledgment to Doug Adkins, Denise M. Anderson, Allan Beaver, Warren Berger, Edward Boches, Steven Brower, John Butler, Peggy Conlon, Hillman Curtis, Sal DeVito, Lou Dorfsman, Valerie Graves, Guido Heffels, Bob Isherwood, Erik Kessels, Shelly Lazarus, George Lois, Jon Maltby, Jim McDowell, Mike Quon, Rich Palatini, Robynne Raye, Paul Renner, Stan Richards, Deborah Rivera, Alan Robbins, Stefan Sagmeister, Carlos Segura, Michael Sickinger, Eric Silver, Jerry Simon, Kevyn Smith, Emmie Vázquez, Gregg Wasiak, and David Weist.

I am grateful to Max Farrow, Lisboa, Inc., Diane and Luke Lois, and Katherine Raymond, I LOVE NEW YORK, for their invaluable assistance in acquiring showcase images. And great thanks to the agencies' staff who helped me acquire all this wonderful work, especially Sarah Brownrigg, Isaac Clemens, Hans Engebretson, Rebekah Fensome, Ellyn Fisher, Christine Gravelle, Tracey Gurr, Rachael Heiss, Jean Howe, Monica Hudson, Hoon Kim, Ann Shannon, Stacey M. Thomas, and Lineke. Thanks to all the clients who granted permission.

It has been my distinct privilege to work with the consummate professionals at John Wiley & Sons. Great thanks to Margaret Cummins, Rosanne Koneval, Jolene Howard, Andrea Johnson, and to copyeditor Sue Warga. My thanks to Andrea Pedolsky, Altair Literary Agency, for representation and guidance. My special thanks to Lowell Bodger, Laurel Bonhage, Rosanne Gibel, Dennis Kuronen, Betsy Kurzinger, Larry Stultz, Toni Toland, and to all the reviewers whose advice bettered this book.

To my esteemed colleagues and dear friends Rose Gonnella, Martin Holloway, Rich Palatini, and Alan Robbins, I say thank you for your help, advisement, and support. To my former professors—Sal DeVito and Bob Mitchell—thank you for your wisdom.

Over the years, it has been a privilege to work in advertising, to teach, and to come in contact with great talent. I am grateful to my former students, who are out there creating ads and public service advertising with impact, for making me proud by winning awards and hiring other Kean University grads. Thanks to the Alcantara and Freire family, Shawn Q. Anderson, Mary and Murray Badner, Dr. Michael Balogh, Donald Fishbein, Lillian Fishbein, Diane Benedict Ryan, Karina Leon, Chris Navetta, Mario Navetta, Dr. Martha Nochimson, Dr. Richard Nochimson, Richard Nord, Nancy Novick, and Michael O'Keefe for helping with this project. Special thanks to Kean University alumnus Adam C. Rogers for his engaging cover design.

To my family and friends, loving thanks for asking about the book and then actually listening. Thank you, Hayley, my darling daughter, for pointing out the value of humor and timing in TV spots that we watched together, over and over again, and for your contagious creativity. To my handsome husband, Harry, thank you for those romantic tangos. Finally, heartfelt thanks to my beloved parents, Betty and Hy Landa, who taught me most of what I know about creative thinking.

Introduction

Teaching advertising is an inspiring and challenging endeavor. Ideation, design, writing, and social responsibility are taught simultaneously. Students must become critical and creative thinkers very quickly, learning to design and write their creative ideas.

Without fail, every semester I want to hand over in a bundle all the information and insights into advertising that I possess, so that my students can immediately start creating ads with impact. I remind myself that it will take a few weeks for my students to get the notion that an idea propels an ad and that together design and copy visually communicate the idea.

At the same time as I'm teaching ideation, writing, and design, I'm hoping that research and discussion will expand my students' views of the world. We talk about social responsibility and creating ads that, in both text and subtext, are respectful of people's humanity. (Every effort was made to record as accurately as possible the dates, titles, and credits of historic works, given limited records from the period. Rather than list an inaccurate date, title, or credit for any work, some information has been intentionally omitted.)

The architecture of this book is transparent, like that of a good Web site, where someone can enter at any point and know what's going on. The suggested sequence most closely follows the logical order of teaching this subject: idea formulation, designing, media. When I teach, I first emphasize concept development, and during critiques I discuss both concept and design. Once students have grasped ideation, I focus on visual and verbal communication. By mid-semester, my students are designing intelligent ads.

I emphasize:

Get attention.

Keep the viewer's attention.

Be ethical.

Be relevant.

Serve as a call to action.

In order for my students' work to be fresh, I always teach what my mother, Betty Landa, taught me about creativity: "Look at what everyone else is doing and do something different." To push the freshness of my students' designs further, I teach them what my father, Hy Landa, taught me about independence and personal style: "Do your own thing." Use what is unique to you, and your work will reflect it.

In all my books on creative thinking, my parents' wisdom has been emphasized. In essence, the message is: be yourself, appropriate, and fresh. Of course, in advertising, being yourself means tapping into your client's brand's or cause's distinct personality as well as your own uniqueness, and understanding what is relevant to your audience. My parents also taught me to be sympathetically conscious of others; and I teach my students to be socially responsible.

My teaching methodology has an excellent track record: my former students are out there working as award-winning art directors, copywriters, and creative directors.

I asked Warren Berger, author, and ad expert, what he considers cutting-edge advertising. Here is Berger's response: "Anything that tries to do something new or different—something that zigs when everybody else is zagging. Sometimes people mistakenly think that 'cutting-edge' means 'outrageous' or 'ironic' or 'hip.' But if everybody is being outrageous or ironic (as is the case in many current ads), then it would be more cutting-edge to go in a different direction—perhaps toward innocence. The bottom line is, you have to try something that does not look like any other ad that is out there."

With these considerations in mind, it should be clear that teaching and learning advertising are part of an involving and adventurous voyage. I have written *Advertising by Design* to serve as a guide and seat belt for the voyage. Enjoy the process.

part one

Informing, Persuading, and Provoking

How Advertising Works

1

A Brief History of Advertising

A creative revolution. It sounds powerful, and it was. In the 1960s, the advertising profession and the work it produced changed, and the change was a watershed. A new breed of leadership arose, and their advertising philosophies were very creative: more endearing, wittier, more respectful of the audience, and less of a hard sales pitch, with no trace of hucksterism.

Before this creative period, advertising solutions varied greatly, from the offensive con to the repetitive hard sell. Mostly, the advertising profession had to try to distance itself from its early history of hucksterism (selling patent medicines that didn't work) and guilt-inducing emotional appeals. Good advertising is not deceptive, stimulates the economy and competition in commerce, and offers choices and information to the public. Advertising is in its greatest role when created for public service—it can help save lives, teach responsible behavior, and benefit society in many other ways. In addition, advertising is a great cog in the engine of capitalism, one of the world's most successful and admired economic systems.

This brief overview of advertising history is in no way meant to be a substitute for a full study; my offering does not include, as any full history would, the influences of current events, social climate and issues, politics, music, and art on the topic of advertising. For example, the social and political climate of the 1960s had a profound influence on the creative revolution in advertising. In this one brief chapter, my goal is to put the theories and methodologies in this book into a broader context.

In the Very Beginning

One could mark the beginning of (an ancient version of) advertising with a sign selling wine from ancient Babylonia, or with trade fairs in ancient China during the Western Zhou Dynasty, both occurring about three thousand years ago, or perhaps with signs from ancient Pompeii, during the first century AD, announcing sporting contests, theater performances, and drinking establishments. (Around the second century BC, paper was introduced in China; printing would later flourish in Europe, and another type of printing was invented in China.) In ancient Greece, there were walking and talking advertisements in the form of criers, who were often accompanied by musicians.

However, it was the invention of the Gutenberg printing press by Johannes Gutenberg in 1448 in Germany, and its popular rise in Europe that allowed the widespread distribution of information to the public—the beginning of mass media. From then on, printed information could be easily distributed. By the late fifteenth century, the first English-language announcement appeared in the form of a handbill (which one could consider an advertisement) promoting the availability of a book. Soon thereafter, great quantities of posted advertising announcing information and hawking goods hung in the streets of London.

In 1625, the first ad appeared in a newspaper in England. It was in England that the first modern mass medium—newspapers—carried advertising. The year 1704 marked the appearance of the first known newspaper advertisement in America, in the *Boston Newsletter*. Unlike today's newspaper ads, early newspaper advertisements were limited to one section of the newspaper. Most were simple announcements. In order to attract readers' attention, many newspaper advertisements repeated a line of copy several times. One could think of this as the predecessor to the ad slogan and a later advertising giant's notion of the power of repetition in successful advertising solutions. Eventually advertisements would appear throughout the newspaper, as they do today.

Art directors and illustrators can thank Benjamin Franklin for adding illustrations to newspaper advertisements in the *Pennsylvania Gazette* around 1728, to better attract readers' attention. Franklin was also responsible both for moving advertising to the front section of the newspaper and for the first American magazine ads, around 1742.

Although most of advertising's history happened in England and America, it was in France that the first, very early incarnation, of an advertising agency was opened around 1630, by Théophraste Renaudot. In 1659, Henry Walker opened an agency in London. Advertising in newspapers had become an accepted part of commerce by the beginning of the nineteenth century in both England and America.

In 1843, Volney Palmer opened the first American advertising agency in Philadelphia, and the American visual landscape would never be the same. By the late nineteenth century, both Canada and Japan had their first advertising agencies, and others would quickly follow.

At first, advertising agencies did not write or design the advertisements; they merely placed the ads. But by the end of the nineteenth century, agencies were preparing the copy and creating the illustrations. Francis Wayland Ayer, owner of N.W. Ayer, the Philadelphia agency, is credited with changing the agency's role by offering copy preparation and illustrations. Early advertising agencies served several functions for their clients. Of interest in the context of this book are copywriting, sloganeering (writing slogans), and the illustration of ads.

Millions of dollars were spent to draw consumers' attention to the increasing number of brand names and marks, as well as real estate and other goods and services. With the introduction of packaged goods and brand names into the marketplace, advertising and graphic design would take on great importance, first creating personalities for these brands and introducing new products, and later differentiating the brands from one another.

Advertising, unquestionably, drew people's interest. For example, in 1898, the N.W. Ayer agency created the slogan "Lest you forget, we say it yet, Uneeda Biscuit," to launch the first prepackaged biscuit, Uneeda, produced by the National Biscuit Co. (today a company called Nabisco).

In the late nineteenth century, the invention of color lithography had great impact on advertising. In Italy, France, and Germany, and later on in England, posters were a widespread form of engaging, colorful advertising. Well-respected fine artists, such as Henri de Toulouse-Lautrec, and equally respected graphic designers, such as A. M. Cassandre, created posters as advertisements.

During the second half of the nineteenth century, Shanghai was the commercial center of China. At that time, advertising in both China and Hong Kong was influenced by Britain, although traditional Chinese styles of art were incorporated into it.

The Art of Advertising: Theories and Media

At the beginning of the twentieth century, many American brands, such as Kellogg's, Crisco, and Woodbury soap, were advertised. Many more brands would appear in the coming decades.

What was the best way to sell these brands? Within agencies, different theories arose about what constituted effective advertising. Certainly, advertising agencies were vying for clients, and each one touted its own ad theories and methods as most successful. Some claimed advertising to be a science; others thought it to be an art. From a contemporary perspective, one can easily see that there are many factors involved in why a consumer chooses one brand over another or why a person is motivated to act on behalf of a social cause; the advertising profession has yet to quantifiably prove any theory or method.

What is pertinent to this book's content begins with some modern theories of the twentieth century. As brands proliferated, it became clear that one had to do more than create a brand identity. How do you keep it in the consumer's mind? Do you advertise a functional benefit? Or do you appeal to the consumer's emotions? Is advertising a science? Is it the art of persuasion? Is it the art of endearment?

One of the main strategies touted by twentieth-century ad pioneers was "reason-why copy," which essentially means that you provide a good, sensible argument—a reason why one should buy a brand; many consider this approach a hard sell. Claude Hopkins (1866–1932), of Lord & Thomas/Chicago, who warned us of plaque to advertise Pepsodent toothpaste, was an advocate of reason-why advertising. Published in 1923, Hopkins' *Scientific Advertising* emphasized the importance of knowing your client's product in order to produce solid reason-why copy—a reason to believe a claim and a scientific explaination of the product. Hopkins is credited with the theory of preemptive advertising, claiming a unique selling point for your brand before the competition does. Also, Hopkins believed in advertising promotions, such as free samples, coupons, mail order, and premiums.

Stanley Resor (1879–1964) and Helen Lansdowne Resor (1886–1964), of J. Walter Thompson Co./New York, were advertising's premier married couple. Stanley Resor was a major agency head. Helen Lansdowne Resor, considered a great copywriter, introduced the revolutionary idea of sex appeal, which is obviously an emotional appeal. When in 1911 she wrote "The skin you love to touch" for Woodbury's facial soap ads, published in the *Ladies' Home Journal,* she changed everything. Resor was also the first woman to present advertising to the client, to Procter & Gamble's representatives.

In 1915, the "Penalty of Leadership" ad ran for Cadillac, establishing Theodore F. Mac-Manus (1872–1940), of D'Arcy MacManus Benton & Bowles/St. Louis, as the leading proponent of another school of advertising theory, the atmospheric approach, which is a far softer way of selling than the reason-why platform. The atmospheric platform communicates an impression about the quality and prestige of the brand. MacManus believed in appealing to the audience's imagination, and the emphasis in the atmospheric platform is on conveying the pleasure the brand could provide a consumer. Certainly, MacManus' theory worked for brands such as Cadillac. It would be more difficult to use the atmospheric platform for laundry detergent. Raymond Rubicam (1892–1978), of Young & Rubicam/New York also was a proponent of atmospheric advertising theory; he used beautiful art images along with evocative sales pitches to attempt to influence the prospective consumer.

James Webb Young (1886–1973), of J. Walter Thompson/New York, who believed in testimonials and rational benefits, in 1919 wrote a now famous ad headline for Odorno deodorant: "Within the curve of a woman's arm." This controversial ad had the temerity to bring up body odor, and used an emotional appeal—it played to the reader's fear of social rejection.

After World War I, radio would play an important role in advertising. In 1922, AT&T's station WEAF in New York aired the first radio commercial for a Long Island real estate firm, the Queensboro Corporation. This radio spot resulted in thousands of dollars of revenue for the client. A few years later, corporations began to sponsor radio programs. In 1928, Lucky Strike cigarettes sponsored a show called *The Lucky Strike Dance Orchestra* (later called *Your Hit Parade*), which aired on thirty-nine NBC stations.

Without imagery, radio presented a new challenge to advertising professionals, who began to realize the role that music, sound effects, rhythm, pace, and entertaining content could play in advertising that was purely aural. Companies such as Kraft, Chase & Sanborn, and Fleischmann sponsored radio programs. Sponsorships were the way advertising manifested itself in broadcast media. (Today, we are seeing a significant return to sponsorship, but in different forms.)

What would eventually become the Advertising Council (www.adcouncil.org), a public service advertising organization, began in 1942 as the War Advertising Council, which was organized to help prepare voluntary advertising campaigns for wartime efforts. In part because of the efforts of James Webb Young, who believed in the power of advertising to benefit the public, the Advertising Council would go on to contribute social advertising that unquestionably added to the greater welfare of society.

In 1941, NBC's WNBT began telecasting. Bulova sponsored the first TV spot, showing a watch that ticked for sixty seconds as the open and close time signals for the day's programming schedule. By the mid-twentieth century advertising had a new darling child—television program sponsorship. By 1954, CBS had become the largest advertising medium in the world, making mass media advertising the norm. The new medium of television really took off in the 1950s, when a postwar America was ready to become ardent consumers (as well as enthusiastic television viewers).

In 1948, David Ogilvy (1911–1999) opened his agency, Ogilvy & Mather Worldwide/New York. A great ad creates "brand personality," claimed Ogilvy. That's what attracts consumers, not the minute differences among products. Ogilvy's Hathaway man and Rolls-Royce had brand distinction. Ogilvy also believed in the power of facts and well-thought-out copy. He was a proponent of respecting the consumer's intelligence. Ogilvy's agency set a visual style that would dominate print advertising until the creative revolution of the 1960s, when a new visual style would come into vogue.

Bernice Fitz-Gibbon (1894–1982), a retail advertising pioneer, thought the key to great retail advertising was live action—events such as dance lessons and fashion shows. On behalf of Macy's, she told us that "it's great to be thrifty." In 1954, Fitz-Gibbon opened her own ad agency and hired many women.

Create a "unique selling proposition"—a selling point that communicates a singular message—and repeat it over and over again so that it sticks in the consumer's mind, and you have the answer, according to Rosser Reeves (1910–1984), of Ted Bates & Co./New York, who worked on campaigns for Anacin, Listerine, and Colgate. In 1961, his *Reality in Advertising* solidified his reputation.

Shirley Polykoff (1908–1998), of Foote, Cone & Belding (FCB)/New York, recommended simply having a "direct conversation with the consumer." One could see her as the originator of the modern-day idea that it is essential to seem as though your ad is striking

1-1
"Lemon"
1959
Agency: DDB/New York
Client: Volkswagen

This is a classic DDB layout. The photograph is the main visual element; the line sits underneath the photograph, and the copy under the line. Prior to this ad, cars were not typically shown against an unadorned background. Even more daring and unusual was to use the word *lemon* in conjunction with a car. Its provocative nature led readers to go on to the copy to learn that "a scratched chrome plate on the glove compartment made an entire car unfit for shipping"; VW picks the lemons before any car is shipped. DDB's style of advertising was appealing, and turned intelligent advertising away from a hard sell towards endearing a brand to the consumer through wit and charm.

1-2a, 1-2b
Levy's Jewish Rye
1950s
Agency: DDB/New York
Art Director: William Taubin
Copywriter: Judy Protas
Client: Henry S. Levy's & Son, Inc.

The neighborliness and wit of this campaign tempted many who had never thought of trying Jewish rye to buy it.

up a conversation with the consumer, rather than talking at the consumer. When Polykoff wrote the now famous lines "Does she . . . or doesn't she? Only her hairdresser knows for sure" and "Is it true blondes have more fun?" she combined a natural way of writing with sexual suggestiveness to make us realize that hair color meant far more than its practical application. Polykoff was in the ad business when very few women were copywriters or art directors; she was the only female copywriter at FCB in 1955. When there was a woman on staff, she usually worked on "women's products," such as hair color or soap.

The Creative Revolution

It is Bill Bernbach (1911–1982) who is credited with changing the advertising profession through the creative revolution. Bernbach was a copywriter who had the great fortune to realize the power of visuals as well as the potentially synergistic relationship between words and image. Also, Bernbach was lucky enough to work, early on in his career, with one of the greatest American graphic designers, Paul Rand, which undoubtedly fueled his respect for the power of visuals and for designers.

Bill Bernbach thought advertising was fundamentally creative persuasion and that persuasion was an art. His influence was extensive, and his ads are still studied and revered today. Bernbach opened his own agency, Doyle Dane Bernbach (DDB)/New York, pairing copywriters with art directors in the belief that the art director and writer should generate ideas together. Before this approach, art directors were thought of more as designers or artisans than as full partners in the ideation process. His creative teams were "dream teams"— Bob Gage and Phyllis Robinson, Helmut Krone and Julian Koenig, Bill Taubin and Dave Reider. DDB's work was based on generating big ideas—the concept would be communicated through a synergistic relationship between the words and the visual.

DDB's campaign for Volkswagen's Beetle in the 1960s persuaded America to love small cars (figures 1-1, 4-9). DDB's ads were ironic and witty, and they endeared their brands to consumers. Hard sell was replaced with intelligence and respect for the consumer's intelligence. Some other well-known campaigns were created for Levy's Jewish rye (figures 1-2a, 1-2b) and Avis. DDB's ads were elegantly designed, usually with big visuals filling the top two-thirds of the page, with a small-size typographic line under the visual followed by body copy. DDB's visual style would become the industry creative standard for decades, until it was replaced in

the late 1990s by a new visual standard: the entire page as the visual, with the line somewhere in there (as you will notice in many of the contemporary ads in this book).

DDB set a completely new standard for art direction and writing. As Warren Berger writes in *Advertising Today,* "Now, suddenly, there were ads with an unspoken message and a complex personality; ads that were capable of engaging you in a dialogue, and that challenged you to keep up with their level of wit and intelligence."[1]

Employed at DDB were some of the most brilliantly creative art directors and writers of the twentieth century, including Bob Gage, Helmut Krone, George Lois, Mary Wells Lawrence, Phyllis K. Robinson, and Julian Koenig. Some of them, including Lois, Koenig, and Wells, left DDB to open their own creative agencies.

McCann-Erickson, for Coca-Cola Co., had its finger on the pulse of a generation with "I'd like to teach the world to sing." And in 1965, John Hegarty (now chairman of Bartle Bogle Hegarty/London and New York) started in advertising as a junior art director at Benton and Bowles in London. An example of Hegarty's early work from 1968 is "Noah's Ark" for El Al Airlines (figure 1-3). Hegarty would go on to have great influence in the international advertising community.

Leo Burnett (1892–1971), Leo Burnett Co./Chicago, would say that a memorable character or icon sells. Some creative professionals would wholeheartedly agree with Burnett, the creator of some of the most recognizable icons in ad history. Burnett gave the world Charlie the Tuna, the Jolly Green Giant, the Pillsbury Doughboy, and Tony the Tiger. His Marlboro man, though it unfortunately persuaded too many people that smoking was cool, went on to become one of the most famous icons in the world.

1-3
"Noah's Ark"
1968
Agency: John Collings & Partners/London
Art Director: John Hegarty
Designer: John Hegarty
Artist: Roy Carruthers
Copywriter: Lindsay Dale
Client: El Al Israel Airlines

Hegarty's wit is clearly evident in this early work.

In 1960, George Lois (b. 1931) and Julian Koenig opened their own ad agency, Papert, Koenig, Lois/New York. Lois and Koenig's success as a creative team led them to establish a creative agency of their own that would lead the way for other creatives. As Lois writes in *Mad Ave:* "One of the mantras of this new generation of talent was 'simplify'—slice off the fat and leave only the meat. The new ground rule was to grab viewers' and readers' attention via clean and evocative cause-and-effect concepts. . . . The role of the art director had transformed that of design artisan to that of shaper of ideas. The new creative teams of the 1960s overturned the common perception of advertising as hucksterism, hidden persuasion, and subliminal manipulation."

George Lois saw the adman as an artist, where the creative idea should "stun 'em and cause outrage." His legendary ads for Wolfschmidt vodka were funny and provocative (see figures 1-10a, 1-10b). Lois is one of the few art directors to be able to use the product as the main visual and still make the ad look like great graphic design or art. Able to move between the creative worlds of advertising creative direction and graphic design, Lois is responsible for two of the most brilliant and famous magazine covers ever: the *Esquire* cover depicting boxer Muhammad Ali as Saint Sebastian, and the *Esquire* cover with Andy Warhol drowning in a can of Campbell's soup. Later on, Lois would open another agency, Lois Holland Callaway/New York. Lois fully understood the power of celebrity to endorse products. In his book *Sellebrity,* he recounts stories of "angling and tangling with famous people." (See George Lois Showcase, pages 15–17.)

In 1966, Mary Wells Lawrence (b. 1928) opened her own agency, after receiving fame and acclaim for her work at DDB and Interpublic's Jack Tinker & Partners. Lawrence was the first woman to head a major agency, and her great creative mind gave rise to many famous ad campaigns for clients such as Braniff International Airways, Alka-Seltzer, Benson & Hedges, and the New York State Department of Economic Development. Lawrence's agency wrote, "I LOVE NEW YORK," and we still do. She looked at what all other airlines were doing and made Braniff different; her personal flair and daring extended into her ad concepts.

Carl Ally (1924–1999) left Papert, Koenig, Lois to open his agency, Ally & Gargano, with art director Amil Gargano (b. 1933) in New York. They wanted to create the best possible ads for society, not just the client. The agency stood behind potent claims and named competitors; they are famous for successfully linking Volvo with safety.

Not all advertising emanated out of advertising agencies; some brilliantly creative ads were created by in-house designers and art directors at corporations. One master graphic designer and art director, Lou Dorfsman, worked for CBS for over forty years. (See Lou Dorfsman Showcase, pages 18–21.) At CBS, Dorfsman worked with the great William Goldin, corporate art director, who had a profound impact on broadcast advertising. Herb Lubalin, one of the great American graphic designers, also created advertisements for pharmaceutical corporations and other types of products, such as this print ad for Land Rover (figure 1-4; see also figure 7-23 in Chapter 7). Gene Federico, who broke with formulaic fashion advertising, had a great influence on fashion advertising.

In America, much of what followed the watershed creative period of the 1960s and early 1970s was marked by a style that was built on the DDB school of thinking, with clever, smart copy and visuals based on ideas. In the 1970s, McCann-Erickson gave us "It's the real thing. Coke." DDB was still creating great ads for Volkswagen. American agencies such as Carl Ally, whose clients included Fiat, and Scali, McCabe, Sloves, whose client roster included Volvo, gained acclaim.

England in the 1970s was a creative hotbed of advertising, with agencies such as Collett Dickenson Pearce (CDP), BMP, and Abbott Mead Vickers. CDP created memorable print ads for the Parker Pen Company, Pretty Polly, Gallaher, and the Metropolitan Police.

1-4
"Goes Anywhere . . .
Does Anything . . . Land Rover"

Designer: Herb Lubalin
Client: Land Rover
Courtesy of the Herb Lubalin Study Center of Design and Typography at the Cooper Union School of Art, New York, and the Lubalin Family

In 1976, Davidson Pearce Berry and Spottiswoode created this award-winning direct mail piece for the International Wool Secretariat, promoting flameproof wool (figure 1-5); created by David Little and Brian Lodge, it still looks fresh today. In 1979, the creative team of art director Jim Downie and copywriter Tony Cox of Hall Advertising, with photography by Tony May, created a haunting poster for the Scottish Health Education Unit (figure 1-6). Film director Ridley Scott made his early mark in England's advertising world with TV spots that resembled mini-films for Hovis and Benson & Hedges. DDB opened an office in London, as well. Film director Tony Scott, Ridley Scott's younger brother, also directed award-winning television commercials in England.

Perhaps as a reaction to the creative revolution of the 1960s, in the 1970s an emphasis was placed on accountability, market research, and positioning brands (comparing one brand to another). It was in the 1970s that we had the "cola wars" and other intense rivalry among brands reflected in advertising. There was also an increase in television advertising, which became the favorite medium for both clients and creatives. Creative directors, copywriters, and art directors began to see television advertising as an opportunity to create mini-movies.

1-5
Direct Mail Ad
1976
Agency: Davidson Pearce Berry and Spottiswoode/London
Art Director: Brian Lodge
Copywriter: David Little
Client: International Wool Secretariat

Very strong direct mail pieces, such as this one, have an opportunity to create a one-on-one conversation with the reader.

1-6
"Grave"
1979
Agency: Hall Advertising/London
Art Director: Jim Downie
Copywriter: Tony Cox
Photographer: Tony May
Client: Scottish Health Education
© Art Director: Jim Downie/Photographer: Tony May

This startling image quickly drives home the message that smoking kills. The design of the coffin played off a well-known English brand of cigarettes.

WHY DO YOU THINK
EVERY PACKET CARRIES A GOVERNMENT HEALTH WARNING?

Issued by the Scottish Health Education Unit

On a positive note, in the late 1960s and 1970s, advertising began to reflect diversity, both in its advertisements and within its workforce, albeit meagerly. In America, besides the pressures exerted on the industry to reflect the diverse nature of the American population, there were pressures exerted by watchdog groups, such as Action for Children's Television (ACT), a U.S. consumer group founded in 1968, and government regulatory agencies, such as the Federal Trade Commission, as well as advertising's own National Advertising Review Board, to adopt completely ethical practices. Ralph Nader, a prominent consumer advocate, sounded many alarms in the 1960s that led to consumer protection regulations. Interestingly, the first American consumer group, the National Consumers League, had already been formed in 1899.

In the early 1980s, thanks to the ad campaign created by George Lois, MTV gained popularity and influenced the look of television advertising. The 1980s was host to a variety of great ads, including the Partnership for a Drug-Free America's "This is your brain on drugs" campaign and Nike's "Bo knows" campaign. Fallon McElligott gave the ad world the great campaign for *Rolling Stone* magazine "Perception/Reality," which would redefine the brand and set a standard for creative thinking. It would force the ad world to realize the power of visually driven ads founded on a big idea. The TBWA Absolut ad campaign would add a new visual layout, one in which the image becomes central, simple, and iconic. Despite these exceptions, however, up until the end of the 1980s visual style was, for the most part, still based on the DDB visual style.

In the mid- to late 1980s mergers of advertising agencies into international conglomerates diluted the creative thrust. The advertising profession changed as large, prominent agencies joined together to form conglomerates. In the face of all the mergers, some independent creative agencies opened in places that were not associated with New York's Madison Avenue elite ad agencies, not even with Chicago or London. Communications technology, such as fax machines and computers, allowed clients to reach out to creative agencies not located in New York, such as the Martin Agency in Richmond, Goodby, Silverstein & Partners in San Francisco, and Fallon McElligott in Minneapolis.

In 1982 Wieden + Kennedy (W+K) opened in Portland, Oregon, with one important local client—Nike. On behalf of Nike, Dan Wieden (b. 1945) and David Kennedy (b. 1940) inspired us to "just do it." Shunning research and the usual ad tools, W+K became advertising trend makers, mixing pop culture and inspirational messages with an emphasis on brand spirit. W+K is an independent agency, known for its somewhat subversive ad-think; this reputation comes from meta-advertising campaigns with such famous directors as Spike Lee.

The work of Jay Chiat (1931–2002) and Lee Clow (b. 1942) at Chiat/Day/Los Angeles places ideas over technique; the agency created ads that felt as large as movies and as powerful as great posters. They gave us ads that could pass for MTV or independent short films. Director Ridley Scott and Chiat/Day created "1984," one of the greatest television commercials of all time, for Apple to introduce the Macintosh.

In England, BBH would redefine the Levi's brand with print and a mini-epic TV spot shot by director Tony Scott. Abbott Mead Vickers created a definitive brand campaign for *The Economist* consisting of a short headline on a red background with white type and a white keyhole that represented a passage into the world of information. Agencies such as Bartle Bogle Hegarty, Boase Massimi Pollitt Partnership, Leagus Delaney, Lowe Howard Spink, Collett Dickenson Pearce, and Saatchi & Saatchi would take center stage. Great creative talents such as John Hegarty and Tim Delaney would become ad stars. In 1987, Boase Massimi Pollitt Partnership (now BMP DDB) would give us the brilliant "Points of View" TV spot for *The Guardian* (figure 1-7). When this spot opens, the camera offers a particular point of view: we see a young man with a shaved head—a skinhead—running toward an older man in a suit.

1

2

3

1-7
"Points of View"
1987
Agency: BMP DDB/London
Photographers: John Webster, Frank Budgen, Paul Weiland
Client: The Guardian

Seeing from both points of view, as does *The Guardian,* is critical to understanding the full story.

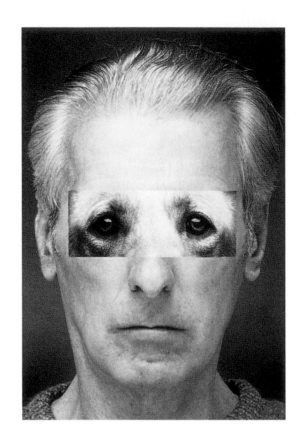

NO SURGEON IN THE WORLD CAN HELP
THIS BLIND MAN SEE. BUT A DOG CAN.

Try going blind.

Walk to the corner of the street with your
eyes closed.

Post a letter with your eyes closed.

Buy a loaf of bread with your eyes closed.

Discover how the simplest tasks become
a nightmare with your eyes closed.

Now walk to the corner of the street and
post a cheque with your eyes wide open.

THE GUIDE DOGS FOR THE BLIND ASSOCIATION
Department 3, 9 Park Street, Windsor, Berkshire SL4 1JR.

1-8
1987
Agency: Saatchi & Saatchi
Client: The Guide Dogs for the Blind
Association, UK
(The Guide Dogs for the Blind Association,
Hillfields, Burghfield Common, Reading RG7
3YG)
Web site: www.guidedogs.org.uk

By replacing the eyes of a man with
those of a dog, this ad poignantly
gets across the message that a dog
can help a blind man see.

A Few Noteworthy American Advertising Slogans

1912 "When It Rains It Pours" (Morton Salt)

1929 "The Pause That Refreshes" (Coca-Cola)

1933 "Breakfast of Champions" (Wheaties)

1942 "Loose Lips Sink Ships" (U.S. Security of War Information)

1948 "A Diamond Is Forever" (DeBeers)

1961 "The Toughest Job You'll Ever Love" (Peace Corp)

1963 "We Try Harder" (Avis)

1971 "You Deserve a Break Today" (McDonald's)

1972 "A Mind Is a Terrible Thing To Waste" (United Negro College Fund)

1988 "Just Do It" (Nike)

1990 "Friends Don't Let Friends Drive Drunk" (National Highway Traffic Safety
Administration (under the U.S. Department of Transportation)

1993 "Got Milk?" (California Milk Processor Board)

2003 "What Happens Here, Stays Here" (Las Vegas Convention and Visitors
Authority)

From that angle, we assume that the skinhead is attacking the other man. Then the spot fades and reopens to reveal another point of view, one in which we see that the skinhead is actually saving the older man by pushing him out of the way of falling debris. Showing both points of view expertly illustrates that *The Guardian* covers issues from both sides.

For the Guide Dogs for the Blind Association, Saatchi & Saatchi would create a print ad as unforgettable and poignant as a Magritte painting (figure 1-8).

By the late 1980s, there was a realization that people weren't that interested in reading ads—a quick glance was going to be it. The times seemed to call for a more visually driven ad world, where creating a visual style for a brand was more important than a specific ad claim about functional benefits, reason-why, or unique features. For example, Lowe & Partners/SAS, for Mercedes, used a rubber duck with the Mercedes logo positioned in the eyes; Dentsu Young & Rubicam in Tokyo symbolized Volvo's safety by shaping a Volvo out of a safety pin. Visuals would have to do the work that visuals and copy previously did together. Visual analogies, recognizable symbols, and unusual images would all become part of the creative visual vocabulary in the 1990s.

The television remote control had an interesting effect on advertising. Advertising professionals realized that their TV spots had better be as entertaining as possible, with less emphasis on product information, so that television viewers wouldn't zap through them or change channels. In part, the remote control led to creating ads that didn't look or sound like typical advertisements, in order to ensure that they would be viewed.

A related school of thought touted getting "under people's radar," ambushing people with guerilla advertising tactics. Early proponents, such New York's Kirshenbaum and Bond, created now-legendary guerilla campaigns for clients—for example, stenciling advertising on sidewalks. They wrote *Under the Radar,* which claims you have to create ads that don't look typical so that your ad goes undetected as advertising by an ad-weary and savvy audience.

As with television and radio, new technologies such as the Internet would again bring new media to the advertising industry, introducing such formats as promotional Web sites, Web banners, and Internet films. Agencies specializing in interactive advertising (or interactive marketing) would emerge as important partners or allies of traditional agencies. More and more agencies would open wings that specialized in ethnic markets, and more independent ethnic agencies would open shop.

In the twenty-first century, other marketers and agencies paved the way in new media, with Jim McDowell, executive marketing director of BMW North America, and the Fallon agency creating BMWfilms for the Internet. Miami's Crispin Porter Bogusky and Partners and Kerri Martin, marketing communications manager for MINI, put MINI on the American map with both traditional and nontraditional campaigns. In countries not usually credited as advertising hotbeds, such as Holland, Germany, Brazil, and South Africa, independent agencies like KesselsKramer in Amsterdam and Heimat in Berlin create campaigns that stun and provoke thought. Famous agencies with international locations, such as BBH in Asia and Saatchi & Saatchi in Brazil, create campaigns that gain acclaim and attention.

Tenets

Reason-why copy

Scientific advertising

Atmospheric platform

Unique selling proposition and repetition

Sex appeal

Brand personality

Events

Sexual innuendo

Memorable icons and characters

Persuade them with creative ideas

"Stun 'em and outrage 'em"

Give it flair—make it daring and different

Stake a claim

Revere creative concepts

Inspire

Be ironic

Get under the radar

What does it take to create great advertising? Revolutionary advertising? Studying the history of advertising gives us a clue to the answer. Knowing your audience's needs and desires can lead to a great ad. Combine that with an education in advertising design, graphic design, and insight into people, toss in critical and creative thinking, ethical behavior, and you've got an excellent chance to create a great ad.

In this book you will read great comments about advertising and design from Denise M. Anderson (DMA), Steven Brower (*Print* magazine), Jon Maltby (Blast Radius), Rich Palatini (Gianettino & Meredith), Robynne Raye (Modern Dog), Paul Renner (Wieden + Kennedy), Deborah Rivera (Alexander Richardson), Carlos Segura (Segura Inc.), Michael Sickinger (Firmenich), Kevyn Smith (Peel Interactive), Jerry Simon (DVC), and Stefan Sagmeister (Sagmeister Inc.). Fascinating interviews offer advice, wisdom, and comments on the advertising profession from some of today's leading advertising and marketing professionals—John Butler, Valerie Graves, Bob Isherwood, and Erik Kessels.

Notes

1. Warren Berger, *Advertising Today* (London: Phaidon Press, 2001), p. 45.

2. George Lois and Bill Pitts, *The Art of Advertising: George Lois on Mass Communication* (New York: Harry N. Abrams, Inc., 1977), p. 27.

SHOWCASE George Lois

George Lois' advertising and graphic design career is an example of the range one individual in the field of visual communications can possess. Lois, listed among the top one hundred people of the century in advertising by *Ad Age,* is an exemplary advertising and graphic design thinker (figures 1-9, 1-10a, 1-10b, 1-11, 1-12, 1-13).

Lois leads the creative department at Good Karma Creative, New York, and is the recipient of innumerable awards, including membership in the Art Directors Hall of Fame. His clients included Wolfschmidt vodka, Xerox, Allerest, MTV, Maypo, Wheatena, and Edwards & Hanly, and his *Esquire* covers remain unrivaled.

1-9
Agency: DDB/New York
Art Director: George Lois
Client: Kerid

In 1958, Lois was a rookie art director at DDB. When he created this image for an ad for Kerid ear drops, other senior art directors found the image shocking. Lois had created a memorable, dynamic image.

"You're some tomato.
We could make beautiful Bloody Marys together.
I'm different from those other fellows."

"I like you, Wolfschmidt.
You've got taste."

Wolfschmidt Vodka has the touch of taste that marks genuine old world vodka. Wolfschmidt in a Bloody Mary is a tomato in triumph. Wolfschmidt brings out the best in every drink. General Wine and Spirits Company, N.Y. 22. Made from Grain, 80 or 100 Proof. Prod. of U.S.A.

1-10a, 1-10b
Wolfschmidt
1962
Agency: Papert, Koenig, Lois
Art Director: George Lois
Copywriter: Julian Koenig
Client: Seagram

One week after the Wolfschmidt bottle was seen "talking up" a tomato, another ad appeared where the bottle was seen trying pretty much the same with an orange. Week after week, other fruits and vegetables—limes, olives, lemons—appeared with the Wolfschmidt bottle. Playing off male/female interaction, using cinematic jargon associated with the likes of Bogart, these ads anthropomorphize the objects, lending a sexy, masculine personality to Wolfschmidt. Although I profess not showing the product as the main visual, this campaign clearly makes the case that anything done with great intelligence, nuance, and wit works. This is one of the most famous campaigns in ad history; it exemplifies ads that endear themselves to the audience.

1-12
"John, Is That Billy Coughing?"
1961
Agency: Papert, Koenig, Lois/New York
Art Director: George Lois
Copywriter: Julian Koenig
Client: Pharmacraft

Not only does this ad have no product shot, it has no logo, no product ingredients, and no people holding cough syrup. A darkened bedroom and two voices are conjured up to let us know what people actually give their children when they're coughing.

1-11
1960
Agency: DDB/New York
Art Director: George Lois
Client: Goodman's Matzoh

Along with this gutsy ad comes a legendary tale about George Lois. The Goodman family patriarch said, "No, thanks," when the DDB account representative offered this poster, which was to run in New York subways just before the Jewish Passover holiday. Upon hearing this news, Lois asked Bernbach for an opportunity to sell the ad to the patriarch. Bernbach agreed, and Lois went to see the A. Goodman & Sons company executives. Lois explained that everyone in New York would understand the word *kosher* written in Hebrew letters. Goodman still refused. Lois writes: "Time was running out. I had to make a final move. I stepped through an open window and shouted at him, 'I'm leaving.' They gaped at me as though I were some kind of *meshugenah*. I was poised on the outer ledge three floors above the pavement like a window washer. I gripped the raised sash with my left hand and waved the poster with my free hand. I screamed from the ledge at the top of my lungs, 'You make the matzoh, I'll make the ads!'" Goodman & Sons bought the ad, and without knowing it, Lois had just raised the status of advertising art director to brash artist and gave himself the reputation of *enfant terrible*.

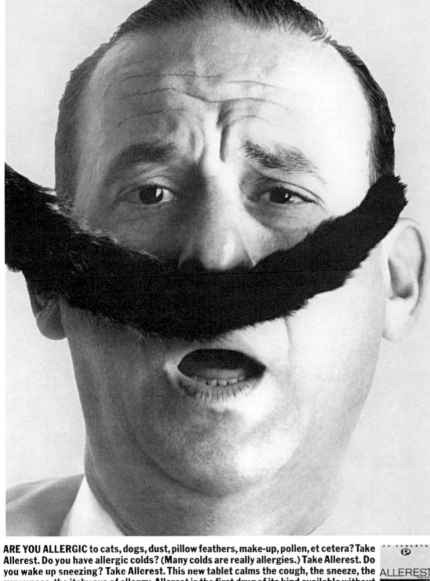

ARE YOU ALLERGIC to cats, dogs, dust, pillow feathers, make-up, pollen, et cetera? Take Allerest. Do you have allergic colds? (Many colds are really allergies.) Take Allerest. Do you wake up sneezing? Take Allerest. This new tablet calms the cough, the sneeze, the runny nose, the itchy eye of allergy. Allerest is the first drug of its kind available without prescription; no cold tablet can work as well. Ah-ah-ah-choo! I better TAKE ALLEREST.

WHAT ALLEREST HAS: ALLERGY SPECIFICS DOCTORS PRESCRIBE. PHENYLPROPANOLAMINE HYDROCHLORIDE 25 MG. CHLORPHENIRAMINE MALEATE 1 MG. & METHAPYRILENE FUMARATE 5 MG. CALCIUM ASCORBATE 37½ MG.
WHAT ALLEREST DOESN'T HAVE: UNLIKE COLD AND SINUS TABLETS, NO ASPIRIN, NO ANALGESICS. (SOME PEOPLE ARE ALLERGIC TO THEM.) NO CAFFEINE, NO BARBITURATES, NO STIMULANTS, NO HABIT FORMING DRUGS.

1-13
"Are You Allergic"
Agency: Papert, Koenig, Lois/New York
Art Director: George Lois
Copywriter: Julian Koenig
Photographer: Carl Fischer
Client: Pharmacraft

A surprising visual not only grabs attention but makes a point about allergies to cat dander.

Lois advises:

The ad solution has to at least surprise, be seemingly outrageous.

It has to be totally memorable.

It has to be memorable with one viewing, with one glance.

It has to sell.

It should change popular culture.

As senior vice president and creative director at CBS, in charge of the CBS design image, Lou Dorfsman created an extensive body of work spanning forty years. Dorfsman's oeuvre includes graphic design, advertising, art direction, creative direction, and brilliant typographic design (figures 1-14, 1-15, 1-16, 1-17, 1-18). Dorfsman's work has influenced many graphic designers and art directors, especially in the field of broadcasting visual communications.

Many of the advertising solutions in this showcase reveal Dorfsman's fine wit, extreme intelligence, and artistry with typography. Dorfsman could tell an entire story though typographic design.

Now Dorfsman is the design director of the Museum of Television and Radio, New York City. He holds honorary doctorates from Long Island University and New School University (affiliated with Parsons School of Design), has received the highest honors from professional organizations, and has won numerable important awards for visual communications.

he laughs best ($) who laughs last

Some people started laughing right off the bat when they heard we planned to concentrate on comedy this season. They were sure it wouldn't work. These days they're not laughing so hard—but the nation's viewers are, and so are the sponsors of our comedy programs. The audiences attracted by the average comedy program on the three networks this season tell the story: Network Y—7.3 million homes...Network Z—8.9 million homes...CBS Television Network, 9.5 million homes.* Moreover, in the latest Nielsen report three of our funniest shows are in the Top 10—and two of them are brand new this season.† But the thing that keeps all our advertisers smiling is that the CBS Television Network attracts the biggest average audiences in every category of entertainment, laughs or no laughs.

CBS Television Network

1-14
"Ha Ha Ha"
Art Director/Designer: Lou Dorfsman
Client: CBS

With an extremely inventive typographic bar chart, Dorfsman wins the viewer's attention. Lou Dorfsman's work for CBS pushed typographic design in advertising to new heights. In this ad, Dorfsman used a bar chart to illustrate the fact that CBS had the best three comedy shows.

1-15a, 1-15b
"Exhilarate!" "Captivate!"
Art Director/Designer: Lou Dorfsman
Client: CBS

Dorfsman used typography
alone to communicate a
message, turning the
typography into the art.

This Fall, the CBS Television Network will again chalk up the biggest attendance record in football. The same go-go-go spirit that first brought professional football home to a nationwide audience (the late National Football League Commissioner Bert Bell attributed the game's phenomenal rise to this network's pioneering coverage) is also responsible for many other CBS Television Network sports firsts. First to give the nation a front row seat at international competitions through exclusive coverage of the 1960 Winter and Summer Olympics. First to use video tape in sports, making it possible to rerun thoroughbred races, crucial golf rounds and scoring football plays as soon as they are over. First to televise the whole incredible range of sporting events from rugby to auto racing, from sky diving to figure skating—through the introduction of the weekly Sports Spectacular series. And throughout the year, this network continues to bring a hundred million television fans such major events of every season as the college bowl games, the Triple Crown, the UN Handicap, the PGA and Masters golf tournaments, and baseball's Major League Games of the Week. Sports play an exhilarating, exciting part in the powerful CBS Television Network line-up, which again this season has the balance, depth and quality to **DOMINATE**

Women are watching more daytime television than ever before and watching more of it on the CBS Television Network than on any other. And with good reason. Day after day they can anticipate exciting new chapter in their favorite daytime dramas—among the longest running programs in television. In fact, back in 1950, this network was the one to innovate the whole idea of daytime television, opening up to housewives a wonderful world of entertainment and information throughout the day: A world that could titillate them with inventive games. A world where they could watch CBS News' distinguished correspondents elucidate the crucial issues of our time. A world in which a Captain Kangaroo could fascinate not only children but mothers as well. In short, a world of daytime programming that would captivate the biggest audiences in network television, as it has for the past three consecutive years. There's no question about it: when it comes to having a way with women, advertisers can always depend on the CBS Television Network to **Dominate**

1-16
"Worth Repeating"
1964
Art Director/Designer: Lou Dorfsman
Client: CBS

Using quotation marks as a graphic element, Dorfsman turned a mere quote into a brilliant design. There is no need for visuals when the type becomes an interesting visual in itself.

The Columbia Broadcasting System turned in a superb journalistic beat last night, running away with the major honors in reporting President Johnson's election victory. In clarity of presentation the network led all the way... In a medium where time is of the essence the performance of CBS was of landslide proportions. The difference... lay in the CBS sampling process called Vote Profile Analysis... the CBS staff called the outcome in state after state before its rivals. JACK GOULD, The New York Times (11/4)

Worth | Repeating

◉ CBS News

1-17
"Of Black America"

1968

Art Director/Designer: Lou Dorfsman
Client: CBS

To represent the subject of a CBS series titled *Black History: Lost, Stolen or Strayed,* Dorfsman's idea was to symbolize struggle for full citizenship through half of the American flag painted on a African American man's face.

1-18
"Expensive . . . by Design"

Art Director/Designer: Lou Dorfsman
Client: Dansk

Besides his role at CBS, Dorfsman created ads for other clients, including a large body of work for Dansk.

Allan Beaver was a founding partner, vice chairman, and chief creative officer of Levine Huntley Schmidt and Beaver. In 1995 he cofounded Beaver Reitzfeld Inc. in New York City. (See figures 1-19, 1-20, 1-21, 1-22, 1-23.)

Allan Beaver began his career as a graphic designer for CBS. Almost immediately upon entering the advertising business, he began winning awards, including many gold medals, in all major advertising shows.

Beaver has been on the American Association of Advertising Agencies Creative Committee and the board of the Partnership for a Drug-Free America.

The advertising industry has voted him among the top one hundred creative people in the United States and has included him in the volume *Who's Who in Advertising*. Over the years, Beaver has produced award-winning work for such clients as Subaru cars, Jockey underwear, Maidenform, Matchbox toy cars, General Foods, Remington shavers, and many others.

1-19
"Get the Lead Out of Your Pants"
1968
Agency: DKG/New York
Creative Director: Peter Hirsch
Art Director: Allan Beaver
Copywriter: Marshall Karp
Photographer: Cailor/Resnick
Client: Talon Zippers

An interesting visual of raised metal, as well as a play on words, communicates the benefit of dyed-to-match nylon zippers.

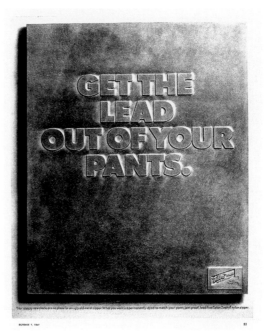

1-20
"Newton's Law"
1970
Agency: DKG/New York
Creative Director: Peter Hirsch
Art Director: Allan Beaver
Copywriter: Larry Plapler
Illustrator: Charles Slackman
Client: Talon Zippers

Beaver uses a comparison of Newton's law of gravity to explain the benefit of a Talon zipper, which *will* stay up. This is a fun way of saying, "Your zipper will stay up when it should."

LET YOUR FATHER'S FACE BE A LESSON TO YOU.

Take a good look at that barbed wire disaster area some morning.

Poor guy, in his day it was the "safety" razor or nothing. And while it gave him a close shave, it was also making his beard tougher. Which of course made shaving tougher.

But all his suffering isn't in vain, if you learn something from it.

Even if you've been shaving 6 or 7 years, it's not too late to break your beard in right. Start shaving our way and your beard will be just as shaveable in 10 or 20 years as it is today.

But as you've heard your father say a thousand times, electric shavers don't shave that close.

That was until the Remington *Lektro Blade*™ shaver.

Its blades are honed to such a fine edge, they have to be replaced. Like the blades in a razor. (Suggested price for replacement blades, $1.95.)

Thanks to this disposable blade concept, the Remington *Lektro Blade*™ shaver gives you every bit as close a shave as you get with a razor.

Without the discomfort of a razor.

So get our electric shaver before you end up with a face like your father's.

Class dismissed.

1-21
"Let Your Father's Face . . ."
1971
Agency: DKG/New York
Creative Director: Peter Hirsch
Art Director: Allan Beaver
Copywriter: Larry Plapler
Photographer: Cailor/Resnick
Client: Remington Shavers

Inviting human interest, this ad gets you to read all the body copy.

EVERYTHING IN THE WORLD SHOULD BE MADE THIS GOOD. ONLY BIGGER.
MATCHBOX.

1-22
"Everything in the World . . ."
1980
Agency: Levine Huntley Schmidt & Beaver/New York
Creative Director/Art Director: Allan Beaver
Copywriter: Larry Plapler
Photographer: Cailor/Resnick
Client: Matchbox Cars

With humor, this ad points out the benefit of Matchbox's construction. (Also see figure 4-22.)

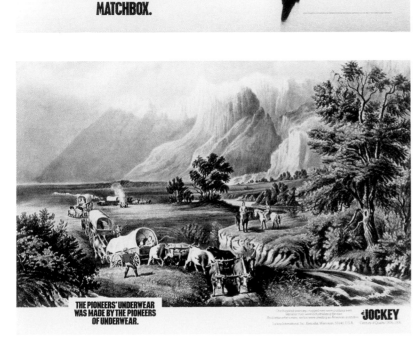

THE PIONEERS' UNDERWEAR WAS MADE BY THE PIONEERS OF UNDERWEAR.
JOCKEY

1-23
"Pioneers"
1981
Agency: Levine Huntley Schmidt & Beaver/New York
Creative Director/Art Director: Allan Beaver
Copywriter: Larry Plapler
Photographer: Bettman Archive
Client: Jockey

Using a panoramic landscape—and the style of American landscape painters of the nineteenth century—this ad demonstrates the idea that Jockey underwear is authentic and first in its class.

The Smokey Bear campaign is the longest-running Ad Council campaign, serving to remind people of the critical importance of outdoor fire safety and wildfire prevention. With so many more wildfires today, Smokey Bear's message is more important than ever (figures 1-24, 1-25, 1-26, 1-27, 1-28, 1-29).

1-24
1944

This is one of the first posters starring Smokey Bear.

SMOKEY SAYS—
Care <u>will</u> prevent
9 out of 10 forest fires!

Smokey Bear, an enduring American icon and character, is based on a real baby bear that a ranger crew found after a wildfire in New Mexico.

On August 9, 1944, the first poster of Smokey Bear was prepared. The poster depicted a bear pouring a bucket of water on a campfire. Smokey Bear soon became popular, and his image began appearing on other posters and cards. In 1952, Smokey Bear had enough public recognition to attract commercial interest. An Act of Congress passed to take Smokey out of the public domain and place him under the control of the Secretary of Agriculture. The Act provided for the use of collected royalties and fees for continued education on forest fire prevention. (www.smokeybear.com/vault/history.asp)

1-25
1956

Here we find the headline as a carved wood sign.

1-26
1959

In this children's-book-like illustration, Smokey Bear and his animal companions remind us how to prevent fires. The lines of copy are part of the illustration.

1-27
1960

Here Smokey addresses us, the readers, and asks "Why?" as we look upon the damage that has been done.

1-28
1973

Appealing to our emotions and concern for wildlife, Smokey reminds us that young animals live in the woods. The relationship of type to visual is representative of the early 1970s.

1-29
1987

With a somewhat surrealistic visual style, this visually driven ad catches our attention.

A Public Service of the U.S.D.A. Forest Service, and your State Foresters.

In the 1970s, the State of New York decided to promote tourism to help offset a recession, and asked the New York City ad agency Wells, Rich and Greene to take on the task of creating a travel and tourism ad campaign. The agency asked esteemed graphic designer Milton Glaser to design the logo. The "I LOVE NEW YORK" campaign was born; Glaser's logo, the brand identity, and the Wells, Rich and Greene ad campaign are renowned in the history of advertising. Not only did the campaign promote tourism, it resonated with a definitive New York spirit and is an example of great emotional branding (figures 1-30, 1-31, 1-32, 1-33, 1-34, 1-35, 1-36, 1-37, 1-38).

The campaign made its debut with an array of celebrities—Broadway, music, and film legends, including Carol Channing, Frank Sinatra, and Frank Langella—endorsing New York.

I LOVE NEW YORK is an official State of New York brand, and it remains New York's tagline today. In the November 2000 issue of *Report on Business* (in partnership with the London *Financial Times*), the I LOVE NEW YORK logo was judged number 24 of the world's top 50 logos.

In this showcase is a range of historic advertising solutions for the State of New York (Courtesy of I LOVE NEW YORK). The I LOVE NEW YORK® mark and photographs are owned by and used with permission of the New York State Department of Economic Development.

1-30
"NYS Belgium"
1969

Part of a larger campaign, this ad predates the "I LOVE NEW YORK" campaign, reminding us that New York State has all the old-world charm of countries such as Belgium, Greece, and Morocco.

1-31
"I LOVE NEW YORK" logo
1976
Designer: Milton Glaser

Commissioned by ad agency Wells
Rich and Greene/New York, this logo,
by one of America's legendary
designers, has become world-famous.

1-32
"I LOVE NEW YORK"
Fall Foliage Poster
1977

Using beautiful illustrations of
leaves and a very soft sell, this
poster reminds the viewer that New
York State is lovely in autumn.

1-33
"I LOVE NEW YORK" State Fair Poster
1979–1980

This sumptuous poster is a good example of typography and layout from the late 1970s to the early 1980s.

1-34
Catskills Poster
1982

This visually intriguing poster, with type characteristic of the early 1980s, captures the personality of the Catskills.

1-35
1983

Using a cinematic style of the 1980s, this spot illustrates all the sensual pleasures of a summer in New York State.

Empire State Plaza, Albany October 8th

1-36
"I LOVE NEW YORK"
Fall Festival Poster

Not only does this poster advertise New York, it has a visual style associated with many prominent New York graphic designers and illustrators of the 1970s and 1980s.

1-37
"I LOVE NEW YORK"
Spring Flower Festival Poster
1983

Small-scale copy complements charming floral illustrations arranged on a grid.

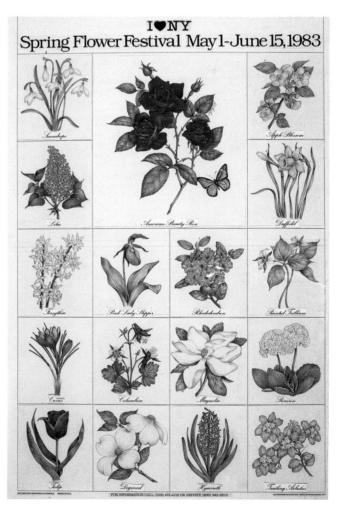

2

The Biz: Structure, Strategy, and the Creative Brief

What Is Advertising?

Advertising differentiates brands and causes, ultimately sells brands, and calls people to action. An *advertisement* is a specific message constructed to inform, persuade, promote, or motivate people on behalf of a brand or social cause. An *ad campaign* is a series of coordinated ads, in one or more media, that are based on a single overarching strategy or theme.

Most people think of advertising as all forms of paid promotional communication conveyed by a mass medium, such as television, radio, the Internet, or print. An advertisement is usually paid mass communication; I say "usually," because guerilla advertising does not pay for media placement, and public service advertisements (PSAs) usually run in donated media. Today, the definition of advertising has been expanded to include an array of other media, both commercial and social advertising, and both paid and unpaid ads. The definition is an evolving one.

Clients include manufacturers and service firms, resellers (retailers, wholesalers, distributors), government, social organizations, and charities.

The Ad Agency

An advertising agency is a business that provides clients with creative, marketing, and other business services related to planning, creating, producing, and placing advertisements.

In the late 1980s many prominent advertising agencies merged together into conglomerates. Today there are several major conglomerates, such as the Omnicom Group, Interpublic Group, WPP Group, Havas, Publicis Groupe, and Dentsu, among others.

Of course, there are many independent agencies throughout the world. An independent agency is a single agency owned and operated by individuals and not part of a conglomerate.

Types of Agencies

Full-service agencies offer a full range of business and creative services related to the advertising process, including planning, creative ideation and design, production, implementation, and placement. Some full-service agencies also handle marketing communication, such as public relations, promotional design, interactive advertising, and direct marketing, or are in partnerships with companies that provide those services. Clients choose full-service agencies because these organizations are able to handle any aspect of the client's marketing needs.

Creative boutiques are known for their focus on creative work. They are usually small, and they often attract clients who prefer to work directly with the principals of an agency. These agencies don't have the layers of bureaucracy or overhead of large, full-service agencies.

Some companies prefer to produce part or all of their advertising, branding, direct marketing, and promotional design themselves. Such companies own and operate their own *in-house agencies*.

Other types of agencies include *global agencies,* with international offices and reach, and *interactive agencies,* specializing in new media.

Who Is the Audience?

Whoever is on the receiving end of a commercial or public service communication, either a group or an individual, is the audience. A target audience is a specific group of people or consumers targeted for an advertising or public service message or campaign.

Arnika's team understood their audience, and based on that developed a strategy and ad concept for Dickies clothing (figure 2-1). Arnika defined the problem this way: Dickies clothing isn't fancy or flashy, but it has started to appeal to a hipper, more urban, youthful market. While this is financially beneficial to the clothing manufacturers, they must con-

Agency Services

Creative services (idea generation, art direction, copywriting, sometimes branding and graphic design)

Account services

Marketing services

Media planning and buying services

Production services

Public relations

Promotion

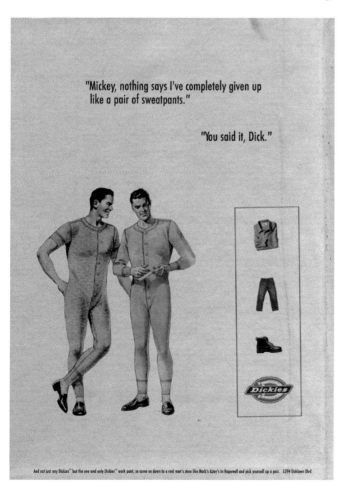

2-1
Dickies
Agency: Arnika/Richmond
Creative Director: Mark Fenske
Art Director: Michael Ashley
Copywriter: Chris Thomson
Client: Mark & Jay's Big & Tall
© 2002 Arnika LLC

Visuals that are reminiscent of 1950s American men combined with offbeat humor create a brand spirit for Dickies.

tinue to appeal to their core group of buyers, working-class men, while keeping a "cool" image for their newer audience. The solution Arnika came up with was a campaign that effectively portrays Dickies as a functional brand to its core market and as a quirky fashion brand to its younger market.

The goal of one advertising campaign for Steve Ford Music was to broaden the client base (figure 2-2). The agency that developed the campaign, Hadrian's Wall, comments: "Steve Ford Music does music for commercials, so their client base is ad agency creatives and producers. . . . Steve Ford Music recognized the need to reach new creative agencies; those that are doing advertising that consumers and industry opinion leaders are talking about. . . . The campaign chosen was conceptually strong, and reflected Steve Ford Music's slavish dedication to music in an engaging, memorable way."

2-2
"Guard Dogs"
Agency: Hadrian's Wall/Chicago
Creative Director/Copywriter: Kevin Lynch
Art Director: Mollie Wilke
Photographers: Oman, Stock
Client: Steve Ford Music
© 2002

"Steve Ford Music has been one of the most successful music houses in Chicago, in part due to the lavish dedication they have to creating music. This ad shows how this one-track mind would hurt them should they pursue other careers."

In today's complex marketplace, advertisers often choose to target groups of people, whether the groups are defined by age, interests, or ethnicity. There are advertising agencies that specialize in particular ethnic markets, such as the African American market, the Asian American market, or the Latino market. For American Airlines, Zubi Advertising created this ad (figure 2-3) aimed at the Latino market. Emmie Vázquez, Zubi's creative director, comments: "This ad is part of a campaign that also includes TV. These ads work under the premise that a simple gesture—outstretching your arms—can trigger the desire to fly (on American Airlines) to see your friends and family."

¿Será que quieres volar?

AmericanAirlines®
Ponte cómodo

2-3
American Airlines "Brazos" Campaign
Agency: Zubi Advertising/Coral Gables
Senior Art Director: José Reyes
Senior Copywriter: Alberto Orso
Art Buyer: Jorge Chirino
Associate Creative Director: Héctor Fabio Prado
V.P. Creative Director: Emmie Vázquez

"This approach, both creative and strategic, strikes an emotional chord with the Hispanic market and instills a sense of comfort that is both emotional and physical." The copy reads: "Could it be that you want to fly?"

Audience Categories

The scope of an audience can be global, international, national, regional, or local. *General household consumers* are the largest audience. The *business audience* comprises corporate or business organizations. The *trade audience* consists of specific trade groups. The *government audience* includes government officials and employees. *Professionals,* such as physicians, teachers, lawyers, psychologists, and other professionals with advanced degrees, training, or certification, are another category of audience.

2-4

"Our Vaccine Doesn't Fit All Cats Either"

Agency: Colle + McVoy/Minneapolis
Creative Director: Annette Bertelsen
Art Director: Liz Otremba
Copywriter: Jay Walsh
Photographer: Dublin Productions
Client: Pfizer Animal Health
© 2000

Making an analogy to a cat that doesn't fit into a pet carrier, this ad for feline vaccines grabs the viewer's attention with a large, provocative photograph.

2-5a, 2-5b

"Sushi"
"Chocolates"

Agency: Mad Dogs & Englishmen/New York
Creative Director: Guy Seese
Art Director: James Dawson Hollis
Copywriter: Craig Miller
Photographer: Steve Hellerstein
Client: Corcoran Real Estate
© 1992

Using analogies that turn real estate into artful delicacies appeals to the sophisticated consumer.

For example, Colle + McVoy's eye-catching ad for Pfizer is aimed at veterinarians (figure 2-4). And ads for Corcoran Real Estate are aimed at consumers, establishing a very sophisticated, fine spirit for the brand (figures 2-5a, 2-5b). The key audience for the inventive ad below, part of a campaign for Penguin Books, was authors (figure 2-6).

2-6
"Girls" Poster

Agency: Mustoes/London
Creative Director: Alan Morrice and Paul Diver
Art Director: Dean Hunt
Copywriter: Simon Hipwell
Client: Penguin Books

"The obvious approach would have been to develop a trade campaign targeted at authors and agents. However, we believed that this wouldn't give Penguin the step change required. Instead, we decided to create a campaign that looked and felt like a major consumer campaign."

Types of Media

CONVENTIONAL MEDIA

Broadcast

TV

    Major network

    Independent station

    Cable

Radio

    Network

    Local

Print

Magazines

Newspapers

    National

    Statewide

    Local

Direct Mail

Support Media

Outdoor

    Billboards (outdoor boards)

    Transit

    Posters

Ambient (near or at point of purchase)

New Interactive Media

Promotional Web sites

Social cause Web sites

Web films

Web commercials

Banners

Online guerilla or viral marketing

Home-shopping broadcasts

Interactive broadcast entertainment
    programming

Kiosks

CD-ROM

Internet

Intranet

UNCONVENTIONAL MEDIA

Logos on sidewalks

Wild postings (on scaffolding,
    temporary walls, etc.)

Coffee cup sleeves

Metro cards

Stickers

Stampings (sidewalks, walls, surfaces)

Room keys

Doorknob hangers

Taxi ads

Wine corks

Bathroom stalls

Supermarket carts and floors

PREMIUMS

Calendars

Logo clothing

Novelties, such as pens, mugs

OTHER

Point-of-purchase displays

Event sponsorship

Exhibit sponsorship

Site sponsorship

Television sponsorship

Product placement in television
    programs, music videos, films

Types of Ads

Commercial Messages

Commercial advertising sells brands by informing consumers about brands, endearing brands to consumers, promoting brands, and brand building. These types of messages can take the form of single advertisements, campaigns, or brand building in any conventional medium: TV, radio, the Web, print, direct response. They can also be found in unconventional media—that is, guerilla advertising formats. Integrated campaigns employ various media in a coordinated fashion.

Public Service Advertising or Social Advertising

The definition of public service advertising varies from country to country. Here's a general definition: public service advertising is advertising that serves the public interest. According to the Ad Council (www.adcouncil.org): "The objectives of these ads are education and awareness of significant social issues in an effort to change the public's attitudes and behaviors and stimulate positive social change."

PSAs are created by various advertising agencies around the world for a great variety of social causes. Mostly the media consider PSAs a service to the community, and therefore there is no charge by the media to run these advertisements on television, on radio, or in print, though in order to have more control over the media and time placements, some non-profit organizations and government agencies have begun to purchase advertising time and space, in addition to the donated time and space.

Imagine that an ad you created saved a life. Perhaps your ad asked someone to stop a friend from driving while intoxicated. Or perhaps your ad motivated someone to donate blood or food. Public service announcements matter greatly. They promote social responsibility, caring about others, and responsible behavior in terms of the self, others, the family, and society at large. Public service advertisements put creativity to work to benefit society.

Noted author Warren Berger comments:

> They're very important for a number of reasons. Advertising is the only common medium/language now; we all watch different channels and read targeted magazines in a splintered media environment—but the ads cross over and connect with everyone. Therefore when we need to have an important public debate on a social issue, advertising can be a good way to do it.
>
> The problem is, sometimes ads don't do a good, balanced job of educating people on social matters—they're too busy being dramatic and compelling to be fair and balanced. And advertising, by its nature, is sometimes willing to manipulate truth. Still, ads are very important in raising awareness of social issues and problems.
>
> And here's another reason why they're important—PSAs are "the conscience of advertising." It gives ad people a chance to do something they can feel good and proud about. It lets them use their persuasive powers for something more important than selling toilet paper.

Cause Advertising

This is a particular category of public service advertising that is used to raise funds for nonprofit organizations and runs in paid media, sponsored by corporations. What differentiates cause advertising from public service advertising is that its commercial nature is maintained to a degree by its affiliation with a corporation.

Guerilla Advertising

Guerilla advertising (also known as unconventional advertising, stealth marketing, nontraditional advertising, or, when conducted on the Internet, viral marketing) is advertising that "ambushes" the viewer. It appears or is placed in unpaid media—often public spaces where the advertising doesn't belong, such as the sidewalk or on wooden construction site walls.

The Creative Brief

Ideas come from understanding how and why people use a product or service. That's why clients and ad agencies spend so much money on market research and focus groups. For the *Harvard Business Review,* Hadrian's Wall formulated an idea that could demonstrate the benefit of reading engrossing articles in a dynamic business journal (figure 2-7). Not only does the design serve to catch the viewer's attention due to its atypical appearance, but its form and content are completely interdependent. Hadrian's Wall comments: "In focus group after focus group, someone who had never considered the magazine to be 'for them' would become engrossed in an article relevant to them. So how do you convert the people who aren't in focus groups? By making the advertising as intelligent and colorful as the publication itself. In other words, make it a product demonstration on paper. Get people's noses in between the pages, and they'll stay there."

Rich Palatini, senior vice president and associate creative director, Gianettino & Meredith Advertising, explains the how and why of an ad for a ferry company (figure 2-8): "NY Waterway is one of the largest ferry companies in the United States and the leader in the New York metropolitan area. While many perceived it as a necessary transportation commodity, NY Waterway wanted its brand and its growing range of products and services to

2-7

"Compass"

Agency: Hadrian's Wall/Chicago
Creative Directors: Thomas Richie, Kevin Lynch
Art Directors: Thomas Richie, Mollie Wilke
Copywriters: Greg Christensen, Kevin Lynch
Photographer: Dave Jordano
Client: *Harvard Business Review*

"This campaign is built upon the simple belief that if you get people's noses between the pages of *Harvard Business Review,* they tend to stay there."

be more fully understood and appreciated by commuters. The challenge was to convince commuters that NY Waterway ferries were a faster and more pleasant way to get to work."

Market research is usually the first step in the process of developing advertising, though according to Richard Palatini, market research can be an ongoing process in branding. Research might provide a jumping-off point for an ad idea. After market research comes the strategic

WHOEVER SAID "WE'LL CROSS THAT BRIDGE WHEN WE COME TO IT" NEVER COMMUTED TO MANHATTAN.

TAKE THE NY WATERWAY FERRY.
SOMETIMES IT'S BETTER TO BURN YOUR BRIDGES.

Trying to find the cure for the common commute? Check out the NY Waterway Ferry. In less than 8 minutes you'll find yourself in New York City, with free Ny Waterway buses to take you where you need to go throughout midtown and downtown. NY Waterway has frequent departures from multiple locations. Parking is fast and easy... and nothing beats that skyline view. Give us a try. What have you got to lose? Besides the stress of your commute?)

NY WATERWAY®
Take to the water.
1-800-53-FERRY
nywaterway.com

2-8
"Bridge"

Agency: Gianettino & Meredith Advertising/Short Hills
Creative Directors: Rich Palatini/Debby Wolf
Art Director: Rich Palatini
Copywriter: Debbie Wolf
Photographer: Lisa Hermann
Client: NY Waterway

"The strategy was to establish a cultural connection with commuters by engaging them in 'shared thoughts' about how frustrating daily commuting was, and offering them a better alternative."

planning: the overall plan of how to position, market, and advertise a brand or social cause. After that, the creative brief is written, where answers to crucial questions are formulated.

A creative brief is the map of the agency's and client's preparatory mission. Most creative briefs consist of questions and answers aimed at understanding the brand, the objectives of the advertising, the context of the advertising, the audience, and the strategic plan for implementing the objectives.

The answers to the questions are usually based on pre-design research, information about the brand or social cause, and the budget. Most often, a brief is written collaboratively between client and ad agency. The creative brief can be initiated by the client's marketing team, by the ad agency's account team, or by the ad agency's creative director, and may include input from the creative team, strategic planners, the agency's research department, and the agency's media department or related media unit.

Essentially, a creative brief is a strategic plan that both client and agency agree upon and from which the creative team works as a strategic springboard. A thoughtful, clear brief can lead to creative and successful ads.

Sample Creative Brief from The Richards Group/Dallas

The client for this creative brief is Chick-fil-A (figure 2-9).

Why are we advertising? To position the Chick-fil-A chicken sandwich as the best alternative to other fast-food sandwiches and to remind people how much they like them.

Whom are we talking to? Adults, ages eighteen to forty-nine, who are infrequent users or nonusers of Chick-fil-A. They are primarily women, college graduates, and in white-collar jobs. They associate chicken with a healthy lifestyle and believe that quality food is better for you and worth the money.

What do they currently think? "Unless I'm in the mall, I just don't think of a Chick-fil-A. I guess they're pretty good, but I haven't been there in a long time."

What would we like them to think? "I'd rather have a chicken sandwich than a hamburger. And Chick-fil-A makes the best one."

What is the single most persuasive idea we can convey? Every other sandwich is second-rate.

Why should they believe it? Chick-fil-A is simple and wholesome and doesn't take itself too seriously.

Are there any creative guidelines? Outdoor board, 14 × 48.

2-9
Agency: The Richards Group/Dallas
Creative Director: Doug Rucker
Art Director: David Ring
Copywriter: Gail Barlow
Client: Chick-fil-A

This ad uses humor to convey the message "Chick-fil-A is simple and wholesome and doesn't take itself too seriously."

DON'T BE A SALAD TOSSER.

Proper food when you're proper famished.

2-10
"Salad Tosser"
Agency: Mustoes/London
Creative Directors: John Merriman, Chris Herring
Art Director: Mick Brigdale
Copywriter: Kevin Baldwin
Client: Pork Farms Bowyers (Northern Foods)

Case History: Mustoes/London

The London-based agency Mustoes developed a brand campaign for the Pork Farms brand of cold pies and snacks produced by Pork Farms Bowyers (Northern Foods). The campaign would include TV, outdoor, and press (see figure 2-10).

What is the challenge facing the brand? How do you encourage people to continue to eat something that is generally perceived as unhealthy when the mantra of the day is to adopt a healthier lifestyle?

Whose behavior do we need to affect? The general public, especially those who currently tuck into pork pies on a fairly regular basis. Housewives, younger men and women on the go, traveling salespeople, delivery people—people with a busy lifestyle who often have to grab lunch or a snack, and who genuinely enjoy their food. Secondarily, the trade—remind them why Pork Farms is the brand leader and why they should continue to stock their shelves with Pork Farms products.

What is our insight? Despite the health fanatics and the knowledge of what we ought to do, healthier snacks and lunches often don't hit the mark. When you're busy and feeling hungry at lunchtime or even midmorning/midafternoon, you usually crave something that's filling, satisfying, and, yes, usually unhealthy—a salad just doesn't quite fill that hole. A pork pie on the other hand, is filling, is substantial, looks and feels like real food, and leaves you feeling very satisfied when you've eaten one (even if you know it's a bit naughty).

Did we do anything in particular to arrive at this insight? Qualitative research among men and women, who told us that there really wasn't anything quite as filling and fulfilling as a pork pie when you're really hungry. Unlike many sandwiches and other snacks, a pork pie is *real food* that really fills you up.

How do we execute this strategy? The start point is the tagline "Proper food when you're proper famished." Tapping into the male personality of the product and the brand, we created a cheeky male-oriented commercial featuring builders and their lunch boxes. The twist of the commercial was that the majority of the action suggested that the builders were lining up at a urinal, while the reality was that they were unzipping bags containing their lunch. The smallest builder of the group had the most satisfying lunch—a Pork Farms pork pie. This humor tapped into the humor of the time (1998) and was reflected in a series of posters with cheeky headlines poking fun at other foods, as well as challenging consumers as to how well packed their lunch boxes were. The *Sun* even ran a competition based on the contents of people's lunchboxes.

What evidence do we have for success? In spite of the supposed adoption of healthier eating habits, the campaign generated the biggest orders from retailers that Pork Farms has ever had. Unfortunately, the Pork Farms factory burned down, which meant that after the initial burst the campaign was put on hold. Following a rebuild and further investment and new packaging, Pork Farms embarked on a new campaign to relaunch the brand four years later.

Insights and Intuition

Advertising ideas can come from insights into human behavior. In fact, some of the best ad ideas are based on truths about human behavior. When an idea is in accord with reality—true to what's happening out there—then it's more believable and sellable.

"Got milk?" is a great ad idea in part because most people drink milk with something else, not by itself. Said Jeff Goodby, co-chairman and creative director on the Got Milk? campaign, Goodby Silverstein & Partners in San Francisco:

We looked for the truth about milk. We asked people to go without milk for two weeks. "Sure, no problem," they said. They came back and told us how hard it was.

What else goes with cereal? What are you going to do with a fresh-baked chocolate chip cookie?

We arrived at the truth: Milk is never just milk. It is always _____ and milk.

Milk as accompaniment. After that, everything fell into place.[1]

Good ideas are also in touch with the spirit of the age; they reflect the zeitgeist or energy of the time. The visual style of the ads, the tone of the copy, and the actual ad message all speak to people in a contemporary way. How you speak to an audience depends upon the audience.

Ethics

Advertising and ethics can coexist. Certainly, public service advertising helps society and is the advertising profession's greatest contribution to society, one that cannot be denied or overrated. Consumer advertising also can be held to ethical standards. When clients and agency professionals are aware of what is unethical and keep to standards of fair practice and social responsibility, then we can have ethical advertising. There is no exit from social responsibility—everyone is accountable. As John Butler, creative director, Butler, Shine and Stern/Sausalito, reminds us: "We are given a voice, and we have to be responsible in how we use that voice."

What is unethical is almost easier to identify than what is ethical.

Here's an obvious list of don'ts:

Don't use racial, ethnic, gender, age, or religious negative stereotyping.

Don't promote dangerous substances to minors.

Don't degrade or talk down to anyone.

Don't lie or cover up.

Here's an obvious list of do's:

Treat the audience with respect.

Be truthful.

Be responsible.

There are watchdog groups, such as Adbusters, mediawatch-uk, Commercial Alert, the Advertising Standards Authority, and Guerrilla Girls, as well as individual critics such as Jean Kilbourne, whose video "Still Killing Us Softly" is important viewing, and collectives such as Men Organized Against Sexism and Institutionalized Stereotypes (OASIS), which produced the video and slide show "Stale Roles and Tight Buns." The "First Things First Manifesto," originally written in 1964 and updated by Adbusters and six design magazines in 2000, is important to read. AWNY (Advertising Women of New York) aids in ensuring ethical behavior with an award program—The Good, the Bad, and the Ugly—that examines good as well as bad images of women in advertising. Professional groups, such as D&AD in England and the One Club and Art Directors Club in New York, also aid the profession. Of course, there are government agencies that regulate advertising. And consumer advocates and consumers can take the lead against unethical behavior.

All students, novices, and professionals should be aware of criticisms so that advertising can be made more ethical. It's far better to be overly concerned about respecting one's audience and aware of how veiled stereotyped thinking can be than to be unconscious of it.

Notes

1. Used with permission from Jeff Goodby.

part two

What's the Big Idea?

Formulating an Advertising Concept

3

Thinking Critically and Creatively, and Getting Started

Thinking Critically and Creatively

Thinking critically and creatively are two processes you will not learn on the job. Besides your design skills, your ability to think is what will get you hired in the first place, over all the other college grads with portfolios in hand.

With the availability of stock photography, digital photography, computer-generated type, and layout programs, most student work looks pretty slick. What differentiates one student portfolio from another (and one professional portfolio from another, for that matter) are the ideas and the design sensibility. One of the differences between possessing design skills (proficiencies in drawing, imaging, composing, knowledge of software) and having a design sensibility (being perceptive, intuitive, and inquisitive; having flexibility, range, a sensitivity to typographic design, and a willingness to explore) is the power to think creatively. "The most important element in anyone's portfolio is ideas," advised Dan Wieden and David Kennedy at an Art Directors Club, Inc. presentation to students.

Getting Started

There are five basic steps to getting started on an advertising concept.

- *Interpret the problem.* Advertising involves creative problem solving. If your idea is creative and doesn't solve the problem, it's not an effective ad.

- *Understand the creative brief.* A good strategy—as stated in the creative brief—usually leads you right to good ideas. Always stay on strategy.

- *Say it outright.* Don't think in fancy words or pictures first. Whenever I have to write something, I ask myself, "What am I trying to say?" and just write it that way first. Later on, I edit it and punch it up.

- *Know your audience.* What do they think about your brand? Your cause? What do you want them to think?

- *Write your objective.* Write down your goal in one sentence.

The Creative Team

Since the 1960s, the conventional creative team has consisted of an art director and copywriter (writer). Together, the art director and copywriter generate and develop ideas. Then they discuss the specifics of the way the ad will look and what it will say. Eventually, the art director must go design the ad, and the writer writes the main line and body copy. Most often, a creative team reports to either an associate creative director, a creative director, or both. The creative director is the lead or head of a creative team.

There are other ways that agencies form creative teams. Some agencies see other agency members, such as account managers or media people, as critical to a team. Therefore, you can have a team—often called a *brand team*—that comprises an art director, a copywriter, a media person, a strategic person, and maybe even the client.

Other agencies have what are called *project teams,* which include an art director, writer, account director, and strategist or planner. They may or may not work with creative briefs. Part of the purpose of having teams that incorporate more than an art director and writer is to share the responsibility of the agency's product among agency members and help raise the level of commitment and involvement.

I've heard agency heads say that all members of their agencies are creative thinkers, not just the ones who wear the title of art director, writer, or creative director. They say they wouldn't hire anyone who isn't a creative soul, and so anyone in their agencies can be a creative team member, generating ideas and directions for client projects. Clearly, what goes into a team is up to the particular agency and that agency's agenda and philosophy.

A creative team works together, with its members generating ideas together. Every team finds its own way of working best. Some utilize brainstorming techniques, whether traditional ones or their own model.

Brainstorming Technique

There are many ways to brainstorm; here's one.

Put the strategy derived from the creative brief into questions. On individual sheets of paper or cards, write each strategic question and each objective of the creative brief. As team members come up with answers to the questions and ways of achieving the objectives, record all ideas so that all team members can see them.

If the process of idea generation slows or stops, then ask the "What if . . . ?" question. For example, "What if an irritated eye issued an SOS?" If this doesn't generate more thinking, then try the deletion strategy, asking, "What would the world be like without this brand or social organization?" For example, where would people in need turn if there were no food banks? If there were no drum pads, what surfaces would people drum on? If this doesn't spark more thinking, take a break and come back to it in a couple of hours.

After your brainstorming session is over, choose the ideas that you think are most promising. Then start to think of ways to realize them.

Brainstorming Rules of Order

All ideas, from logical to absurd, are encouraged.

Early on, there should be no criticism of ideas.

Generate as many ideas as possible.

Each creative team member should attempt to combine or build on the ideas of the others.

What Makes an Ad

Just like a synergistic reaction between two drugs, where the effect is more than additive, advertising depends upon a synergy of the visual and verbal to communicate with the most power. In other words, the visual/verbal ad equation is: 1 + 1 = 3.

Every successful ad has to have an idea that works successfully with the overarching strategy and brand and manifests itself effectively both visually and verbally.

The Elements of an Ad Explained

An ad, in any visual medium, is almost always a cooperative relationship between words and images. The advertising idea is expressed through the combination of words and images. Working off one another like a great duet, the line and visual are synergistic in each ad of this campaign for Prulink Realty (figures 3-1a, 3-1b).

The main verbal message is called the *line* or *headline*. Most people refer to this line of copy as the headline because in the early days of advertising it usually occupied the top of the page. Today's art directors experiment freely with composition—a line can be positioned anywhere on the page or screen, depending upon your design idea and solution, as in the ad at right for Living Quarters (figure 3-2), where the line is within the photo below the image and the body copy runs up the side of the ad.

3-1a, 3-1b
"Casino"
"Tree"

Agency: Saatchi & Saatchi/Singapore
Executive Creative Director: Sion Scott-Wilson
Art Director: Simon Yeo
Copywriter: Srinath Mogeri
Client: Prulink Realty

The adage "location is everything" is demonstrated by showing how proximity (a pawn shop located next to a casino and a car wash located next to a bird sanctuary) can make your business: "We'll take care of the right place bit."

Put it out of your misery.

Living Quarters at Millenia Plaza grand opening. October 11-13. Stop by. No questions asked.

3-2
"Lake"
Agency: PUSH Advertising/Orlando
Creative Director: John Ludwig
Copywriters: John Ludwig/Gordon Weller
Art Director: Ron Boucher
Photographer: Doug Scaletta
Client: Living Quarters

Disposing of old furniture in a uniquely anthropomorphized way, so that it can be replaced by new furniture, is an attention-grabbing device.

The main visual message is called the *visual* or *image.* Together, the line and visual should communicate and express the advertising message. In fact, in a really good ad, the line and visual, in combination, should have an additive effect, as in BMP DDB's classic ad for Volkswagen (figure 3-3). When the line and visual work off one another, together they have greater meaning. Just like a good comedy team or a musical duet, the sum total of the effect is greater than the mere addition of the separate parts; it is seamless. We call this reaction between visual and line *visual/verbal synergy.* In Buzz Grey's campaign for the Buick Classic, the line and visuals work together to communicate the message of a golf tournament in New York (figures 3-4a, 3-4b).

3-3
"Psychiatrist"
Agency: BMP DDB/London
Client: Volkswagen

If you cover the visual and just read the line, you do not get the full meaning of the ad message, and if you cover the line and look at the visual, you don't get the ad message at all. However, in combination the line and visual yield a greater meaning than either of the parts alone. The composition of this ad was characteristic of the Doyle Dane Bernbach ads for Volkswagen.

Do we drive our mechanics too hard?

For most people, going under a car is the end of their career.

For a Volkswagen mechanic, it's just the beginning.

He starts with the humble spark plug.

And works his way up to the digifant electronic system.

He takes every part apart. And puts it back together again.

Over and over and over again.

Until he can show us where every bolt, every washer and every nut goes.

What every part does.

And how to service every single one of them.

Then we really turn the screws on him.

Because, when he's not working on a Volkswagen, Volkswagen are working on him.

At one of our training schools.

There he spends seven hours a day studying the mechanics of the car.

So, by the end of his apprenticeship, he knows his Volkswagen bumper to bumper and sill to sill.

All this is part of the quaint Volkswagen notion that the service has to be as good as the car itself.

It's the kind of madness that makes us make our cars the way we do.

The sanest things on wheels.

3-4a, 3-4b
"Divot"
Agency: Buzz Grey (Grey Worldwide/NY)
Art Director: Mark Catalina
Creative Director: Robert Skollar
Copywriter: Brian Fallon
Client: The Buick Classic
© 2002

Merging the worlds of golf and New York City creates visual twists.

The usual elements of a print ad are:

Line (headline): main verbal message

Visual: main visual message

Body copy: the text of the ad (supports main message)

Product shot: a photograph or illustration of the product or packaging

Tagline: claim (also called *slogan, end line,* and *strap line*), which embodies the ad strategy

Sign-off: this includes the product shot and claim

Three of the usual elements in a print ad are in Rethink's visually inviting campaign for Clover Leaf (figure 3-5). The visual is the photograph cleverly depicting the benefit of this brand of tuna—chili peppers on fish hooks. The line sits at the bottom of the ad: "Tuna with chili in it." In the bottom right-hand corner of each ad is the product shot. The body copy in Hunt Adkins' ad for Dublin Productions makes for entertaining reading (figure 3-6); the line is at the top of the page, with a main visual in the center of the page that is surrounded by body copy and smaller inset photographs. The logo is at the bottom right-hand corner.

3-5
"Chili"
Agency: Rethink Advertising/Vancouver
Art Director/Designer: Mark Hesse
Copywriter: Rob Tarry
Photographer: Philip Rostrom
Client: Cloverleaf

This tempting visual explains the product.

3-6
"Sadistic Willie"
Agency: Hunt Adkins/Minneapolis
Creative Director/Copywriter: Doug Adkins
Associate Creative Director/Art Director: Steve Mitchell
Client: Dublin Productions

Satire evokes the spirit of the Dublin Productions brand in this ad.

"Come inside" is the tagline for an ad for Borders (figure 3-7), where we are privy to the favorite books, music, and videos of a Little Leaguer. Serving as both line and body copy, Michael's list of favorites resides in the upper right-hand corner, running over the background in the photograph; Michael, our Little Leaguer, is the main visual.

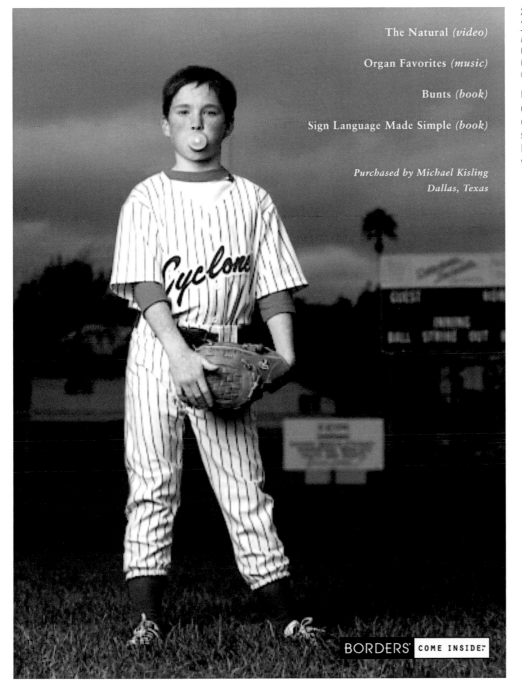

The Natural *(video)*

Organ Favorites *(music)*

Bunts *(book)*

Sign Language Made Simple *(book)*

Purchased by Michael Kisling
Dallas, Texas

BORDERS® COME INSIDE™

3-7
"Little League"
Agency: Butler, Shine & Stern/Sausalito
Creative Team: Hilary Wolfe, Ryan Ebner
Client: Borders
© 2003 Butler, Shine, & Stern

Using a Little League player as a customer—a type of endorsement or spokesperson—creates a relaxed spirit while demonstrating that Borders carries books, music, and videos.

Ingredients That Go into an Ad

Creative Strategy

The *creative strategy* is the statement outlining the guiding principles—a creative platform—for the advertising assignment. This usually is clearly delineated in the *creative brief* or *creative work plan*. The strategy guides the creative director and her creative teams—the art directors and copywriters—who will be formulating the ideas and advertising solutions in the form of single ads or ad campaigns. All ads produced should be in agreement with the strategy. (See more on the creative brief in Chapter 2.)

If you think of yourself as a general in the armed forces, then the strategy is your tactical scheme, your overarching approach to advertising a brand or social cause. It's your plan for action.

Idea

Each ad depends upon a specific idea. The *idea,* which is also called a *concept,* is the underlying unique creative thought; it is the thinking behind an ad or an ad campaign that distinguishes a brand or social cause; communicates a message about the brand or social cause; brands it in the mind of the consumer; and motivates the consumer to purchase the product, try the service, or act on behalf of the social cause or in response to the social cause's message.

An advertising idea is a formulated thought that communicates meaning and promotes action. The ad idea comes as a result of reflecting on the research, strategy, audience, advantages of the client's brand or social cause, intuition, feeling, and visualization.

Working from the creative strategy, the creative team formulates specific ideas that will follow through on the plan. "The big idea has been described as 'that flash of insight that synthesizes the purpose of strategy, joins the product benefit with consumer desire in a fresh, involving way, brings the subject to life, and makes the reader or audience stop, look, and listen.'"[1]

Benefit

When a consumer looks at an ad, the underlying question is: *What's in it for me?* Specifically, the consumer asks: *What will I gain if I buy this brand? What advantage does this brand offer? How will this product or service meet my needs? Why should I donate to this social cause?*

A *benefit* is the specific gain or advantage your ad is claiming. A benefit can be a useful aid, a provided service, a favorable impression or effect, an emotional connection, a premium—anything that the consumer perceives as an advantage over the competition. The way in which one sells or promotes the benefit is called the *appeal*—the link between the audience and the brand or social cause. How the brand appeals to the audience and satisfies their needs or desires can be thought of in functional or emotional terms. At times, ads utilize both functional and emotional benefits and appeals, as in an ad for *Golf & Travel* magazine (figure 3-8) in which the visual and line communicate the idea that this magazine is for people who are passionate about both golf and travel.

Functional Benefits

Functional benefits are the practical, useful, or helpful characteristics of a product or service that aid in setting a brand apart from the competition, such as nutrition, economy, dependability, durability, or handiness. These are tangible benefits. For example, a meal replacement bar may have the benefit of extra protein, or a housecleaning service may claim the benefit of bonded workers. The functional benefit of Visine is that it gets the red out of the whites of one's eyes (figure 3-9). Slim-Fast's functional benefit is that one can lose weight quickly (figure 3-10). By cleverly combining parts of a car or truck with purchased items, GM ads remind us that a percentage of every purchase on a GM-branded credit card goes toward the purchase of a GM car or truck (figures 3-11a, 3-11b). With interesting visuals, an ad for the Lunch Garden restaurant communicates the benefit of a yummy lunch for a reasonable price (figure 3-12). Appealing to one's sense of humor, a fun ad for Post-it Notes acts as a reminder (figure 3-13).

Two Passions, One Magazine **GOLF&TRAVEL** To advertise call: **407.345.5514**

3-8
"Martini"
Agency: PUSH Advertising/Orlando
Creative Directors: John Ludwig, Julio Lima
Copywriters: Rich Wahl, John Ludwig
Art Directors: Ron Boucher, Julio Lima
Photographer: Vincent Dente
Client: *Golf & Travel*

The visual conjures a sense of adventure, appealing to the emotions; the functional benefit is the combination of subjects covered by the periodical.

3-9
"SOS"
Agency: Taxi/Toronto
Client: Visine

Using the red veins in the eye to issue a distress call (SOS), this ad explains the benefits of Visine.

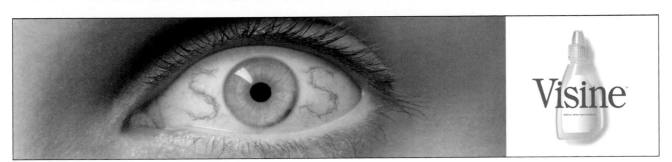

3-10
"Broken Cake"

Agency: Grey Worldwide/Toronto
Creative Director: Marc Stoiber
Art Director: Shelley Weinreb
Copywriter: Shawn McClenny
Photographer: Philip Rostron
Client: Unilever Canada

This ad uses humor and the idea that brides need to fit into their wedding dresses quickly to promote the product, Slim-Fast.

3-11a, 3-11b
"Golf Clubs"
"Swingset"

Agency: Mullen/Wenham, MA
Chief Creative Officer: Edward Boches
Art Director: Michael Ancevic
Copywriter: Stephen Mietelski
Photographers: Stuart Hall, Bruce Peterson
Client: GM Credit Card
© Mullen

The tagline in this campaign rounds out the communication, ensuring that we understand the functional benefit of the GM credit card while appealing to the emotions with an anticipatory feeling.

Spaghetti bollognese for 175 F

LUNCH GARDEN *restaurant*
GOOD COOKING, THE WAY YOU LIKE IT

3-12
"Spaghetti"
Agency: Euro RSCG Brussels
Creative Director: Veronique Mermous Hermans
Art Director: Minou van de Kerckhove
Copywriter: Frederik Dewispelaire
Photographer: Hans Kroeskamp
Client: Lunch Garden
© 1998

Surprising visuals catch the viewers' attention so that they'll get the message about the lunch specials.

Post-it®. Reminds you of what you already forgot. **Post-it** Notes

3-13
Post-it Notes
Agency: Grey Brasil
Creative Director: Fernando Luna
Art Director: Ulisses Agneli
Copywriter: Fulvio Oriola
Photographer: Fernando Moussan
Client: 3M
© 3M

Emotional Benefits

Emotional benefits are not based on a tangible characteristic of a product or service; they are based on passions, responses, feelings, and reactions, and are subjectively experienced. People's motives for consumption might be based on meeting emotional needs, such as gaining self-esteem or finding pleasure, relieving guilt or fear, or fulfilling a wish. For example, anti-acne medication that diminishes scarring may improve self-esteem, or purchasing comprehensive homeowner's insurance may alleviate fear. As one campaign shows, purchasing a Vespa may be just what you need (figures 3-14a, 3-14b). An ad for Oxfam appeals to both our intellect and emotions, offering the emotional benefit of helping others (figure 3-15). Rider After-Sport Footwear allows the consumer a "time to slide," appealing to our sense that we deserve a break after exerting competitive energy (figure 3-16).

3-14a, 3-14b
"Soul Patch"
"Friends Move"

Agency: McClain Finlon/Denver
Creative Directors: Gregg Bergan, Jeff Martin
Art Director: Dan Buchmeier
Copywriter: Eric Liebhauser
Photographer: Jeff Martin
Client: Vespa

The lines humorously explain the emotional benefits of buying a Vespa, while the cropped close-ups illuminate the beauty of the product design.

3-15
"Make Trade Fair"

Agency: KesselsKramer/Amsterdam
Art Director: Erik Kessels
Copywriters: Dave Bell, Lorenzo de Rita
Photographer: Hans van der Meer
Client: Oxfam International

"Oxfam is calling on world leaders to put an end to a trading system that allows rich countries to profit at the expense of the world's poorest people."

3-16
"Runner"

Agency: PUSH Advertising/Orlando
Creative Director: John Ludwig
Copywriter: Gordon Weller
Art Director: Ron Boucher
Photographer: Doug Scaletta
Client: Rider Sandals

The three-dimensional illusion of the photograph hanging from the locker heightens the visual impact.

3-17a, 3-17b
"Tickets"
"Keys"
Agency: Sawyer Riley Compton/Atlanta
Web site: www.brandstorytellers.com
Creative Director: Bart Cleveland
Associate Creative Director/Copywriter:
Al Jackson
Art Director: Laura Hauseman
Photographer: Parish Kohanim
Client: Elliott City Infiniti
© 2002

Supports

Supports are reasons to believe the benefits you're asserting. For example, if you're claiming that a moisturizer makes skin glow, then the support would be the key ingredient in the moisturizer, such as seaweed extract or vitamin E. In essence, a support backs up your claim. A series of engaging ads for the Q45 Infiniti supports the claim of more horsepower in a variety of ways (figures 3-17a, 3-17b). An inventive ad for Canon provides detailed explanations of why you get the claimed benefits (figure 3-18); for example, it asserts that the Canon is adaptable, and supports the benefit claim with an explanation stating that it is compatible with over fifty EF lenses.

In this campaign, the visuals support the claim, "The Q45. Now with more horsepower," as well as invite the viewer to interact a bit. "Tickets" depicts two toll receipts from the same day—one from the Massachusetts Tollway Authority and the other from the Golden Gate Bridge.

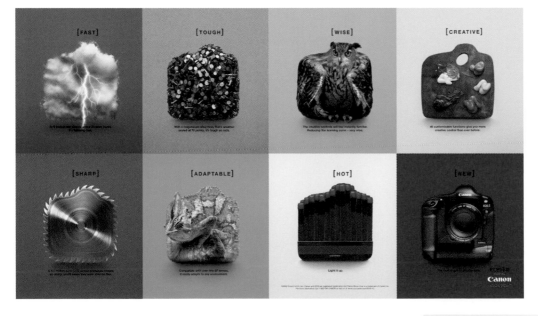

3-18
"Adaptations"
Agency: Grey Global Group/New York
Client: Canon USA

If you're going to tout benefits, showing them as fascinating visuals invites a much wider audience.

What an Ad Has to Do

Get attention

Keep the viewer's attention

Be ethical

Be relevant

Serve as a call to action

Design, Execution, and Media

Your design is the visible representation of your ad idea or concept. Regardless of the medium or format—print for magazines or newspapers, direct mail, poster, billboard, TV, Web, kiosk, guerilla advertising—designing an ad is key to successful communication. The *design* of an ad is the arrangement of the ad's parts into a composition that has graphic impact and communicates to a mass audience.

In print, a design usually includes the line, visual, body copy, and sign-off. At times, one or more of these elements may not be included. There are times when an ad doesn't need body copy—for example, an ad for chewing gum doesn't really need to explain much more than what is communicated through the line and visual. Or if the main visual of an ad is the product, then there is no need for a product shot.

Regardless of medium, you can have a good idea with a poor execution. In print, your execution determines how well your design communicates your idea. Your choices of type, arrangement, style, and imagery may all aid or detract from message communication. How well your words and visual combine to communicate your message is paramount. If you analyze the quality of the photography, the font choices, the visual style, and the tone of the copy in Butler, Shine & Stern's ad for Garageband.com, you'll see how appropriate all the creative decisions are for the target audience (figure 3-19).

How do you make sure someone notices your outdoor board? How about hanging a chair lift from it (figure 3-20), as did Cultivator Advertising & Design for Keystone Resort? Cultivator also created another surprising concept for Colorado's Wildlands—"a hand-charred poster campaign hung across the state to heighten awareness for Colorado's drought" (figure 3-21).

3-19
"Nirvana"
Agency: Butler, Shine & Stern/Sausalito
Creative Team: Jason Stanfield/Ryan Ebner
Client: Garageband.com
© 2003 Butler, Shine & Stern

A photo of a garage perfectly illustrates the idea of the start of a successful band. Garageband.com is the Web site for Garageband Records, a new record label that signs bands based on reviews from music lovers.

3-20
Keystone Resort Outdoor Board
Agency: Cultivator Advertising & Design/Boulder
Creative Directors: Tim Abare, Chris Beatty
Art Director: Chris Beatty
Copywriter: Tim Abare
Sculptor: David Bellamy
Client: Keystone Resort

3-21
Colorado Wildlands Drought Awareness Outdoor Board
Agency: Cultivator Advertising & Design/Boulder
Creative Directors: Tim Abare, Chris Beatty
Art Directors: Chris Beatty, August Sandberg
Copywriter: Tim Abare
Client: Colorado Wildlands

The quality of your visual—the quality of the photograph (clear versus grainy), the quality of the typography (appropriateness of font, kerning, interline spacing, readability, legibility), color choices (color can add to legibility and appropriateness), and (on the Web) user-friendliness—can contribute to or detract from successful communication.

Critique Guide

Before you let anyone else see your work, critique it yourself. Here's a helpful guide.

- *Goal fulfillment.* Did you achieve your goals or did you go off strategy?

- *Appropriate solution.* Is your idea appropriate for your client's brand, context, and audience?

- *Appropriate execution.* Is your execution, both design and tone of copy, appropriate for your client's brand, for the context, and for the audience?

- *Communication.* Is your message clear? Concise? Can necessary information be easily gleaned? Did you communicate a functional or emotional benefit?

- *Interest.* Is there an interesting message? Is there a gripping and distinctive visual style?

Critique Method

The following critique method is that used by Sal DeVito, cofounder and creative director of DeVito/Verdi in New York. When I studied advertising under DeVito at the School of Visual Arts, New York, he employed a critique methodology of teaching that greatly clarified things for me. DeVito has said, "In the advertising class I teach, I've created a list of critiques that go with the types of predictable ads students create, which I paste up on the wall. . . . Most ads can be placed under one of these critiques. And every now and then you get a good one that doesn't go with any of these critiques."[2]

When you use these categories, be brutally honest. If your final ad falls into one of these categories, rethink and redo.

Sounds like advertising

Too damn cute

Sounds like bullshit

I've heard it before

Dull

Good idea but needs a stronger execution

Notes

1. John O'Toole, *The Trouble with Advertising: A View from the Inside,* 2nd ed. (New York: Times Books, 1985), p. 63.

2. Sal DeVito, "La Vida DeVito," *One: A Magazine*, vol. 6, no. 2 (2002), p. 8.

chapter 4

The Big Idea

Points of Departure:
Where Do Big Ideas Come From?

Every advertising creative professional talks and dreams of "the big idea." The idea is the unique thinking behind an ad or an ad campaign, usually based on an emotional or functional benefit, or on brand spirit or style. The idea distinguishes a brand, endears it to the consumer, and motivates the consumer to run out and buy the brand or act on behalf of a social cause.

When trying to generate an idea, you have to start somewhere. Here are a few springboards to ideation. Remember, these are catalysts.

Visual Analogy

Let's say you're advertising personal computers, and the brand and advertising strategy positions your brand as the fastest in a price category. What type of argument most effectively convinces someone that your computer brand is fastest? If you simply stated your argument, the consumer would have to take your word for it. (Saying something outright usually isn't a very interesting approach.) A demonstration might work. Or you could use a visual analogy. Showing a shooting star moving at the speed of light just might get across to me how much faster your computer processes information than the competition.

A visual analogy is a comparison based on similarities or parallel qualities. For example, a motorcycle and a jet are both types of transportation, and we may infer that they are parallel in their ability to rapidly accelerate. We use visual analogies "in order to *clarify*, to make it easier to understand," says Dr. Richard Nochimson, professor of English at Yeshiva University. Analogies tend to be more memorable as well, as Mullen's witty ads for Boeri helmets illustrate (figures 4-1a, 4-1b). Saatchi & Saatchi's "Button" ad shows the unique benefits of a Sony product via analogy (figure 4-2).

4-1a, 4-1b
"Bunnies"
"Worm"

Agency: Mullen/Wenham, MA
Chief Creative Officer: Edward Boches
Art Director: Mary Rich
Copywriter: Stephen Mietelski
Photographer: Craig Orsinni
Client: Boeri Helmets

Humorous analogies show a clever chocolate bunny and a worm, who protect their respective skulls, reminding us: "Remember to ski and snowboard responsibly."

4-2
"Button"

Agency: Saatchi & Saatchi/Madrid
Executive Creative Director: César Garcia
Creative Directors: Miguel Roig, Oksy
Art Director: Amabel Minchan
Copywriter: José Luis Alberola
Photographers: Nahuel Berger, Gonzalo Puertas
Client: Sony España
© December 2000

The unique feature of programming with only one button is visually explained by the analogy of a shirt with a one-button closure.

Visual Metaphor

"'You're a tiger!' she murmured in his ear." In this sentence, replacing *man* with *tiger* suggests virility. In advertising, everything from the cliché of a dewy rose to designate moisture-rich skin to the indelicacy of a toilet bowl to suggest foul breath is employed. In ads by TBWA/Brazil for wireless Internet access, metaphors express the idea that other brands are slow and complicated (figures 4-3a, 4-3b).

When you use one thing to identify another, that's a metaphor; for example, a fire is a metaphor for hot sauce. Substituting one kind of object for another suggests a likeness or similarity between them. In language, a comparison between things is a simile—for example, "My love is like a rose." A metaphor would read "My love is a rose." To call attention to the plight of children with asthma, a PSA uses a simile to describe and communicate to others the extreme struggle children with asthma experience in trying to breathe (figure 4-4).

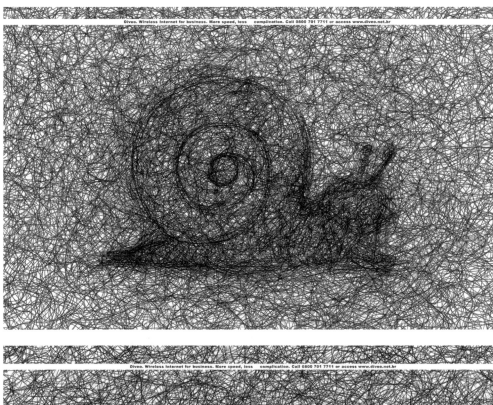

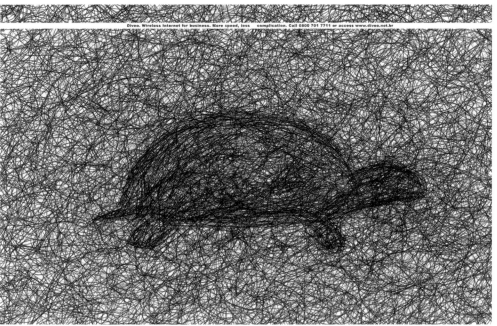

4-3a, 4-3b
"Rabiscos"
Agency: TBWA/Brazil
Creative Director: João Linneu de Paula
Illustrator: Erevan Chakarian
Client: Diveo Wireless Internet
© 2001/2002, TBWA\Worldwide

These metaphors for slowness are linearly depicted to express complication. The copy reads: "Diveo Wireless Internet for business. More speed. Less complication."

Metaphors have the potential to transcend the commonplace, yet be immediately understood, as shown in the motivational ads at right (figures 4-5a, 4-5b). Visual metaphors may seduce the audience into looking at an ad. By contrast, usually, when the product itself is the "hero" and is prominently featured as the main visual in a conventional manner, the ad is not subtle or seductive. Instead it shouts, "I'm trying to sell something! Beware the sales

4-4
Agency: The Kaplan Thaler Group, Ltd.
CEO/Chief Creative Officer: Linda Kaplan Thaler
Creative Directors: Jack Cardone, Michael Grieco
Art Director: Marco Cignini
Client: Childhood Asthma, Environmental Protection Agency, and the Ad Council

Using a simile written by a child suffering from asthma heightens the emotional level of the communication, in hopes of inspiring the audience.

"I FEEL LIKE A FISH WITH NO WATER."

–JACOB, AGE 5
DESCRIBING ASTHMA

You know how to react to their asthma attacks. Here's how to prevent them.
1-866-NO-ATTACKS | EVEN ONE ATTACK IS ONE TOO MANY.
For more information log onto www.noattacks.org or call your doctor.

♻EPA

pitch!" Metaphors can serve another purpose: they can act as a more attractive representation of an idea when the actual product or service might be off-putting.

Visual metaphors can invite the reader to work a little bit, to interact with the ad; the reader is engaged by thinking. If the visual metaphor is interesting, on strategy, and accessible (but not clichéd), the reader is more likely to notice the ad, be engaged, and interact.

4-5a, 4-5b
"Rope"
"Hand"
Agency: Loeffler Ketchum Mountjoy/Charlotte
Creative Director: Jim Mountjoy
Art Director: Doug Pedersen
Copywriter: Curtis Smith
Photographer: Jim Arndt
Client: Outward Bound

Combining the use of metaphors with a natural look makes for an inspiring message.

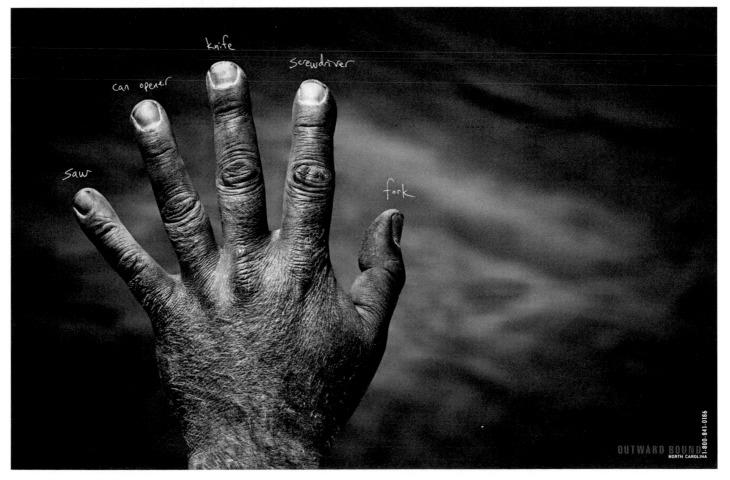

Life Experience

Entertainers such as Bill Cosby, Ellen DeGeneres, Paul Reiser, Ray Romano, and Jerry Seinfeld base their observational comedy on little everyday occurrences—ones that happen right under our noses. We relate to their humor because we can remember similar experiences. These are the little events and moments that make up an individual life—the disappointment over a fallen ice cream cone, wanting more than one bag of peanuts on an airplane, filling in a sentence for your spouse, waiting on line to get a table at a restaurant.

Drawing upon life experience may be one of the richest techniques for finding ideas. There is nothing funnier or more interesting than the actual way people do what they do. Ideas can be based on the tiniest things we do: how we eat a sandwich cookie, how we tug at our underwear, how people will hold out for things, how we squirt mustard. Paul Renner, of Wieden + Kennedy/New York, bases many of his ideas on his own life experience as well as his observations of others (see the foreword). A campaign for Ayotte custom drums amusingly illustrates what people will do in the absence of something they need or really desire (figures 4-6a, 4-6b).

Musing on anything from relationships to basketball may generate an idea. In the process of examining how we interact, function, and behave in various situations, you may find a way to sell a brand or promote awareness for a social cause. Being an ardent observer of human behavior, animal behavior, interpersonal dynamics, and other life mysteries can definitely yield ideas to which people might relate. Basing ideas on personal life experience or observing others can help make your ads relevant to others' lives.

In advertising, when you draw upon common experiences—funny, sad, bittersweet— people usually relate. People should react: "Yep, that's how it is!" That's exactly what Colle + McVoy's PSAs do for the League of Women Voters "Vote" campaign (figures 4-7a, 4-7b);

4-6a, 4-6b
"Yellow Pages"
"Mouse Pad"

Agency: Rethink Advertising/Vancouver
Art Director: Ian Grais
Copywriters: Chris Staples/Andy Linardatos
Photographer: Hans Sipma
Studio Artist/Typographer: Brent Mulligan
Client: Ayotte

These ads play on the idea of people who were holding out for this brand—drumming on anything and everything. Photographing the yellow pages and mouse pad in what look like actual living and working spaces adds to the sense that this is someone's life experience.

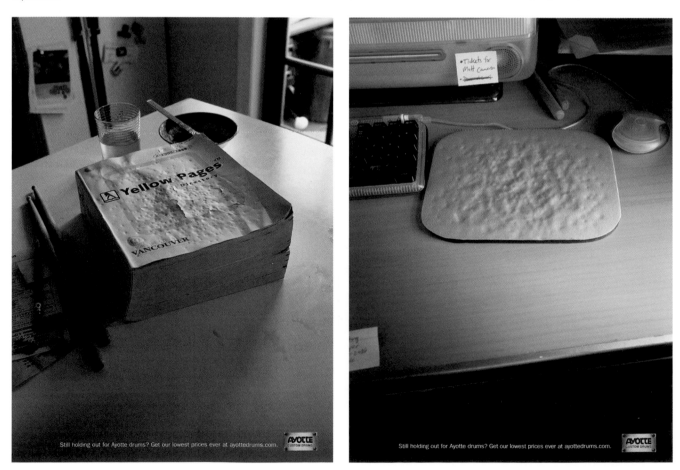

by relating to its audience—picking up on the choices people make every day—this campaign successfully got young voters out in record numbers in Minnesota. An ad can make an experience a communal event, making us feel that we've all participated. Their reality is our reality, and we feel a kinship with the brand or cause being advertised.

Eccentric Points of View

Looking at things—at life—from odd angles, both literally and conceptually, can be a great point of departure for ideation.

Look at things from different perspectives:
Below
Above
Inside
Weird angles
A bug's-eye view
A giraffe's perspective

Look at things through:
Water
Fog
Frosted or tinted glass
Smoke

Look at things as if you were:
A fly, with compound eyes
An alien from another planet
A child
A one-thousand-year-old person

Look at things as if you:
Had a partial view
Were looking from behind a ceiling fan
Had multiple simultaneous vantage points

Using an odd angle adds to the sense of excitement experienced in training for aerobatic flight (figure 4-8).

4-7a, 4-7b
"Fan"
"Pizza"
Agency: Colle + McVoy/Minneapolis
Creative Director: John Jarvis
Art Director: Liz Otremba
Copywriters: Eric Husband, Dave Keepper
Photographer: Curtis Johnson
Client: League of Women Voters

"This campaign sought to compel young and first-time voters with the argument that an election was yet another opportunity to express their opinion—something every young person is prone to do."

4-8
Agency: Hunt Adkins/Minneapolis
Creative Director/Copywriter: Doug Adkins
Art Directors: Mike Fetrow/Mike Murray
Client: Aerobatic Flight Program

Using odd angles might fascinate consumers who are engaged by the extreme nature of aerobatic flight training.

The Problem Is the Solution

At times there are products with features that may be perceived as disadvantageous. For example, in the 1960s, when Volkswagen Beetles appeared on the American market, small (and atypically shaped) cars were perceived as a negative characteristic. Leading American brands were large, graceful, and grand. The now-famous ads created by Bill Bernbach and his creative team at Doyle Dane Bernbach changed our thinking about car size by creatively convincing us to "think small" (figure 4-9). Small was cooler. Small was more modern. You take what is perceived as a negative and turn it into a positive—so much that others may have to follow your lead. People pick up on the difference and start viewing the leading brand's style or qualities as obsolete or somewhat negative.

When Avis's advertising proclaimed, "We try harder," acknowledging that they were the number two car rental company, they became the little engine that could. Bernbach used a circumstantial situation—Avis's position behind Hertz, number one in the car rental category—to an advantage. Avis rentals greatly increased. For years, in various ad approaches, Listerine's medicine-like taste has been turned into a positive attribute. The ads claim its taste is part and parcel of Listerine's efficacy in killing germs.

A Darned Good Reason

When you give the consumer a reasonable rationale, the consumer's reaction might be, "That makes sense! I should use *that* brand because of that particular reason."

Providing a rationale for a functional benefit can turn consumers into believers. For example, keeping your body parts is a good reason to get checkups or conduct breast or testicular self-examinations, as seen in messages from the Canadian Cancer Society (figures 4-10a, 4-10b). PSAs often offer us good reasons to enlist certain behaviors and stop others.

This point of departure is used for specific brands as well as for commodities, such as meat, plastic, and oranges. For example, plastics manufacturers, in their TV spots, make a case for the functional benefits plastic offers, listing the many advantageous uses of plastic. These spots counter the criticism of plastic by environmental advocates. In everyday life, we come up against all kinds of obstacles that many products, services, and organizations help us overcome. Dishwashers clean our dishes. Sunblocks protect skin. Food banks collect food and distribute it to the needy. There are actual reasons to use products or services or aid causes, and that is what this orientation banks on. You're giving the consumer indisputable reasons to need *your* client's brand, to support *your* client's cause. Elucidation can take various forms, as shown in an unusually teasing ad campaign for Britart.com by Mother, a London agency (figures 4-11a and 4-11b).

4-9
"Think Small"
1960
Agency: DDB/New York
Creative Director: Bill Bernbach
Client: Volkswagen

DDB's visual style set a new creative standard in the 1960s.

What's worse than getting kicked in the balls?

Getting kicked in the ball.

Every guy in class has already checked them out.

You should too.

4-10a, 4-10b
"Testicle"
"Breasts"
Agency: Rethink Advertising/Vancouver
Art Director: Martin Kann
Copywriter: Andy Linardatos
Photographer: Robert Kenney
Studio Artist/Typographer: Jonathan Cesar
Client: Canadian Cancer Society

Drives home the point about the necessity of checkups, but does it with humor. PSAs often offer us good reasons or rationales to enlist certain behaviors.

Here are some other good reasons made famous in advertising:

- *When you can't brush, chew Wrigley's Extra sugar-free gum.* You just ate, and brushing your teeth is impossible, but you want fresh breath and clean teeth, so chew Extra instead. That's a real-life problem with a proposed solution—and a darned good reason to chew Extra (see figure 8-2).

- *You deserve a break today.* The ad claim is offering a practical suggestion, a reason to believe it's okay to view McDonald's as a dinner restaurant alternative, and giving you permission to make life somewhat easier for yourself. It's a good argument based on the reality of a working parent.

- *It's abundantly clear that you need roadside assistance—it's 53,000 steps to the next city, or you might have to use your kid's roller skates to get back to town for assistance.* Now there's an incentive to subscribe to membership with the BCAA (figures 4-12a, 4-12b).

- *Kids.* Kids are a good reason to make sure you have the multipurpose cleanser OxiClean in the house, as it works for all types of stains (figure 4-13).

4-11a, 4-11b
"Bridge"
"Junction"
Agency: Mother/London
Client: Britart.com
© January 2000 Mother/London

These tongue-in-cheek ads communicate a very good reason to buy from Britart.com—it sells art you can actually buy!

4-12a, 4-12b
"53,000 Steps"
"Key"

Agency: Rethink Advertising/Vancouver
Art Directors: Ian Grais, Andrew Samuel
Copywriter: Ian Grais
Photographer: Dave Robertson
Studio Artist/Typographer: Brent Mulligan
Client: BCAA

Both ads elucidate the need for membership in BCAA.

4-13
"Sleeve"

Agency: McClain Finlon/Denver
Creative Directors: Gregg Bergan, Jeff Martin
Art Director: Jeff Martin
Copywriter: Gregg Bergan
Client: Orange Glo International

OxiClean's claim "Millions believe for a reason" encapsulates the strategy: that this cleanser works well.

Comparison

Comparing your current boyfriend to your former boyfriend can get you into hot water. Comparisons can be mean-spirited and often uninteresting. For example, at the end of the twentieth century we witnessed fast-food chain wars (McDonald's fried burgers versus Burger King's broiled burgers) and cola wars (Coke versus Pepsi).

Any way you look at it, taste is a personal thing. Ask yourself why you prefer one flavor to another. Comparing foods or beverages based on taste is not a strong premise.

On the other hand, comparing a product or service to something different from it—a feeling, a sensation, another type of experience—can be a strong premise; it has the potential to be extremely effective and memorable. We associate the product with the desirable experience. Comparing a dated old photo of a location to a current image of the same spot, a campaign by Eisner Communications makes the point that the Nature Conservancy is preserving precious places around the world (figures 4-14a, 4-14b).

This point of departure is similar to an analogy, but it speaks more to how something might feel or taste. If I bite into a York peppermint pattie, I'll feel the sensation of skiing down a snowy mountain or of standing under a cool waterfall. I get an added-value experience! An ad for Daffy's says, "If I buy my clothes at Daffy's, then I'm getting the same designer clothing as in retail stores but saving a lot of money," but by using a price comparison, it says it humorously and gets our attention (figure 4-15).

4-15
Agency: DeVito/Verdi/New York
Client: Daffy's

Using sharp wit, these well-known comparative ads for Daffy's turn the functional benefit of buying at a discount retailer into classic comedy.

THE SUGGESTED RETAIL PRICE OF THIS SHIRT IS $125. WE HAVE A SUGGESTION FOR WHOEVER SUGGESTED IT.

Designer clothes 40-75% off, every day. New York City, Manhasset, L.I. & New Jersey.

DAFFY'S
CLOTHES THAT WILL MAKE YOU, NOT BREAK YOU.

4-14a, 4-14b
"Mountain Lake"
"Rain Forest"
Agency: Eisner Communications/Baltimore
Executive Creative Director: Steve Etzine
Associate Creative Director: Mark Rosica
Photographers: Alan St. John, Andy Drumm
Client: The Nature Conservancy
© April 2000

The nuances of the execution make this comparison resonate.

Exaggeration

Ketchup so good, you bite the plate where the ketchup was sitting. A handbag so beautiful, a thief steals the bag and throws the valuable contents away. A car so sturdy, even a monster truck can't crush it.

Making an overstatement or enlarging the truth beyond bounds can express just how terrific/tasty/fast/creamy/rich/low-calorie/easy-to-use/edgy a product is. Overemphasizing a product's quality drives home a selling point quickly. The Best Behavior brand of designer handbags is so desirable that a thief wouldn't even want the contents of the handbag; she'd take the handbag and throw the contents away (figures 4-16a, 4-16b). Of course, the exaggeration has to be understood as an exaggeration. Reversing our expectation, Heinz ads suggest that their ketchup is so good, we'd want more ketchup than main course (figure 4-17). Using exaggeration to make a "so good that . . ." point can be comical and unforgettable, as in an ad for Optique by The Richards Group (figure 4-18). As shown in a series of clever ads for Volkswagen (figures 4-19, 4-20), the exaggeration must be so extreme that we don't believe the actual events depicted in the ads, but we get the point: this product is so good that . . .

This point of departure can be used in so many different ways that it's almost inexhaustible.

4-16a, 4-16b
"Stolen Handbag I"
"Stolen Handbag II"

Agency: Leo Burnett/Denmark
Creative Director: Charlie Fisher
Art Director: Nete Borup
Copywriter: Thomas Fabricius
Client: Best Behavior
© February 2001

These handbags are so desireable that thieves stole the handbags instead of the contents.

4-17
Agency: Leo Burnett/Paris
Creative Directors: Christophe Coffre, Nicolas Taubes
Art Director: Pascal Hirsch
Copywriters: Axel Orliac, Laurent Dravet
Photographer: Frank Goldbrown
Client: Heinz Ketchup

This ad suggests that one would rather eat a plateful of ketchup than a spare main course, seen here in a clever reversal of quantities.

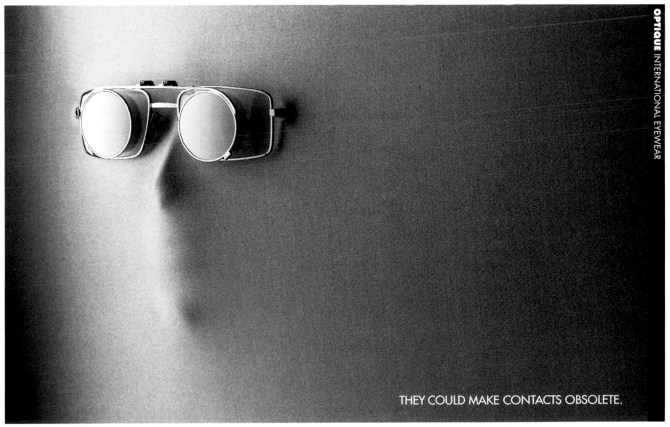

4-18
Agency: The Richards Group/Dallas
Creative Director: Todd Tilford
Art Director: Brian Burlison
Photographer: Robb Debenport
Client: Optique

The tough new Polo. (VW)

4-19
"Big Truck"
Agency: BMP DDB/London
Photographer: Gary Simpson
Agent: Vue
Client: Volkswagen New Polo

Exaggeration—so tough that a monster truck can't squash it.

Polo L. £8,240 (VW)

Surprisingly ordinary prices (VW)

4-20
"Wedding"
Agency: BMP DDB/London
Photographer: Paul Reas
Agent: John Wyatt Clarke
Client: Volkswagen

VW's price is so low that the photographer misses the wedding shot to focus on the car ad.

Authenticity and Being First in Its Class

The genuine article is often preferable to the imposter. Authenticity, in advertising, can mean suggesting a product is one of three things:

- *Genuine*—the product is not an imitation, but bona fide; for example, processed cheese that is made with milk, not oil, or kosher hot dogs that are truly kosher.

- *Original* to a certain place—Russian vodka, American blue jeans, Italian spaghetti sauce, African kente cloth, Idaho potatoes, Israeli figs.

- *First in its class*—when something is the first branded product in its category, people tend to believe it's best.

Arnie Arlow, the former creative director at Margeotes/Fertitta + Partners, who created a campaign for Stolichnaya vodka based on Russian art and the line "Freedom of vodka," said, "Since Russia is considered the birthplace and home of vodka and associated with the finest-quality vodka in the world, we decided to use authenticity as our concept."[1]

Many people value "the real thing"; people associate "the genuine article" with brands that were first in their class. In Butler, Shine & Stern's ad for Specialized mountain bikes—the first production mountain bikes ever made—this "first in class" value is highlighted (figure 4-21). Using another approach, an ad for Matchbox toy cars conveys the idea that these model cars are so well made, they can be compared to genuine cars (figure 4-22).

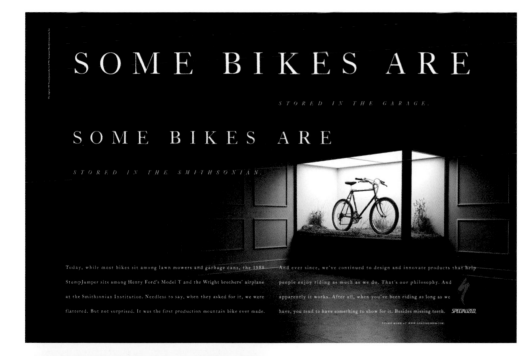

4-21
"Smithsonian"
Agency: Butler, Shine & Stern/Sausalito
Creative Team: John Butler, Arty Tan, Ryan Ebner
Client: Specialized
© 2003 Butler, Shine & Stern

The angle and lighting of the photograph contribute to the idea of the bike as art object in a museum setting, and so first in its class of products.

4-22
"We Sell More Cars . . ."
1979
Agency: Levine Huntley Schmidt & Beaver/New York
Creative Director/Art Director: Allan Beaver
Copywriter: Larry Plapler
Photographer: Cailor/Resnick
Client: Matchbox Cars

Pitting the toy cars against real cars makes the toys seem more authentic. The composition of this handsome classic ad is characteristic of the visual style of the decade—a large visual at the top of the page with the line underneath.

Motivation and Inspiration

Go create (Sony). Play more (Xbox). Think different (Apple Computer).

Many audiences love motivational speakers, motivational preachers, motivational self-help books, motivational talk show hosts—and motivational advertising.

"Just do it"—get out there and go for it, run, jump! Some women found the Nike ads with this slogan so compelling that they tore them out of magazines and hung them on their walls. "Be all that you can be," another ad said, and when an American enlisted, the U.S. Army made sure she excelled.

This springboard for idea generation is rooted in self-help; the ad idea becomes the stimulus for people to achieve, giving people that push to go after their personal best. People want the ads to act like an inner voice, pushing them to do something.

The ad becomes our personal trainer, motivational coach, preacher. We need incentive; we need a voice to inspire us to "go create," as in a campaign for Sony (figures 4-23 and 4-24). We need drive. Some ads give it to us.

4-23
"Hand"

Agency: Saatchi & Saatchi/Madrid
Executive Creative Director: César García
Creative Directors: Miguel Roig, Osky Canabal
Art Director: Jesus Martín-Buitrago
Copywriter: Santiago López
Photographers: Nahuel Berger, Gonzalo Puertas
Photographic finishing touches: Goyo Gómez
Client: Sony España
© December 2000

This camera is so small that it can't be seen behind a hand, which illustrates a brand advantage. Sony's slogan "Go create" certainly appeals to music buffs as well as technophiles.

4-24
"Free Loader"

Agency: Saatchi & Saatchi/Madrid
Executive Creative Director: César García
Creative Directors: Miguel Roig, Osky Canabal
Art Director: Alberto Quirantes
Copywriter: Juan Fran Vaquero
Photographers: Nahuel Berger, Gonzalo Puertas
Photographic finishing touches: Goyo Gómez
Client: Sony España
© December 2000

The cord hanging straight down from the sky not only captures our attention, but makes the point about downloading.

Just the Facts, Ma'am

Shocking, interesting, or little-known facts can be the basis of an idea. This is where good research can be very helpful. Using facts is informative. (Of course, facts can be presented and interpreted in a variety of ways.)

Using a shocking comparison, Dr. Martin Luther King Jr. and Charles Manson, in conjunction with a statistic, makes the ad "The Man on the Left," produced for the American Civil Liberties Union, an extremely gripping message (figure 4-25). Visualizing this message as a handbill nailed to walls heightens the drama of the call to support the ACLU. The facts can be visualized too, as in a striking ad for the Humane Society of Canada (figure 4-26). TheTruth.com uses facts to expose the truth about tobacco, such as that cigarette smoke contains arsenic.

4-25
"The Man on the Left"
Agency: DeVito/Verdi/New York
Creative Director: Sal DeVito
Art Director: Sal DeVito
Copywriter: Sal DeVito
Client: American Civil Liberties Union

Reading facts, we learn something; we can be enlightened, as with Hadrian's Wall's train and bus wraps for the Illinois Department of Public Health—an unconventional format that uses facts to discourage people from smoking (figures 4-27a, 4-27b). The newly learned fact will, advertisers hope, compel us to change behaviors, support a cause, act, buy a brand.

4-26
"Dog Bite"
Agency: Taxi/Toronto
Client: Humane Society of Canada

Dramatically exhibiting a fact, this ad shows how much thread, wrapped around an envelope, was used to sew a wound sustained from a dog bite.

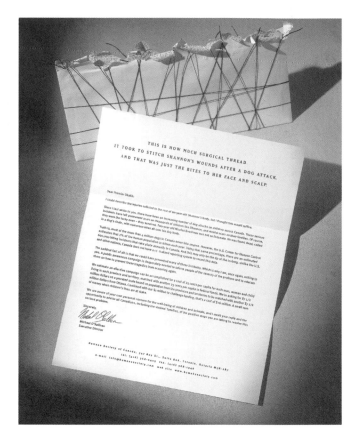

4-27a, 4-27b
"Hearse"
"Lungs"
Agency: Hadrian's Wall/Chicago
Creative Director: Kevin Lynch
Art Director: Mollie Wilke
Copywriter: Greg Christensen
Photographers: Oman/American Lung Association
Client: Illinois Department of Public Health

"These special train and bus wraps combined simple tobacco-related statistics with jarring visual consequences."

Notes

1. Robin Landa, *Thinking Creatively* (Cincinnati: HOW Books, 1998), p. 147.

INTERVIEW Bob Isherwood

**Worldwide Creative
Director, Saatchi & Saatchi**

If I were to give a crash course in the Bob Isherwood school of creative advertising, I'd make the following points. First off, what is meant by the term *creative advertising*? I take it to mean advertising that is more noticeable than the boring norm that surrounds us like wallpaper. I have always subscribed to the view that creative advertising is more effective and cost-efficient than the dull and predictable kind.

My guidelines are the following:

- *Is it original?* I ask this because original ideas cut through and are more memorable than ordinary ones.

- *Is the idea relevant?* In other words, is it based on an insight into the product or the consumer?

- *Does it make an emotional connection with the target audience?* I ask this because if there is no emotional connection, the ad simply will not work.

Another point I would make is that great ideas can be let down in the way they are presented, so craft skills are important. Writers and art directors should have the skills to deliver ideas brilliantly.

Finally, in my crash course I would say that if you want to be the world's best, do your utmost to work with those who already are.

How do you convince a client to take a chance on a daring ad concept?
Help the client understand the context in which their ad will appear. For example, a survey in China recently showed that 84 percent of viewers channel-surf when the ad break comes on. Eleven percent will stick for a few seconds. With that in mind, what would be the purpose of debating the end title in research focus groups if you lost your 11 percent in the opening seconds?

The risk for clients isn't in being noticed. The risk is in being irrelevant and invisible. Everyone's fighting for attention, media owners and your competitors alike. This is an attention economy, and you need striking ideas to cut through.

Research can help reduce risk. For example, many years ago the toothpaste brands were fighting a war based on cleaning and were at parity. One brand commissioned a research project that revealed seven out of ten people were cleaning their teeth before breakfast. In effect, those people weren't using toothpaste to clean their teeth at all. The brand changed its line to "It cleans your breath while it cleans your teeth," and sales went through the roof. Research can eliminate risk for a client by providing up front the insights needed to make our messages relevant.

I've said that ideas are the currency of the future. My friend Dr. Edward De Bono, at the global launch of the Saatchi & Saatchi Innovation in Communication Award, suggested we are leaving the information age and entering the age of creativity. He said, "Competence, information, and technology are all becoming commodities. What will differentiate companies in the future will be value creation, and that demands new ideas."

What does this mean for conventional advertising agencies? At Saatchi & Saatchi, we've taken advertising out of our name; our focus is on building an ideas company. We see our role as transforming our clients' brands, business, or reputation through highly valued ideas, and those may not be traditional advertising.

4-28a, 4-28b
"Trunks"
Agency: F/Nazca Saatchi & Saatchi/Brazil
Creative Director: Fábio Fernandes
Art Director: Sidney Araújo
Copywriter: Victor Sant'Anna
Photographer: João Caetano
Client: SOS Mata Atlântica Foundation
© 1999

4-29a, 4-29b
"Eyes"
Agency: F/Nazca Saatchi & Saatchi/Brazil
Creative Directors: Fábio Fernandes, Eduardo Lima
Art Director: Sidney Araújo
Copywriters: Eduardo Lima, Victor Sant'Anna
Photographer: João Caetano
Client: SOS Mata Atlântica Foundation
© 2001

These visually driven and provocative PSA campaigns remind us of the value of the rain forest.

Our remuneration by Procter & Gamble, the world's largest advertiser, for example, is based not on conventional media spending but on net outside sales. What they want from us are communication ideas that drive sales, not just ads to fill media bookings.

What's your take on designing and conceiving ads?
First, I try to get as many facts about the product and the business challenge as possible. Facts help me get past the intimidation of the blank page. They help narrow or refine the possibilities, which I think is important. For me one of the worst briefs is "you can do anything you want." I need to understand what the problem is to be solved; otherwise how will I know when I've found the answer?

In fact, a good place to begin problem solving (to quote Bob Seelert, our chairman) is to "start with the answer." When I have all the facts I can gather regarding the customer, client product, and goal, I find the ad usually does itself.

4-30
"Beach, Pool and Bar"
Agency: Saatchi & Saatchi/London
Creative Director: Dave Droga
Client: Club 18-30

The sexual suggestiveness of this ad gained a great deal of consumer and media attention.

Often the answer is so simple, you wonder why no one has thought of it before. Simplicity is a key thing for me—simplicity in concept and design, because simplicity cuts through advertising clutter. Along the same lines, in my own work as an art director I design my ads from the inside out. That is to say, let the idea do the art direction for you. I try to avoid affectation in design; it quickly dates your work. Perseverance, I believe, is key. It's a greater attribute than talent.

I have been credited with changing the way Saatchi & Saatchi copywriters and art directors work. What did I do and why?

Let's start with the problem. Our creative people everywhere were complaining that they didn't have enough time to make the work as great as it should be. This was best summed up by one of our creative directors, who said, "I don't have time to think." The reason for this was that our briefing form, based on single-minded propositions, was a tired system developed for a conventional ad agency. What's more, over time, as the role of planning increased, creative teams found themselves relegated to the back end of the job, after all the thinking time had been used up.

Through the Worldwide Creative Board I asked our planning board to come up with a new kind of briefing system that would get our creatives back into the strategic front lines and stimulate more original thinking. The answer was the ideas brief, the starting point of which is the challenge or business problem. The writing of the ideas brief is a collective effort involving all disciplines, including creative, and is done right at the beginning of the project. As a result, creative teams aren't sitting back waiting for a brief before they can do an ad; they're part of the process.

With the challenge as the first box to be filled, people are empowered to come up with solutions to business problems that may or may not revolve around traditional media. The ideas brief destroys an assembly-line process.

I don't think advertising will be replaced by product placement in television programs. Product placement has been with us for a long time. Also, I'm not sure you can build a brand purely through product placement.

What may be an issue is TiVo and similar ad-skipping devices, which are currently driving some advertisers to supplement brand establishment with product placement. In the TiVo environment, the future of advertising will depend on its ability to entertain and amaze, because in this world the consumer has the power to say, "Entertain me, or I won't entertain you." It's a wonderful thing for those who truly believe in creative advertising.

chapter 5

Ad Categories

Understanding ad categories can help you generate and focus ideas.

Demonstrations

In the old days, a door-to-door salesman would throw dirt on a carpet and then demonstrate how well his brand could vacuum up the dirt. What a gutsy demonstration! Exhibiting the merits of a brand to a potential buyer or showing how something works is a demonstration. Naturally, television and the Internet allow for the best types of demonstration, since they incorporate sound and movement. In print media, demonstration is more difficult, but still possible. A demonstration in print can be a single illustration, a diagrammatic illustration, an illustration with call-outs, or a storyboard showing a step-by-step presentation. A demonstration can be presented through typographic design, as in the ad below for Sony batteries (figure 5-1). Or it can be interactive, where the reader is asked to pull a tab or fold the ad. On the Internet, the BMWfilms series stars a driver and his trusty BMW demonstrating the brand's performance capabilities (see figure 11-12).

5-1
"Stamina"
Agency: BMP DDB/London
Photographer: Steen Sundland
Agent: M.A.P. Ltd.
Client: Sony Batteries

This demonstrates what can happen when your batteries die (you hear the nearby child's story instead of your own music).

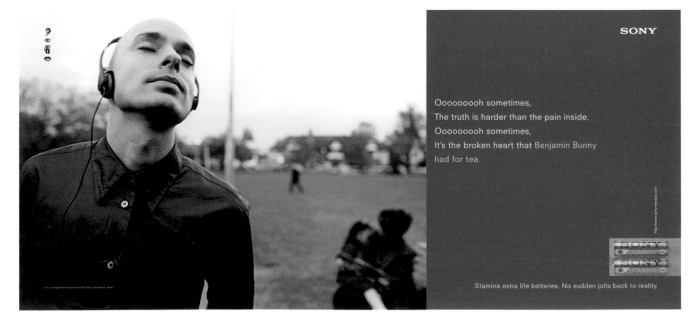

SONY

Oooooooooh sometimes,
The truth is harder than the pain inside.
Oooooooooh sometimes,
It's the broken heart that Benjamin Bunny had for tea.

Stamina extra life batteries. No sudden jolts back to reality.

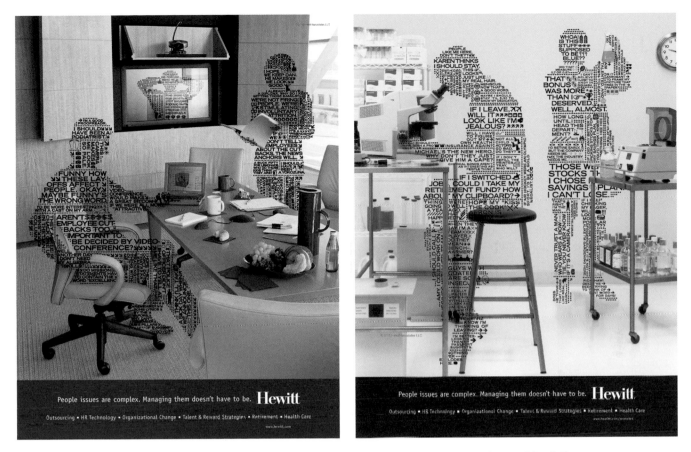

In a campaign for Hewitt (figures 5-2a, 5-2b), a visual demonstration is used to explain something that would take a great deal of explaining in words. Hadrian's Wall creative director Kevin Lynch writes: "Instead of talking about how complicated people and people issues can be, these ads demonstrate it. By showing the thoughts that go through (and distract) an employee's mind every day, the ads show how important a human resource consultant like Hewitt can be."

Endorsements and Testimonials

When Penélope Cruz endorses a fragrance, what does it mean to a consumer? What does it mean when leading male recording artists All-4-One, Backstreet Boys, Clint Black, Coolio, Kenny Loggins, Richard Marx, and Travis Tritt take the lead in encouraging men to speak out against domestic violence? Celebrity endorsements and testimonials run the gamut from politicians to celebrity canines. What do celebrity endorsements mean to us, the celebrity-crazed public? A lot. We like the celebrity; we like the brand.

In many cultures, celebrities have a powerful influence. Many of us, especially teenagers and young adults, look up to famous actors, athletes, musicians, and other public figures. Famous people use their celebrity status to raise money for charities, heighten awareness of social issues, and call people to action for a variety of charitable acts. For example, in the United States, Washington Redskins football star Gus Frerotte, Washington Wizards basketball star Juwan Howard, and Baltimore Orioles baseball star Rafael Palmeiro used their status for a public service announcement for the D.C. Rape Crisis Center.

If Heather Locklear, TV star and sex symbol, thinks Preference hair color by L'Oréal is good enough for her (and remember, she can afford to go to the best salons in the world), then hey, it's good enough for me! If we wear Air Jordans, we'll be like Mike. When a beau-

5-2a, 5-2b
"Video Conference"
"Lab"

Agency: Hadrian's Wall/Chicago
Creative Director: Kevin Lynch
Art Directors: Thomas Richie, Mollie Wilke
Copywriters: Kevin Lynch, Greg Christensen
Typographer: Segura, Inc.
Photographers: Juliana Sohn, Hunter Freeman
Client: Hewitt
© 2002

"Each ad depicts a typical work situation. However, employees are made up entirely of 'thoughts' that go through their heads on any given day, everything from wanting more respect to wishing they had pursued other occupations. The tagline reads simply, 'People issues are complex. Managing them doesn't have to be.'"

tiful celebrity or model endorses a cosmetic brand, do we believe that we will become as beautiful as she if we use it, too? Sociologist Diane Barthel cautions us: "It is one thing to envy their beauty; it is another thing to believe that it comes from a jar."[1]

A major problem involved with using celebrities is that they are all too human; if a celebrity gets into personal trouble and his or her public image is tarnished, the brand being endorsed can be tarnished as well.

When an everyday person endorses a brand, another phenomenon can happen. We identify with that person because he or she is a peer—an average Juan or Jane just like us; we believe what that person is saying. In an ad for the M. D. Anderson Cancer Center, using an individual who survived cancer with the help of Anderson gives the hospital a human voice (figure 5-3). Peggy Conlon, president of the Ad Council, remarks: "The Ad Council typically chooses not to feature celebrities in its public service ads. Our research has consistently shown that people listen to and heed messages that are communicated by people that they can relate to and identify with. Therefore, a real-life testimonial or a message from someone who appears to be ordinary can have the greatest impact. However, sometimes celebrities are featured in public service advertising. The public may pay attention if they recognize a favorite celebrity's voice. In addition, the media may be more inclined to donate media if the ads include a celebrity that is a part of a program on their network."

In Holland, on outdoor boards, photographs of individual average Dutch citizens, including the elderly, young people, women, and men, declared, "Ik ben Ben" (figure 5-4). This was the launch campaign of a new GSM company, Ben, which was targeting the general consumer. In Dutch, "ik ben" means "I am," and Ben is a common name, as well as the name of the mobile phone company. As is typical of the urbane-minded creatives at KesselsKramer/Amsterdam, there is a touch of irony in this campaign.

5-3
Agency: The Richards Group/Dallas
Creative Directors: Jeff Hopfer, Ron Henderson
Art Director: Jeff Hopfer
Copywriter: Ron Henderson
Photographer: Brad Guice
Client: M. D. Anderson Cancer Center

Crossing out the disease with a red line graphically illustrates what the hospital is able to do. Photographing this individual in a natural setting emphasizes his health.

5-4
"Ik ben Ben"

Agency: KesselsKramer/Amsterdam
Art Director: Erik Kessels
Copywriter: Johan Kramer
Photographer: Bert Teunissen
Client: Ben

The endorser's identity becomes one with the brand.

ALBERT BANKS JR., ADVANCED TESTICULAR CANCER.

In the summer of 1979, Albert Banks Jr. was diagnosed with an advanced case of testicular cancer. Today, he's a man who survives by his mother's catfish recipes and a hospital called M. D. Anderson. Because no one has ever more cancer than we have, M. D. Anderson is consistently ranked one of the nation's top two cancer centers by THE UNIVERSITY OF TEXAS *U.S. News & World Report.* Which is why we can offer you, or someone you know, the best MD ANDERSON hope for survival, no matter what form the cancer takes. *Making Cancer History*™ CANCER CENTER

FOR AN APPOINTMENT, OR FOR MORE INFORMATION,
PLEASE CALL US AT 1-800-392-1611, OR ASK YOUR PHYSICIAN. www.mdanderson.org.

een nieuw mobiel netwerk

Declarations

"Buckle up."—U.S. Department of Transportation/National Highway Traffic Safety Administration

"The ultimate driving machine."—BMW

"Friends don't let friends drive drunk."—U.S. Department of Transportation

"Listerine kills germs."

"Stop for pedestrians. Think of the impact you could make."—U.S. Department of Transportation Federal Highway Administration

"Only you can prevent forest fires."—U.S. Forest Service, Smokey Bear

Well, you get the idea: ads declare, proclaim (declare with force), announce (declare something for the first time), or state resolutely that a brand is scientifically proven, tested and retested, stain-resistant, waterproof to the depths of the bottom of any sea, leakproof, sanitary, 100 percent something, absolutely positively shrinkproof (trust us, we washed these pants twelve million times and they still didn't shrink), the best, and any other promise you can think of.

When something is emphatically stated, we tend to believe it. In a campaign for Performance Motors, the declaration that BMW is the ultimate driving machine is inventively reinforced (figures 5-5a, 5-5b).

When you hear the public service announcement emphatically declare, "Friends don't let friends drive drunk," you are called into action to intervene in order to prevent drunk driving. Celebrities including Marc Anthony, 98 Degrees, Brian McKnight, and others, all supporting the message "Friends don't let friends drive drunk," are showcased in TV and radio PSAs to beseech people to heed the message. In one startling campaign, we see the personal effects of people whose lives were ended by drunk drivers (figures 5-6a, 5-6b, 5-6c).

The idea is that people are likely to heed declarations in PSAs. We are responsible for the safety of the eggs in the nest in the forest setting; and when Smokey Bear declares that "only you can prevent forest fires," the nature of the declaration places responsibility on the reader

5-5a, 5-5b
"Reserved"
Agency: M&C Saatchi/Singapore
Creative Director: Shane Gibson
Art Director: Muk
Copywriter: Raymond Quah
Retoucher: Procolor
Client: Performance Motors

"The color print and posters campaign features the new BMW X5 in its natural habitat—off-road. The series of ads depict the car in a reserved space among the most hostile scenery, where it sits in complete confidence."

Amanda Geiger bought these sunglasses
to wear on spring break. She wore them only once
before she was killed by a drunk driver.

Friends Don't Let Friends Drive Drunk.

Este es el reloj que llevaba puesto Stephen Hollingshead, Jr.
cuando se encontró con un chofer borracho.
Murió a las 6:55pm.

Amigos no dejan que amigos manejen borrachos.

These shoes were found 46 yards from
the crash caused by a drunk driver.
Carissa Deason was thrown 30 yards and
not even her father, a doctor, could save her.

Friends Don't Let Friends Drive Drunk.

Photo by Michael Mazzeo

U.S. Department of Transportation

5-6a, 5-6b, 5-6c
"Friends Don't Let Friends Drive Drunk: Sunglasses"
"Friends Don't Let Friends Drive Drunk: Watch"
"Friends Don't Let Friends Drive Drunk: Shoes"
Agency: DDB Worldwide/New York
Photographer: Michael Mazzeo
Client: U.S. Department of Transportation
© U.S. Department of Transportation and the Ad Council

Photographs of the personal effects of people
who were killed by drunk drivers are arresting
images that call us to action.

(figure 5-7). The atypical angle of the photograph in another PSA helps send the urgent message to stop for pedestrians (figure 5-8).

A declaration's believability is affected by the tone and origin of the voice. In other words, who's talking to us? Is the company telling us their brand is great? Or is it a paternal voice? A scientist's voice? Does the voice have an authoritative tone or a maternal one? Naturally, we will more likely trust a maternal or neighborly voice than that of a corporation. Diane Barthel, in *Putting on Appearances: Gender and Advertising,* cautions us to question the "presumption of authority" in the voices in fashion and cosmetic ads.[2]

Certainly, tying a declaration to a humorous concept helps get viewers to accept what is being declared. In the campaign for the U.S. launch of Domtar paper, a twist in a literary excerpt backs up the tagline (figure 5-9).

5-7

"Only You Can Prevent Forest Fires"

Client: U.S. Department of Agriculture, Forest Service; National Association of State Foresters; the Ad Council

This PSA asks us to understand that the forest is home to many.

5-8

Driver Safety

Client: U.S. Department of Transportation, Federal Highway Administration

The atypical point of view of the photograph heightens the emotional appeal.

5-9
**United States Launch
for a Paper Company**
Agency: Hunt Adkins/Minneapolis
Creative Director/Copywriter: Doug
Adkins
Associate Creative Director/Art Director:
Steve Mitchell
Client: Domtar

Unexpected story line twists, along
with the tagline, clarify the ad
concept while making a declaration
about the paper.

and that's when I realized that Old Yeller, my most loyal friend, the dog that had saved my mama and my little brother and me from bears and wolves and wild boars, had rabies. My arms were shaking and my eyes were blurry with tears as I raised my rifle and aimed it right between Old Yeller's big, trusting eyes. And then, as my finger tightened on the trigger, I discovered that my best friend wasn't really rabid at all but had just been eating some soap, so I hugged that big yeller dog and he licked my face and we wrestled around in the grass and then ran off into the sunset together.

THE END

EVERYTHING TURNS OUT BETTER ON DOMTAR PAPER.

DOMTAR
Papers

Slice of Life

Family dinners, washing the car, going to work, playing in the backyard, making dinner, working in an office, petting a dog, doing homework, watching TV—all are potential scenes from everyday life. When a fragment of actual life experience, one with which we are completely familiar, is translated into a very short piece of drama or comedy, the result is slice-of-life advertising. We see people in their everyday circumstances, interacting with a brand, or in need of a product or service. Jane Maas writes, "At its best the 'slice of life' shows you people who look and sound authentic, talking about human problems to which the product provides a solution."[3] A campaign for Backwoods allows us to see people behaving as one would while communing with nature—hiking in the woods, petting a dog—while sending the message that if you enjoy this type of experience, then Backwoods is your kind of store (figures 5-10a, 5-10b). (Also see "Life Experience" in Chapter 4.)

5-10a, 5-10b
"Group Therapy"
"12,035 Step Program"
Agency: Sullivan Higdon & Sink/Wichita
Art Director: Scott Fleming
Copywriter: Steve Hobson
Photographer: Ron Berg
Client: Backwoods
© 2000
Courtesy of Sullivan Higdon & Sink/Wichita, Kansas

In these ads we see large visuals first; then we see the headlines, which make analogies to mental health remedies. It is the cooperative action between the headline and visual that communicates the analogy.

Meta-Advertising

Meta-advertising is self-referential. It can be a commercial about doing a commercial, or one that points out that it's a commercial. In advertising, a "meta" device deals critically with the awareness of the ad as an ad—it admits, "I'm an ad." Meta-advertising is in direct opposition to ads that show a slice of life, ones that try to create the illusion of everyday experience.

Popular Culture

Most advertisers realize that aiming at a very specific audience is the way to go. If you can reach a community of faithful return or heavy users of your brand, then you have a piece of the market. Using elements drawn from popular culture, particular social groups, or a certain cultural milieu may appeal to select audiences.

The "Whassup?" Budweiser TV commercials were based on a short film, titled *True,* by director Charles Stone III. In the Budweiser ads, the question "Whassup?" is answered with "Watchin' the game, havin' a Bud." Drawn from pop culture, the expression "Whassup?" became part of the mainstream lexicon.

Popular culture can be used in a variety of ways, drawing from contemporary music, dance, fashion, or sports. In a TV spot for Fox Sports, creative director Eric Silver created the characters Alan and Jerome, who are urban youth basketball wannabes. Alan and Jerome discuss the players and the game, and finally play the game with the Utah Jazz (see figure 11-7).

Drawing from popular culture can allow people to feel they are part of a larger group, or it can expose them to a group they may find attractive or fascinating.

Fantasy

Wizardry. Jedi. Fantastic creatures. Personal fantasy. What thirteen-year-old boy doesn't find strange settings and grotesque characters appealing? Just look at the vast audience for the Harry Potter stories, Star Wars installments, or Fellowship of the Ring trilogy. If people find this type of fiction or storytelling so compelling in novels and films, why not in commercials or print ads? We can relate to the lone hero; we can "fight the monster," as in Butler, Shine & Stern's startling ad for iFuse (figure 5-11).

Ridley Scott, who directed the masterpiece *Blade Runner,* also directed two of TV's most memorable commercials utilizing fantasy: Apple's "1984" and Chanel perfume's "Share the Fantasy."

Apple's "1984" (agency Chiat/Day) was one of the greatest TV commercials of all time. This commercial, which aired only once to a national audience, during the Super Bowl, was an homage to George Orwell's novel *1984.* The hero in the "1984" TV spot was a lone woman with a sledgehammer who did battle against Big Brother and his dead-looking drone followers.

5-11
"Locker Room"
Agency: Butler, Shine & Stern/Sausalito
Creative Team: Stephen Goldblatt/Josh Stern
Client: iFuse
© 2003 Butler, Shine, & Stern

Using fantasy, this ad appeals to the key youth market, attempting to inspire its audience to free themselves from pop culture. This ad is also a visual surprise.

As the drones (think PC users) watch Big Brother on a huge screen, the female hero (think Macintosh) runs toward the screen and releases the sledgehammer, which smashes the screen. The voice-over says: "On January 24, Apple Computer will introduce Macintosh. And you'll see why 1984 won't be like *1984*."

The TV spot "The Surfer," for Guinness beer, claims that "good things come to those who wait." A BBC reviewer said this TV spot was reminiscent of the "Riders at the River Bruinen" sequence in Tolkien's *Fellowship of the Ring*. The follow-up to "The Surfer" was "The Dream Club," involving squirrels and a philosophical question about the meaning of life. Clearly, there are all types of fantasies.

Misdirection

Misdirection ads start out one way, then suddenly change direction. Thinking the TV commercial is about one thing, viewers are surprised by the real message.

These ads can work for a variety of reasons. One reason is the element of surprise; we are being led one way but are surprised to find ourselves taken somewhere else. Certainly, there is a risk with this type of approach: once you've seen the ad, you know the surprise ending. Of course, if the idea and execution are excellent, then you might not mind seeing it again.

This category is often used to spoof other commercials. Pepsi's agency, BBDO/New York, used a misdirection ad during Super Bowl XXXV, playing on a Viagra commercial featuring spokesperson Bob Dole. In the Pepsi ad, Dole was drinking a Pepsi to get "rejuvenated."

We are completely misled in a satiric TV spot for the Fox Sports Web site (figure 5-12). At first we see a close-up of a man attempting to fasten a baby's diaper with his toes, which leads us to believe that we're watching a heartrending PSA, perhaps about a man triumphing over adversity. Gradually, it is revealed that the man is a sports-obsessed father who is using his fingers on the computer keyboard to visit the Fox Sports Web site!

5-12
"Feet"

Agency: Cliff Freeman & Partners/New York
Creative Director: Eric Silver
Art Director: Kilpatrick Anderson
Copywriter: Kevin Roddy
Director: Rocky Morton
Producer: Nick Felder
Client: Foxsports.com

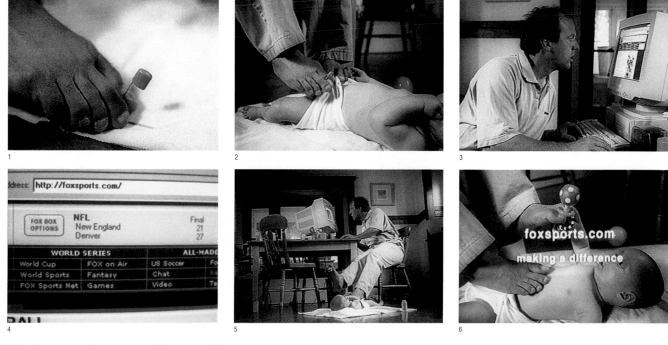

Taking irreverence to an extreme, this commercial leaves the audience completely surprised by the time it's over.

Image or Lifestyle

Fashion. Fragrances. Cars. Liquor. Motorcycles. How can you differentiate one brand of any of these from other brands in their categories?

If most beers are interchangeable (and taste tests prove that most people can't tell their own brand when blindfolded), then the beer must appeal to a certain demographic segment—younger men who drive pickup trucks, or executives who "do lunch"—for other reasons. We all belong to groups or communities, according to the Stanford Research Institute, and each group has a basic lifestyle. Image advertising is based on the idea of promoting a particular lifestyle.

Image ads project an attitude, an aura, a conception of someone's style and persona, which can be anything from bohemian to country cowboy. If we wear that clothing line, then we too can be like those attractive, sexy people in the ads. Very often, when there is no particular functional benefit to which advertisers can point, they employ image advertising

5-13
"Fall in Love"

Agency: Armando Testa/Milan
Creative Directors: Maurizio Sala, Michele Mariani
Art Director: Paola Balestreri
Copywriter: Sonia Cosentino
Photographer: Philippe Cometti
Client: Dismi 92 S.p.A.—Allegri
© 2002

We focus on the fashion, which is surrounded by a textural environment.

Fall in love.

allegri

5-14
"Kiss"
Agency: Butler, Shine & Stern/Sausalito
Creative Team: Nathan Naylor, Ryan Ebner
Client: Anchor Blue
© 2003 Butler, Shine, & Stern

The photomontage style of the art direction has an almost cinematic quality, depicting a youth-oriented lifestyle.

to differentiate products. After all, what are the differences among top-end cosmetics? Fragrances? Cars? In essence, people are purchasing the advertising, the style, the packaging, and the brand. As Randall Rothenberg points out, some clothing and cosmetics companies "are selling pure images, just barely tethered to physical products."[4]

Some image advertising breaks away from the typical, using sophisticated wit and artistic vision not only to get the viewer's attention but also to establish a spirit for the brand, as does the "Fall in Love" ad for Allegri (figure 5-13). Targeting youthful customers, the art direction and concept for the Anchor Blue retail store projects an on-trend lifestyle (figure 5-14).

Adventures and Escapes

Risk, excitement—the seductive power of a good adventure should never be underestimated. Whether it's driving across the country in your new car or experiencing camaraderie in the woods while using your Swiss Army knife (see figure 9-19), the idea of adventuring into nature or a new experience can be used to sell cars, vacations, or perhaps even tea. At the other end of the continuum, the retreat or solitude that an escape provides can seem to have the power to cure or transform. You need an escape *from* something (your petty boss, your screaming kids) and an escape *to* something. Escaping to North Carolina for some natural beauty and peace looks very appealing in ads for tourism in the state (figures 5-15a, 5-15b). For those who "stalk" adventure, a vacation in Nevada might be just the thing (figures 5-16a, 5-16b, 5-16c).

Benefits and Differentiation

Why should I use your brand? What does your brand offer? What's in it for me? Ads that showcase benefits or explain what a brand has to offer have long been a mainstay of ad-think. However, in today's competitive marketplace, where most advertisers believe that visual style and spirit sell a parity product, it's an underlying creative idea that can make an ad touting a benefit stand out, as in an ad for *The Guardian* that plugs one of the periodical's special features (figure 5-17). An ad can also demonstrate a brand's capabilities, as in Lowe's inventive campaign for Olympus that truly invites close scrutiny on the part of the reader (figures 5-18a, 5-18b, 5-18c).

5-15a, 5-15b
"Trail Sign"
"Drive-in Theater"
Agency: Loeffler Ketchum Mountjoy/Charlotte
Creative Director: Jim Mountjoy
Art Director: Doug Pedersen
Copywriter: Curtis Smith
Photographers: Olaf Veltman, Stuart Hall
Client: North Carolina Travel & Tourism

These ads use signage and a theater marquee in a unique way.

5-16a, 5-16b, 5-16c
"Nevada: Bring It On"
Agency: R & R Partners/Las Vegas
Creative Director/Copywriter: Tim O'Brien
Designer: Mike Corbitt
Photographer: Jim Erickson
Client: Nevada Commission on Tourism
2001

The typographic design, choice of photographers, and mood of photographs aid the communication.

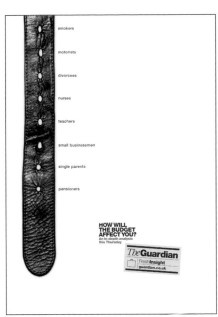

5-17
"Budget Belt"

Agency: BMP DDB/London
Photographer: Alan Mahon
Agent: Horton Stevens
Client: Guardian Unlimited

An analogy is made to
tightening one's belt.

5-18a, 5-18b, 5-18c
"Murder"
"Congresswoman"
"Tourist"

Agency: Lowe/London
Creative Director: Charles Inge
Art Director: Steve Williams
Copywriter: Adrian Lim
Photographer: David Preutz
Client: Olympus

The camera produces such picture quality that
you won't miss a thing. The line plus the photos
convince us of the claim. Also, this campaign
engages viewers' attention by making them
search the photo for the evidence.

Using humor, another ad illustrates the obvious benefits of having a skylight and roof window (figure 5-19). Appealing to people seeking extreme experiences, an ad campaign differentiates Nevada from the typical vacation retreat (see figure 5-16). One brand of diapers is differentiated from its competition because it is for toddlers on the go (figure 5-20). Another ad argues you can get what you need—a quick fix for your home—at Ikea (figures 5-21a, 5-21b).

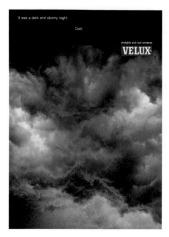

5-19
"Dark and Stormy"
Agency: Loeffler Ketchum Mountjoy/Charlotte
Creative Director: Jim Mountjoy
Copywriter: Curtis Smith
Client: VELUX America, Inc.

The straight visual—a beautiful photo—is complemented by a comic line with a twist (It was a dark and stormy night. Cool.). In combination, they communicate the functional and emotional benefits.

5-20
"Library"
Agency: Forsman & Bodenfors/Gothenburg
Art Director: Kim Cramer
Copywriter: Jonas Enghage
Photographer: Peter Gehrke
Client: SCA Hygiene Products
Product: Libero Diapers

This ad makes the point that the child can walk and is not a baby.

5-21a, 5-21b
"Quick Fix with IKEA"
Agency: Forsman & Bodenfors/Gothenburg
Art Directors: Karin Jacobsson, Anders Eklind
Copywriters: Filip Nilsson, Fredrik Jansson, Hjalmar Delehag
Photographer: Karolina Henke
Agent: Skarp
Client: IKEA Sweden

With visual gags, these humorous ads engage the viewer, explaining the benefit of shopping at Ikea.

Recognition

Smokey Bear. Bibendum, the Michelin Man. McDonald's golden arches. The Volkswagen Beetle. The Energizer Bunny. Carvel's Cookie Puss.

Immediately, we know them.

Memorable characters in ads can be adorable, funny, or even annoying. Often, corporate icons or "spokescharacters" become part of pop culture. Think of Smokey Bear (see the Smokey Bear Showcase in Chapter 1), General Mills' Betty Crocker (who has changed her appearance several times), the Pillsbury Doughboy, Kellogg's Tony the Tiger, Flat Eric (a living yellow puppet for Levi's), Pets.com's sock puppet, and many more. "The power of corporate mascots is that of all icons," writes Tom Vanderbilt. "It becomes a symbol for something larger than the brand itself. It takes mass, impersonal abstractions (i.e., multinational corporations) and condenses them into approachable, charismatic, even cuddly symbols."[5]

In a TV spot for Carvel, KBPWest uses animated characters (figures 5-22). KBPWest says: "Carvel was the best-loved brand in the ice cream category, but had lost saliency with their core target of moms. To reconnect with this audience, we brought back two fondly remembered, creamy, crunchy, and silly ice cream cakes—Cookie Puss and Fudgie the Whale—and made them 'spokes-cakes' for the brand." My five-year-old daughter, Hayley, asked me to replay this Carvel commercial over and over again!

Symbols allow us to quickly identify the brand—think of McDonald's golden arches, Nike's swoosh, the Mercedes-Benz hood ornament, the shape of the VW Beetle. Using a symbol or logo, something we recognize and have come to identify with the brand, directly relates to branding, to establishing a brand presence.

5-22
"Beams Down"
Agency: KBPWest/San Francisco
Creative Director: Jeff Musser
Art Director: Jesse McMillan
Writer: Craig Erickson
Broadcast Producer: Christine Gomez
Client: Carvel
© Carvel

These entertaining animated TV spots "breathed new life and excitement into the business and re-invigorated the franchisees," according to KBPWest. The campaign introduced the line, "We're creamy. We're crunchy. We're Carvel."

Notes

1. Diane Barthel, *Putting On Appearances: Gender and Advertising* (Philadelphia: Temple University Press, 1988), p. 55.

2. Ibid., p. 56.

3. Jane Maas, *Adventures of an Advertising Woman* (New York: Fawcett Crest, 1986), p. 72.

4. Randall Rothenberg, *Where the Suckers Moon: The Life and Death of an Advertising Campaign* (New York: Vintage Books, 1994), p. 14.

5. Tom Vanderbilt, "The 15 Most Influential, Important, Innocuous, Inane, and Interesting Ad Icons of the Last 500 Years (In No Particular Order)," *Print* 54, no. 6 (2000), p. 116.

6

Expression: Make 'Em Laugh, Make 'Em Cry

Make them laugh. Or make them cry. Just make them feel something. If you can emotionally move someone, then you just may have made an emotional connection with your client's brand or cause. Make your ad relevant to the audience. We think, but in the ad world, it's far better to make someone feel.

A few ways to find humor

- Create a visual surprise.

- Do what is unanticipated.

- Be zany.

- Look at something from someone else's perspective— that of a fish, a bus driver, a skydiver, a mortician.

- Turn things around; what is noise to you is music to someone else.

- Ask, "What if...?" What if dogs could fly? What if people could read minds? What if there were no gravity? What if people spoke in musical notes?

- Use physical humor.

- Do something incongruous.

- Be extreme, be outrageous.

- Illuminate a silly human quality or behavior.

- Say it in pig Latin. (Okay, maybe not.)

- Closely examine life's little happenings.

- Be odd (oddvertising).

- Twist it.

There is a vast range of expressive avenues that advertisers use to endear brands and social causes to us, to motivate us to donate to charities, to call us to action. The creative team's job is to find the best way to express a particular ad message. The following are appeals based on emotions, emotional benefits, desires, and needs.

Humor

"How can advertising possibly be creative when it has to pitch a product? Try serving it up with a laugh."[1]

When we associate a brand with something humorous, or when an ad has made us laugh, we're more likely to remember something that has tickled us, and we'll have a good feeling about the brand. Certainly, humor has to be on strategy—that is, it has to make sense in relation to what you're trying to accomplish—and it has to be brand- and audience-appropriate.

What is funny to one person, age group, sex, or other demographic segment may not be funny to another. That's where knowing your audience comes in. To take one example, kids love scatological jokes, but adult women probably wouldn't find them so funny.

And for goodness' sake, have a social conscience. Humorist, actor, and producer Bill Cosby created a paradigm for humanistic humor, which plays off human foibles and common interpersonal experiences rather than negative stereotypes. His humor is about what we all share, what we have in common, rather than what separates us. Humor based on race, sex, age, weight, ethnicity, or religion is not funny; it is unethical.

Recently, odd humor—what some call "oddvertising"—has taken center stage in advertising humor, as in the TV spot "Turkey/Cliff Diving" for Fox Regional Sports, where creative director Eric Silver masters bizarre comedy (see figure 11-5). With some irreverence and a good deal of wit, in the TV spot "Lamp," for Ikea, the announcer says to the viewer, "You're crazy"—there is a self-awareness when the character in the commercial speaks directly to the audience (see figure 11-1). Another type of offbeat humor is utilized in a nostalgic-looking ad for Harper Hardware (figure 6-1). Arnika explains the problem and their solution:

Problem: With expansion of hardware superstores, smaller mom-and-pop hardware stores have become overlooked. Harper Hardware is a community hardware store that combines essential building materials with a comfortable down-home atmosphere.

Solution: Focus on the basics Harper Hardware offers while establishing a fun, nostalgic appeal to the brand's character.

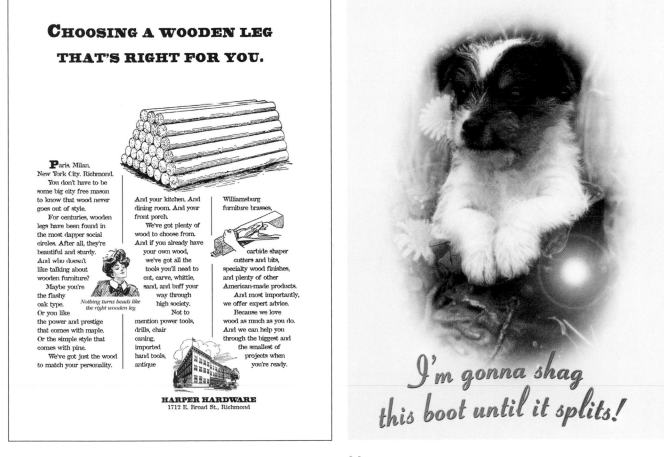

6-1
Harper Hardware Campaign
Agency: Arnika/Richmond
Creative Directors: Jerry Torchia, Mark Fenske
Copywriter/Art Director: Michael Ashley
Client: Harper Hardware
© 2002 Arnika LLC

Playing off the look of early advertisements, the droll humor in this ad points out the functional benefits of shopping at Harper Hardware, such as the expert advice from the staff.

6-2
"Shag"
Agency: Mad Dogs & Englishmen/New York
Creative Director: Dave Cook
Art Director: James Dawson Hollis
Copywriters: Andrew Ure, Craig Miller
Client: Friends of Animals
© 1992

With this ad campaign, Friends of Animals is offering people help with affordable breeding control for their pets.

6-3a, 6-3b, 6-3c
"Roller"
"Stapler"
"Ice Cube"

Agency: Mad Dogs & Englishmen/New York
Creative Director: Dave Cook
Art Directors: James Dawson Hollis, Vivienne Wan
Copywriters: Jaime Palmiotti, James Robinson
Photographer: Kudo Photography
Client: Haribo
© 1992 Haribo

We are drawn into these extremely funny scenes acted out by mischievous little bears, which endear this brand to consumers and give the ads a lighthearted, sardonic stance.

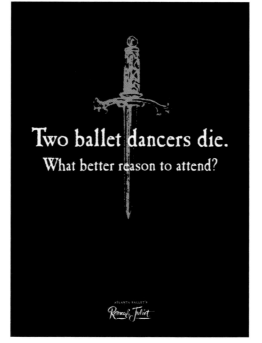

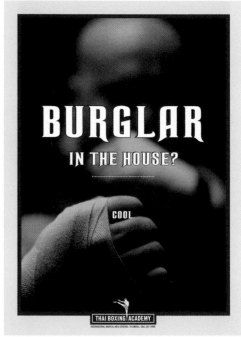

6-4
"Two Dancers Die"

Agency: Sawyer Riley Compton/Atlanta
Web site: www.brandstorytellers.com
Creative Director: Bart Cleveland
Associate Creative Director: Al Jackson
Art Director/Copywriter: Kevin Thoem
Copywriter: Ari Weiss
Client: Atlanta Ballet
© 2001

The color palette, font choice, and graphic dagger help convey the tragic mood of *Romeo and Juliet;* however, the copy adds a slight unexpected twist.

6-5
"Burglar"

Agency: Sawyer Riley Compton/Atlanta
Web site: www.brandstorytellers.com
Creative Director: Bart Cleveland
Associate Creative Director/Copywriter: Al Jackson
Art Director: Kevin Thoem
Photographer: Rick Newby
Client: International Martial Arts Studio
© 2002

Behind the typography, the visual creates a gripping mood designed to express an amusingly confident attitude.

Shocking language contrasts with a sweet image and a soft color palette in an ad for Friends of Animals intended to compel people to act on behalf of their pets (figure 6-2).

Mischievousness finds a home in hilarious ads for Haribo (figures 6-3a, 6-3b, 6-3c). We find our naughty little bears pulling rather awful pranks on fellow bears. Since the bears are much smaller than the common household items used in the spots, such as a hair roller, stapler, and ice cube, scale plays a part in the humor.

In copy-driven ads for a ballet company and a martial arts studio, there is definitely some attitude in the humor. "Two Dancers Die" uses a very unusual tactic to attract a new audience to the Atlanta Ballet (figure 6-4). Another ad, for International Martial Arts Studios, reverses the usual fear of burglars (figure 6-5). (Also see figure 8-6 for an ad from Mustoes with a "quiche-my-ass" attitude.)

Visually driven ads can make us laugh by the outrageousness of their visuals. The special effects and use of exaggeration as a humorous device works extremely well in ads for GT (figures 6-6a, 6-6b). Exaggeration is also used as a device in an ad for A&P (figure 6-7), where the copy and visuals work cooperatively. If you compare the use of exaggeration in figures 6-6a, 6-6b, and 6-7, you can see the range of possibilities this device provides.

Unexpected uses for a potato peeler and a shower curtain rail almost become sight gags in playfully telling ads about the human condition for Ikea (figures 6-8a, 6-8b). Quirky illustrations and type are combined in a humorous ad to communicate the benefit of the Middleton brand (figure 6-9).

6-6a, 6-6b
"Leg Shave"
"Conference Room"
Agency: Crispin Porter + Bogusky/Miami
Creative Director: Alex Bogusky
Art Director: Alex Burnard
Copywriter: Ari Merkin
Photographer: Heimo
Client: GT

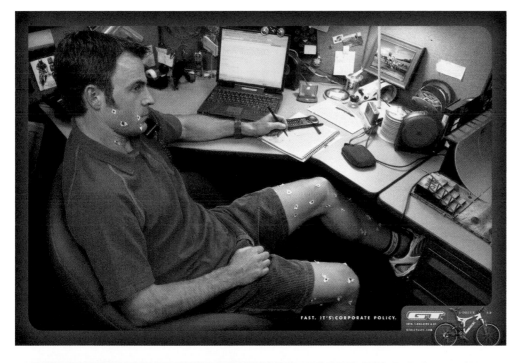

Riotously exaggerated visuals and the line "Fast. It's corporate policy" convey just how fast these bicycles can go.

6-7
"Picnic"
Agency: Rethink Advertising/Vancouver
Art Director: Tony Woods
Copywriter: Brent Wheeler
Photographers: George Simhoni, Jonathan Cesar, Genevieve Smith
Studio Artists/Typographers: Mark Tyler, Brent Mulligan
Client: A&P

This ad uses exaggeration to explain just how seriously A&P employees take their jobs.

6-8a, 6-8b
"Shower Curtain Rail"
"Potato Peeler"

Agency: Forsman & Bodenfors/Gothenburg
Art Directors: Karin Jacobsson, Anders Eklind
Copywriters: Filip Nilsson, Fredrik Jansson, Hjalmar Delehag
Photographer: Karolina Henke
Client: IKEA Sweden

Targeting men, these ads utilize unexpected visuals in a slice-of-life setting.

6-9
"All Six of Them"

Agency: PUSH Advertising/Orlando
Creative Director: John Ludwig
Copywriter: John Ludwig
Art Director: Ron Boucher
Client: Middleton

The linear quality of the type and illustrations correspond and are unified, working together to communicate the benefits of Middleton.

Satire, Parody, and Irony

Satire is a literary or artistic form exposing absurdity and foolishness. Parodies are works that imitate or mock the style of another author, artist, designer, or director. Usually parody is done for comic effect, as in a spoof on before-and-after ads for Lea & Perrins (figure 6-10).

The television show *Saturday Night Live* has satirized TV commercials. Ads can parody TV shows, contemporary events, or even other ads. Musicals are parodied for comic effect. Some ads for Old Navy retail stores are satires using passé television personalities. TV spots for eBay.com parody film musicals, with characters breaking out into song. Ad agency TBWA/Chiat/Day in Los Angeles featured the Energizer Bunny "going and going" in a series of parody TV spots, barging through mock commercials.

Embracing elements of postmodernism, some ads have mocked advertising itself, joking about their own brands and the advertising process and business. For example, Cliff Freeman & Partners' deconstructionist ads for Little Caesars pizza sneered at focus groups, and their Outpost.com ad took a jab at the lengths advertisers go to in order to get your attention

KesselsKramer creates fashion advertising for Diesel that winks ironically at both image advertising and advertising in general (figures 6-11a, 6-11b). "The idea for the models came from the concept of the campaign, which was to take an ironical look at the world of beauty. There is this obsession with staying young and perfect like a doll. We could have heavily air-brushed the images, but photographer Jean-Pierre Khazem was already working with these amazing silicone masks that were perfect for the idea. The masks give this eerie, doll-like perfection that fits with the messages of the campaign. The goal of the campaign, as with every Diesel campaign, is to maintain Diesel's ironic place in the world," says Erik Kessels.

6-10
"Transformation"
Agency: Mustoes/London
Creative Directors: Mick Mahoney, Andy Amadeo
Art Director: Mick Brigdale
Copywriter: Kevin Baldwin
Photographer: Rory Carnegie
Client: Lea & Perrins

Using humor, this subway poster puts a new spin on the "before and after" advertising comparison.

SAVE
YOURSELF /
CLONING

Louise Kemp-Welch (the 1st) born 1893

SAVE YOURSELF /
DRINK URINE

Helen Pickering, born 1890

6-11a, 6-11b
"Save Yourself"

Agency: KesselsKramer/Amsterdam
Art Director: Karen Heuter
Copywriter: Dave Bell
Photographer: Jean-Pierre Khazem
Client: Diesel

We are told how these strangely youthful, nubile models stay so young in these wickedly playful, ironic ads that definitely stand out from other ads in the fashion category.

6-12
"Waterproof Spray"

Agency: Sukle/Denver
Creative Director: Mike Sukle
Photographer: Richard Feldman
Client: Patos

This ad is so sexy, it borders on X-rated fetishism, though it resolutely makes a case for appealing footwear.

6-13
"Beauty Spot"

Agency: Euro RSCG/Brussels
Creative Director: Jean-Luc Soille
Art Director: Minou von de Kerckhove
Copywriter: Frederik Dewispelaire
Photographer: Christophe Gilbert
Client: Peugeot
© 2002

A beauty spot is likened to a turbo tailpipe, lending sexiness to the turbo diesel engine.

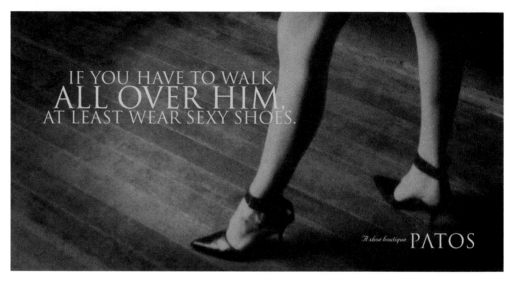

IF YOU HAVE TO WALK
ALL OVER HIM,
AT LEAST WEAR SEXY SHOES.

A shoe boutique PATOS

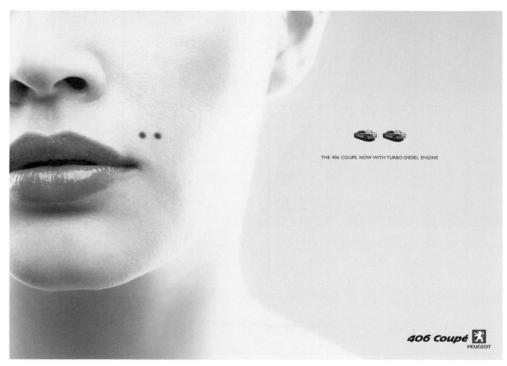

THE 406 COUPE. NOW WITH TURBO-DIESEL ENGINE

406 Coupé
PEUGEOT

Passion, Lust, and Desire

Sex, according to Freud, is a basic drive. Even if you've never studied Freud, it doesn't take much to realize that sex gets people's attention.

Sexually appealing models and sexy ad ideas have been used to sell everything from ratchets to shaving cream. In the 1960s, there was a TV spot for Noxzema shaving cream that used a very sexy blonde who purred, "Take it off. Take it all off!" as a man shaved off his beard with Noxzema brand shaving cream. We've come a long way since then, as evidenced by Sukle's sexy ad for Patos (figure 6-12).

When should you use sex to sell? Or should you ever use sex to sell? It depends upon your ethics. It depends upon your audience and the country. It depends upon your client. In some countries—for example, Brazil and France—frontal nudity is acceptable in ads, and ads are at times overtly sexual. In Europe, sexy ads have even been used as public service messages to convince people to use condoms to prevent the spread of sexually transmitted diseases. In other countries, such as the United States, people tend to be more conservative about nudity in advertising.

Sometimes it's interesting to mix sexiness with humor or the unexpected, as in Euro RSCG's ad for Peugeot (figure 6-13).

Triumph

People love triumph, whether it's the underdog, the hero, the soccer team, or the average person. The distinct advantage of this category is that the audience vicariously shares a moment of glory and feels good about the advertised brand or social cause, as in an ad on behalf of the Canadian Paraplegic Association that asks for help in seeking a cure for spinal cord injuries (figure 6-14).

6-14
"Wheelchair"

Agency: Butler, Shine & Stern/Sausalito
Creative Team: Brad Wood, Ryan Ebner
Client: Canadian Paraplegic Association
© 2003 Butler, Shine & Stern

This visually surprising use of a pictogram creates the illusion of movement and acts as a symbol of working toward a cure for spinal injuries.

HELP CURE SPINAL CORD INJURIES. Send your donation to The Canadian Paraplegic Association, 520 Sutherland Drive, Toronto, ON M4G 3V9. (416) 422-5644. Or visit info@cpaont.org.

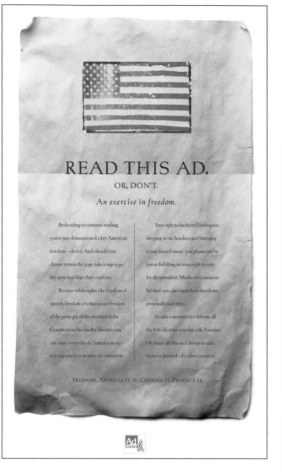

6-15
Campaign for Freedom: "Flag"

Agency: TBWA/Chiat/Day/Los Angeles
Chief Creative Director: Lee Clow
Creative Directors: Duncan Milner, Eric Grunbaum
Copywriter: Chris Adams
Art Director: Liz Soares
Client: Ad Council

With a very clever succinct headline, this ad
explains the cherished freedom Americans enjoy.

6-17a, 6-17b
"Hallowed and Paved"
"Casualties"

Agency: Work, Inc./Richmond
Creative Director: Cabell Harris
Art Director: Chris Just
Copywriter: Maryann Neary-Gill, Danny Boone
Photographer: Karl Steinbrenner
Photo Illustration: Lot 44
Client: Gettysburg National Battlefield Museum Foundation
© 2002 Gettysburg National Battlefield Museum Foundation

"These ads—and all of the collateral material that Work
designed—highlight the importance of the Civil War as
perhaps the defining moment in America's history, and remind
Americans to honor the events and heroes of the past as
guides for our future. In many ways, Gettysburg represents a
second independence day for the United States."

6-16
"America"

Agency: PUSH Advertising/Orlando
Creative Director: John Ludwig
Copywriter: John Ludwig
Art Director: Ron Boucher
Photographer: Shari O'Neal
Client: Boy Scouts of America,
Central Florida Council

Playing off the idea of respecting
the U.S. labor force by buying
clothing made here, this ad is
about the Boy Scouts as a symbol
of American national pride.

Respect and Value

Importance can be placed on many aspects of life—personal character, country, or achievements. An appeal to national pride can be used to communicate a message, as in TBWA/Chiat/Day's very intelligent ad for the Campaign for Freedom (figure 6-15), where the ad is made to look like an American historical decree or document. Another ad treats the Boy Scouts as a symbol of America (figure 6-16).

The Work agency explains their campaign for the Gettysburg National Battlefield Museum Foundation (figures 6-17a, 6-17b):

> The purpose of the project is the need to restore, properly preserve, and present the battlefield, historic relics and documents in a way that will give visitors a deeper, more lasting appreciation of what happened there.
>
> In designing these materials, we wanted to capture the value of history as presented through the stories of the brave soldiers who fought during the Civil War. . . . Our goal in the creative process was to develop creative that encouraged people to take another look at a place they thought they knew.

Pathos and Compassion

An ad based on pathos can move us to pity or summon forth compassion or sorrow. Often, ads for nonprofit agencies or charities utilize this approach in order to motivate us to give money, time, or needed supplies (food, blood, clothing, etc.). At times, the ads are so poignant, with images of starving children, people living in cardboard boxes, or animals who have been tortured or put to death, that we can barely watch them. What the ads are trying to do is create a "sympathetic consciousness of others' distress together with a desire to alleviate it."[2] This approach may appeal to our humanity, as in ads for the Virginia Holocaust Museum (figures 6-18a, 6-18b). About this campaign, the Martin Agency comments: "The museum's curator, Jay Ipson, guided art director Christopher Gyorgy and copywriter Chris Jacobs through the museum and recounted the Ipson family experience of escaping a Nazi death camp in Lithuania. The experience proved to be deeply moving for Gyorgy and Jacobs and began a two-year process to develop advertising that gave people compelling reasons to visit the museum."

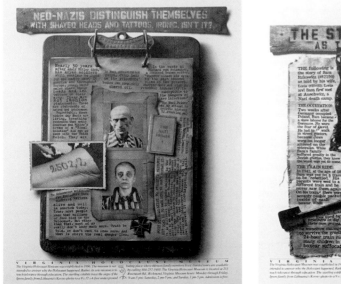

6-18a, 6-18b
"The Story of 82190"
"Neo-Nazis Distinguish"

Agency: The Martin Agency/Richmond
Creative Team: Brad Wood, Ryan Ebner
Co-Creative Directors: Christopher Gyorgy, Chris Jacobs
Art Director: Christopher Gyorgy
Copywriter: Chris Jacobs
Photographer: Kip Dawkins
Studio Artist: Tyson Brown
Photo Illustration: Jeff Satterthwaite, Liquid Pictures/Richmond
Client: Virginia Holocaust Museum
© 2000 Virginia Holocaust Museum, 2000 East Cary St., Richmond, Virginia

"While it was a rewarding and life-changing experience, it was also the most frustrating campaign I've ever written. The topic is so broad and so emotional that condensing it down to four posters felt trite to me. The museum quickly reminded me, however, that if we got people to stop and think, we've done our job," said Chris Jacobs, copywriter on this campaign, who is now with Cole Henderson Drake in Atlanta.

"The Holocaust had always been an academic exercise for me until this," said Gyorgy. "When I held a piece of Hitler's stationery in my hands, it was a surreal experience—I had never been that close to pure evil. The museum features dozens of artifacts from Nazi Germany that tell the Ipson family Holocaust story in a hauntingly real way. My goal with the art direction was to preserve the visceral detail of the items and to give people a glimpse of what the museum had to offer."

"The posters literally made me cry," said curator and Holocaust survivor Jay Ipson.

For the same museum, Arnika created a brochure (figure 6-19). Arnika comments: "This brochure needed to raise money and awareness for the Holocaust Museum's new location. The museum had no budget, but had to compete for donations at a time when everyone was trying to raise money immediately after 9/11. We knew the piece would have to work very hard to stand out. In the end, the brochure helped the museum raise $4 million toward the construction of the new facility."

By forcing us to share the suffering of others, an ad may compel us to take action. Appropriating the spot on the Oreo cookie where the brand mark normally resides, an ad asks for donations for the San Francisco Food Bank (figure 6-20).

6-19
Tolerance Brochure
Agency: Arnika/Richmond
Creative Director: Michael Ashley
Art Director/Designer/Illustrator: Michael Ashley
Copywriters: Dinesh Kapoor, Michael Ashley, Matt Blum
Client: Virginia Holocaust Museum, Richmond, VA
© 2003 Arnika LLC

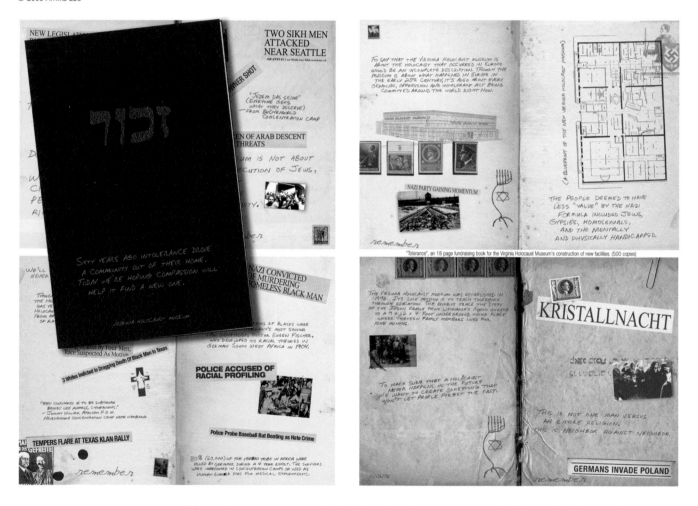

Using contemporary events combined with photographs and imagery on the subject of the Holocaust, this brochure powerfully illustrates why we should never forget any type of persecution based on race, religion, or ethnicity, and why we all need this museum.

It's more than just food.

THE SAN FRANCISCO FOOD BANK 1-800-870-FOOD

6-20
"Oreo"
Agency: Butler, Shine & Stern/Sausalito
Creative Team: John Butler, Ryan Ebner
Client: San Francisco Food Bank
© 2003 Butler, Shine & Stern

Borrowing interest from an existing product, this ad rebrands the idea of food as hope.

6-21
Agency: Giovanni, FCB/Rio de Janeiro
Client: Sociedade Síndrome de Down

Banking on our preconceived notions about people with Down syndrome, this spot makes a very important point about reevaluating our thinking.

Fear

In advertising, all sorts of fears can be used to motivate people to take action. The fear of leaving our families unprotected may prompt us to purchase life insurance. Fear of being socially ostracized may prompt us to use deodorant, mouthwash, dandruff shampoo, acne medication, age-defying cream, hair coloring, and a host of other products. Fear of losing one's job might motivate one to use the "right" brand of computer or overnight carrier. Fear of contracting AIDS motivates condom use. Is it ethical to use fear to motivate a viewer? Using fear on behalf of social causes seems justifiable.

Shock and Changing Our Expectations

Banking on the viewer's expectations—the belief that something is going to happen in a particular fashion—and defying those expectations can lead to some very dramatic communication. In a PSA for the Down Syndrome Society, we see wait staff working in a restaurant (figure 6-21). When we hear a plate drop, we fully expect it was dropped by the server with Down syndrome, but it was not. Quickly and keenly, this important message points out our misconceptions.

Readers at first are shocked by an ad for the National Sports Center for the Disabled (figure 6-22). Seeing a disabled young person labeled with a sign reading "Push Me" is very shocking—until we read further and discover the actual meaning of the headline.

To warn people about the extreme dangers and consequences of prolonged sun exposure, Heimat uses unusual images that bring us to our senses (figures 6-23a, 6-23b).

6-22

"Push Me"

Agency: Sukle/Denver
Creative Director/Art Director: Mike Sukle
Photographer: Jay Dickman
Client: National Sports Center for the Disabled

Shock tactics are enlisted in the good service of social advertising.

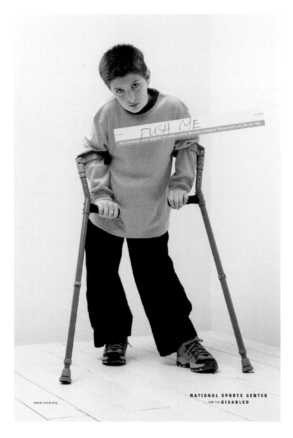

6-23a, 6-23b

"Rucken" ("Back")
"Streifen" ("Stripes")

Agency: Heimat/Berlin
Client: ADP

In the first ad, seeing the cancerous melanomas that are a result of tanning being sprinkled on a beautiful torso is frightening, but also serves as a reminder to us to prevent skin cancer. In the second, tanned skin may seem appealing, but eventually years of exposure to the sun leads to skin cancer; in the last stripe of color we see the skin color of a corpse.

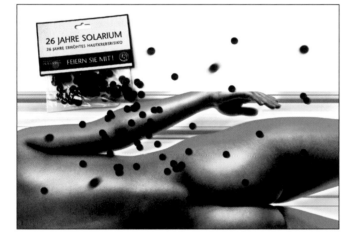

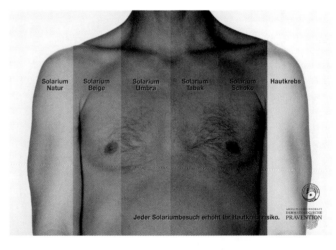

6-24

"E-mail"

Agency: Sawyer Riley Compton/Atlanta
Web site: www.brandstorytellers.com
Creative Director: Bart Cleveland
Associate Creative Director/Copywriter: Brett Compton
Art Director: Rick Bryson
Photographer: Andy Anderson
Client: James Hardie Siding Products
© 2003

Our emotional connection to home is visualized by arrangements of family photos on beautifully painted walls.

Association

When a stranger walks by and you get a whiff of the fragrance he is wearing, the scent reminds you of a long-ago boyfriend. The smell of the ocean on your skin provokes memories of summers at the beach. People form mental connections between responses. Linking memories with a person, place, or thing is common. (In fact, associational devices are used to improve memory.) Our tendency to form mental connections between brands and memories is what this category of ads can bank on, encouraging emotional bonds between the consumer and the brand.

Images of "coming home," associating home with the good things in life, are vehicles used in campaigns for many different products. Some things may change (we may someday vacation on the moon), and some things have changed (we correspond via e-mail), but there is still no place like home. In one ad, James Hardie Siding Products reminds us to maintain and care for the home we love (figure 6-24).

In a TV spot for HP Sauce (figures 6-25), we see a young woman associate coming home with comfort food—a bacon sandwich with HP sauce. Mustoes Qualitative Research quotes one consumer as saying, "When I come home from holiday, the first thing I do is put the kettle on and have a nice cup of tea and a bacon sandwich." Added the researchers, "This comment summed up the general view—that there are certain foods that capture the feelings of security, safety, and indulgence of coming home. Bacon sandwiches and HP Sauce are two of those foods—which happen to also complement each other perfectly."

6-25
"Bacon Sandwich"
Agency: Mustoes/London
Creative Director: John Merriman
Art Director: Mary Sue
Copywriter: Rosie Elston
Client: HP Foods

This TV spot associates HP sauce with a snack—a bacon sandwich—and depicts it in a comforting and homey way.

Notes

1. John Lyons, *Guts* (New York: AMACOM, 1989), p. 252.

2. Merriam-Webster dictionary definition of *compassion*.

INTERVIEW John Butler

Creative Director, Butler, Shine & Stern/Sausalito

Do you think humor in advertising works?

I don't think that we ever attack an assignment by saying, "How funny can we make this one?" I think it's just common that people remember stuff that makes them laugh, as opposed to a smart, thoughtful line or idea. Humor is universal, and it's an easy way to connect to your audience. But it's not the only way. We try to keep it balanced. We start out trying to find something that's both relevant and interesting about a brand, something smart and thoughtful usually, and if we can't find that, we'll generally just go for the crack-up.

How do you continually come up with ideas?

We have a proprietary computer program here that does it all for us. We just type in the client's name and a few words from the brief, and it spits out campaigns. It's great!

Okay, seriously, there's just no way to answer that. I think every great author or filmmaker gets asked that as well at some point, and no one ever has an answer for it. I think the important thing is to not think about advertising 24-7; you need to get out and experience things or you have no reference point to write from. The best thinkers in this business have a lot of other interests, and you see it in their work. We have artists and musicians and photographers and writers of things other than ads working here. If it's 9 p.m. and I'm walking out the door, and I pass someone still sitting here, I try to make him or her leave. Unless it's a new business pitch—then we do crank 24-7 usually.

What's your ideation process?

We try to absorb ourselves into a brand when we are working on a brief. We get out and experience our client's brands as much as possible. For Specialized, we rode. Mt. Tam is in our backyard, so we just made sure we were on it frequently enough to know what the heck we were talking about. There's a PlayStation, an Xbox, and a Game Cube sitting downstairs that always have three or four people on them (hey, wait a minute . . .), and Anchor Blue keeps us pretty busy hanging out with skaters and bladers as well. We've even had people put on silly hats and act as counter girls/boys serving up food to understand what our client's business was all about.

We do a number of groups and one-on-ones with consumers in our own focus group facility here at the agency. We also have a proprietary (really, this time) publication called *In-Flux* that exists in magazine form as well as online, that identifies trends in pop culture, fashion, and sports. In a lot of ways, *In-Flux* is really the starting point for everything. All employees are exposed to a number of different stimuli like this; it keeps all of us sharp and plugged in. (I actually said "plugged in"—someone shoot me.)

Do you have to consider the brand as a whole and its brand essence campaign when you create an ad campaign?

Brands are funny things. Just like people, they are constantly evolving. Nike is probably the best example of this. You have to know what your brand represents, but constantly be aware that this may not be consistent with what consumers are taking away on their own. Sometimes we hear the comment "That's just not us," and I generally counter with "How do you know?"

How do you utilize predesign research? Postdesign research?

If you mean do we do research before we start on a project, to help us define our communication strategy, the answer is yes. We get some preliminary thinking in front of as many

POINT OF DIFFERENTIATION #27:

WHILE MAINTAINING HIGHLY TARGETED AFFLUENT VIEWERS, COMEDY CENTRAL HAS ACHIEVED 15 STRAIGHT QUARTERS OF RATINGS GROWTH.

CONCLUSION:

OUR ORIGINAL AND DIVERSE PROGRAMMING IS POPULAR AS EVER.

AND, WITH THE INCREASED REVENUE, WE'LL FINALLY BE ABLE TO REMOVE THE ASBESTOS IN THE DAYCARE CENTER.

SOUTH PARK

THE DAILY SHOW WITH JON STEWART

[X] DIFFERENT [X] BETTER [X] ESSENTIAL [X] UNIQUE

THE ONLY PLACE YOU'LL FIND THEM IS HERE.

FOR MORE INFORMATION CONTACT
DAVID KOHL AT (212) 767-8645 OR
GARY MERRIFIELD AT (248) 723-0020

6-26
"Asbestos"
Agency: Butler, Shine & Stern/Sausalito
Creative Team: Jerome Marucci, Alex Grossman
Client: Comedy Central
© 2003 Butler, Shine & Stern

Using the illusion of a three-dimensional clipboard, this ad attracts us and then retains our attention with humor.

consumers as we can to determine what "baggage" a brand has already, or to simply make sure that we aren't bringing our own baggage into the process. We try to determine what consumers know and think about a brand before we start mucking with it. After the fact, we try to do some qualitative research to determine if consumers are taking away what we set out to accomplish.

What's your philosophy about advertising?
It has to be likeable. It has to inform and inspire. It has to have some emotional hook to it that makes consumers interact with it. It can't talk down to the consumer. There's a great quote, I can't remember who said it, but it's hanging on my door: "He who writes the sto-

ries defines the culture." I think that pretty much sums it up. We are given a voice, and we have to be responsible in how we use that voice.

Butler, Shine & Stern regularly does creative work pro bono—why?

Two reasons. One is purely selfish, the other is more philanthropic. Early on, because of the Sega experience we had at Goodby and our age, we were looked at as the young, in-your-face, edgy, Gen X guys who would knock one out of the park for you if you needed to communicate to the sixteen-to-twenty-four age group. Public service let us show a different side to the place, and we figured if we couldn't bring them in the door with our charm and wit, we'd better make sure that the reel was diverse. So I'd be lying if I just said it was just because we wanted to give something back." But we are concerned with this world we live in, and we try to do something for the community every year. As local as possible. We've done work for the San Francisco Food Bank, the Marin Homeless Shelter, the AIDS Memorial Quilt, and are currently doing some work for the Firefighters National Trust, an organization that makes sure that donations go directly to the family members of fallen firefighters. If it's something we believe in, we'll generally do it.

part three

The Visual and Verbal Expression of an Idea

Design and Copy

7

Graphic Impact: Design Principles

The Design Process

Sketches

Once your research is completed, you sketch to give form to your ideas.

Many people create thumbnail sketches—small rough sketches—during the initial stage of the design process. Some use a pencil or marker; some create their thumbnails right on the computer. Either way, it's an important phase. Many students are tempted to create one bigger design on the computer, but that's a danger in that it tends to inhibit the generation of other solutions, exploration, and experimentation.

Experimentation

It's in the initial design stage that you can wildly explore. Try anything and everything that serves your advertising idea and the client's brand. Part of the fun of being an art director or designer is experimenting.

Intuition and Feelings

Another part of being a creative professional is trusting your "inner artist," that little voice suggesting the most creative solutions. Trusting your talent, your training, and your creative hunches is what makes you a creative individual.

Creativity and Risk

Most children are creative; they make random associations, mix metaphors, combine things into new arrangements. Somehow we lose that to rational thought as we become adults. Fear—the fear of taking risks and appearing foolish—also causes us to lose our creative inclination. Risk taking is good; it stretches a designer's limits. Stay open-minded.

Roughs

Once you've created a good number of thumbnails, it's time to turn a few of them into roughs. Thanks to computer technology, most roughs don't look rough; they look like slick, professionally printed pieces. The advantage to this is that you can very clearly see what the piece will look like. The disadvantage is that this same finished look seems to inhibit reworking things. Don't be seduced by the slickness—keep designing. Keep working on the arrangement, and especially on the typography.

Depending upon the advertising agency or design studio, you may show either thumbnails or roughs to your creative director. You'll get her input and then go back to designing some more. You'll probably get input from others as well, including your partner, the copywriter, and perhaps an associate creative director or other team members.

Comps

Once your creative director has approved your design, you create final comprehensives (comps) to show your client. After your client gives his input, you'll probably have to do some additional designing. It's rare that a client says, "That's perfect! Let's print it." More often than not, the design process involves redesigning.

Composition: Critical Principles of Design

You may have terrific advertising ideas in your head, but to be an art director, you need design skills and the sensibility to communicate your ideas. Line, color, shape, type, texture, form, pattern, light, space—the elements of design visually interact to shout or whisper ideas and emotions. Design for advertising has a main thrust; combined with words, it stimulates perceptions in order to sell products, services, and ideas.

The way you create, select, and arrange everything—the type, visuals, and graphic elements—in an ad or graphic design piece is design. It's the composition or arrangement. The design is part and parcel of your concept, your idea, and helps to communicate the idea.

Format

Whether it's a magazine ad or a computer screen, whatever substrate you start out with is the *format,* a vital element in two-dimensional design. Brochures, posters, video screens, and outdoor boards are just a few of the many formats designers use.

Formats come in a variety of shapes. Most are rectangular. There are standard rectangles (for example, a standard-size magazine page), which are not extremely long in any one direction, and elongated rectangles, which are much longer in one direction, either vertical or horizontal (such as a magazine spread of two facing pages or an outdoor board). For example, a poster for Spyke Beer is an elongated vertical format (figure 7-1). The shape of the format influences the use of the other formal elements, such as line and shape, as well as compositional decisions. Designing on a computer screen, a standard-size rectangle, is a different experience from composing and designing on a folded brochure that opens into an extended horizontal.

How do you learn to compose within differently shaped formats well, appropriately, and to your advantage? The best way to learn about the inherent energy and distinctions of formats is to explore them, play with their boundaries, and design within them.

7-1
"Lab Rats"
Agency: Butler, Shine & Stern/Sausalito
Creative Team: Haj Audo, Mike Shine
Client: Anheuser Busch/Spyke
© 2003 Butler, Shine & Stern

This interesting composition makes great use of an elongated format.

Balance

Viewers need to feel or sense balance in order to comfortably engage with the arrangement and to believe the design is complete. A design that is poorly balanced might frustrate viewers, making them feel uncomfortable and possibly dismiss the message. Combining the principles of balance with other design principles will ensure that your compositions function harmoniously and deliver the message you intend.

Symmetry

A symmetric design uses similar or identical elements arranged on two sides of an imaginary horizontal or vertical axis so that each side of the composition is a mirror image of the other. The resulting arrangement is orderly and feels stable. Symmetry works favorably because of the strong sense of stability it projects. This feeling can be tapped to contribute to or reinforce the expressiveness of a design.

Asymmetry

An asymmetric design has a balance of visual weights, but the arrangement is not formalized around a central axis. Asymmetry relies on a complex positioning and interaction of dissimilar elements to arrive at a sense of equilibrium throughout the arrangement. Any composition that is balanced and not symmetric is asymmetric. The asymmetric design challenges the viewer to search and discover the compositional balance. The balance created through an asymmetric composition is not as obvious as a symmetric one. Asymmetry's dynamic nature commands attention as well as actively engages the viewer. Asymmetric designs can help express a feeling or define your message. Compare the compositions in two cleverly creative ads in the same campaign—one is symmetric and the other is asymmetric (figures 7-2, 7-3). In another ad in the campaign, "Where Did We Park the Car?," the visual is almost symmetric; however, the line is positioned at the left, balanced by the claim in the upper right-hand corner and the product name in the lower right-hand corner, making the composition asymmetrical (figure 7-4).

Here's the key: whether on paper or computer screen, a viewer who is comfortable and engaged with a composition is likely to remain interested.

7-2
"Freezers"

Agency: Forsman & Bodenfors/Gothenburg
Art Directors: Anders Eklind, Andreas Malm, Mikko Timonen
Copywriters: Johan Olivero, Filip Nilsson
Photographer: Henrik Bonevier
Client: Volvo Cars Sweden

This humorous ad utilizes a symmetric composition to make a point about Volvo's ability.

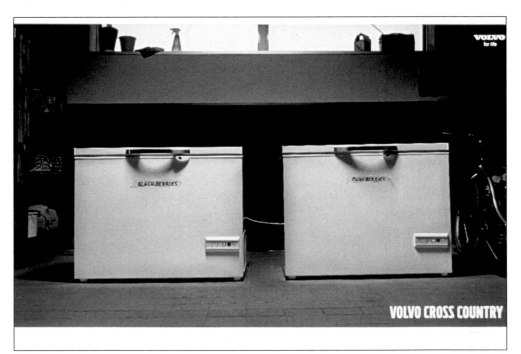

7-3
"Seat Belt"

Agency: Forsman & Bodenfors/Gothenburg
Art Directors: Anders Eklind, Andreas Malm, Mikko Timonen
Copywriters: Johan Olivero, Filip Nilsson
Photographer: Jesper Brandt
Client: Volvo Cars Sweden

Equating driving in a convertible to getting a tan on the beach, this ad's amusing drama is enhanced by the asymmetric composition.

7-4
"Where Did We Park the Car?"

Agency: Forsman & Bodenfors/Gothenburg
Art Directors: Anders Eklind, Andreas Malm, Mikko Timonen
Copywriters: Johan Olivero, Filip Nilsson
Photographer: Sjöberg Photo Agency
Client: Volvo Cars Sweden

Using humor, this ad illustrates a vehicle's ablity to go through extreme terrain.

Positive/Negative Shapes and Space

In a successful positive/negative relationship, the positive (visuals, type, graphic elements) and the negative (space between and around positive elements) are interdependent and interactive. No space should go unconsidered. *Dead space* refers to blank areas that are not actively working in the overall design; this does *not* mean that all blank space must be filled. (Most visually unsophisticated clients would prefer that you fill every available space, believing that they are getting more design for their money.) A designer must be constantly aware of the blank spaces and make them work in the design, as does designer Paula Scher in the poster "Dancing on Her Knees," created for the Public Theater in New York (figure 7-5). Notice the way the leg in this poster leads to the title of the play, *Dancing on Her Knees*. Directing the viewer's eyes with the placement of elements—that is, how one element leads to another—also helps establish a visual hierarchy (discussed in the next section). Actively dividing the space contributes to a dynamic composition. Both positive and negative shapes become active in a symmetric poster by Luba Lukova (figure 7-6); acting as both a nuclear cloud and a backdrop between the figures, the black shape is forceful. Considering all the space actively forces you to consider the *whole* space. Think of it as holistic design.

7-5
"Dancing on Her Knees"
Studio: Pentagram/New York
Creative Director/Partner: Paula Scher
Client: Public Theater

Not only does the background become an active participant due to the color and division of space, but one element directs our eyes to the next.

7-6
"War Is Not the Answer"
Studio: Luba Lukova Studio
Designer: Luba Lukova
Client: AIGA Orlando
© Luba Lukova

Lukova treats all space, both positive and negative, as active—yielding very dramatic communication.

AIGA Orlando presents **Luba Lukova**
November 12th, 2002 • 6:30pm-8:30pm • at the Orange County Regional History Center's Grand Ball Room

war is not the answer

Visual Hierarchy

What's the main message? What's the ad trying to tell me? Sell me? Where can I buy it? Whom do I call?

From every ad, a reader tries to glean information. If an ad does not have a visual hierarchy, then the reader will have a very difficult time getting information, and will probably give up trying. For example, in Butler, Shine & Stern's ad for Valor Tours, there is a great deal of information and four images (figure 7-7). Without a visual hierarchy, we wouldn't be able to get the advertising message easily. First we look at the center, boxed headline; second, at the biggest photograph; third, at the smaller two photographs at top; then we go on to the body copy; and finally, we move to the bottom right-hand corner. More importantly, if there is no visual hierarchy, the ad will, in almost all cases, look chaotic and not attract readers in the first place.

In an ad, the most important information is the message communicated by the combination of the line (headline) and visual. However, the viewer's eyes can go to only one place at a time, so the designer should arrange all the elements within the composition to allow the viewer to move effortlessly from one element to another. Even though it is the cooperative action of the headline and visual that communicates the ad message, the viewer will tend to look at one before the other. Either the visual or the line should be the focal point.

After that, some people read the body copy, and most people, if engaged by the main message, look at the sign-off (claim, logo, or product shot). Certainly, the goal is to design such a compelling ad that the reader takes in all the information, including the body copy. In posters that advertise events, there is additional important information that must be accessible, such as the date, time, and location of the event. In public service advertising there is usually a phone number or Web address. *All* information must be arranged into a visual hierarchy.

The art director or designer is responsible for arranging all the elements so that there is a main focus or focal point, which is usually the main ad message, and then subsequent information. What do you want the reader to see first? Second? Third? Fourth? In Richter 7's dramatic ad for WCF, there is a clear visual hierarchy (figure 7-8). First we see the hand, second the headline, third the subheadline, then the body copy, and finally the logo.

7-7
"Japanese"

Agency: Butler, Shine & Stern/Sausalito
Creative Team: Brad Wood, Ryan Ebner
Client: Valor Tours
© 2003 Butler, Shine & Stern

Often, the art director must include a great deal of information in one ad. That's when visual hierarchy is key to communication.

It's the designer's job to control the order in which type and visuals are seen by the reader, even when there is a great deal of type, as in Hunt Adkins' ad for American Skandia (figure 7-9). In this ad, first we read the headline; then our eyes move to the left-hand column. The visuals inset into the body copy help move our eyes from column to column and then finally to the sign-off of the logo and tagline.

7-8
"Four Out of Five"
Agency: Richter 7/Salt Lake City
Creative Director: T. C. Christensen
Art Director: Ryan Anderson
Copywriter: Eric Gutierrez
Photographer: Tyler Gourley
Client: Workers Compensation Fund

This is a great example of the art director being able to steer the viewer's eyes very effectively from one element to another in the composition.

7-9
Financial Services Company
Agency: Hunt Adkins/Minneapolis
Creative Director/Copywriter: Doug Adkins
Associate Creative Director/Art Director: Steve Mitchell
Photographer: Joe Lampi
Client: American Skandia

The layout conveys the message "Trust us," in essence saying, "We know what we're talking about," and the wit makes an investment company feel friendlier.

In a magazine ad, creating a meaningful hierarchical relationship between the main line (headline) and visual is a delicate balancing act. The designer must consider:

- Format
- Scale (size relationships between type and images)
- Weight of type
- Size of all the type, including the line and body copy
- Arrangement (composition)
- Color and value

7-10a, 7-10b
"Pity"
"Stare at It"
Agency: Carmichael Lynch/Minneapolis
Creative Director: Brian Kroening
Art Director: James Clunie
Copywriter: Michael Atkinson
Photographer: Ron Crofoot
Client: American Standard

The design and concept behind this campaign changed consumers' perception of American Standard from institutional to stylish.

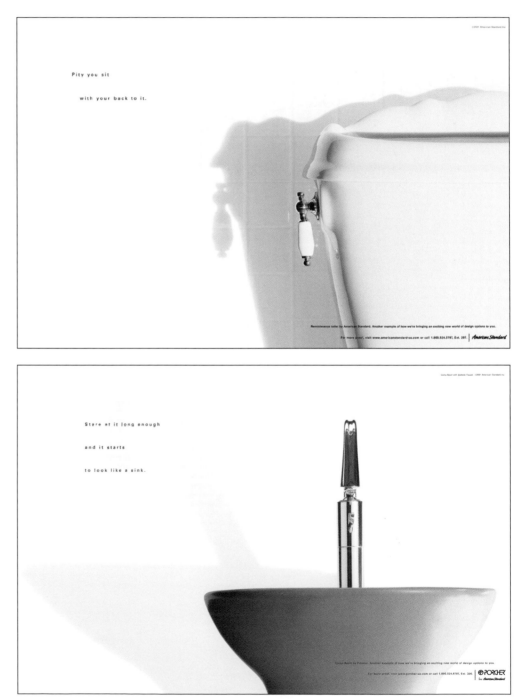

In an ad that has no or very little copy—where the entire message is communicated by the visual—the visual must have a main focal point and, if necessary, secondary and perhaps additional levels of focal points. Turning bathroom fixtures into beautiful art objects, ads for American Standard use the fixture as the main focal point (figures 7-10a, 7-10b). If a visual is carrying the entire responsibility of communicating the ad message, then it must be carefully created or selected, with care given to the visual hierarchy of the elements in the image. In an ad where there is copy and no visual, visual hierarchy is paramount.

Unity and Variety

A design must hold together. A design has *unity* when the elements look as though they belong together. How does a designer get the entire ad or Web site or direct mail piece to work as a whole, to look unified?

One of the most important factors affecting unity is *correspondence,* that is, connections among all the elements. When elements, such as color, texture, a font, imagery, and direction, are repeated, then correspondence is established. Our eyes and mind expect some type of repetition; we have various types of memory, hierarchical perception, pattern recognition, and associative processes. Mike Quon uses flat shapes to create both the positive forms (dove and war plane) and the background shapes and a font that is perceived as flat shapes to create correspondence among all the elements in the stirring "Peace Poster" (figure 7-11). In the "Printed Woman" exhibition poster, flat shapes with white lines that describe details

7-11
Peace Poster
Agency: Designation/New York
Art Director/Designer: Mike Quon
© Mike Quon 2002

Unity is established in this poster by utilizing a similar vocabulary of forms and by establishing flow from one element to another.

within them are combined with hand lettering in white, establishing unity between the visual and the typographic design (figure 7-12).

There are many ways to create unity in the design of a single ad. Elements may be repeated in the design. Color alone can create an amazingly powerful correspondence throughout a design. Integrating elements so that they seem completely united greatly contributes to flow,

7-12
"The Printed Woman"

Studio: Luba Lukova Studio
Designer: Luba Lukova
Client: La MaMa e.t.c.
© Luba Lukova

Often, Lukova uses her own hand-drawn lettering to ensure that the type and visual act in concert, to communicate expressively.

7-13
"Hands"

Agency: Butler, Shine & Stern/Sausalito
Creative Team: Nathan Naylor, Mike Shine, Nicole Michels
Client: Il Fornaio
© 2003 Butler, Shine & Stern

The visual and type, in this ad, are conceived together to contribute to flow and unity.

Some of the main ways to achieve unity:

Correspondence

Thematic processes

Repetition of an element in slightly altered form at various points in the design

Type alignment

Continuity (family resemblance among elements)

Flow or movement by arrangement of elements

as in the "Hands" ad for Il Fornaio (figure 7-13). Flow is the ease of movement from one element to another in a composition.

Establishing unity within a campaign (a series of ads) is a similar process. One must have corresponding elements in the ads, such as color palette, fonts, type alignment, and compositional templates, as in Hunt Adkins' entertaining campaign for the Minnesota Twins (figures 7-14a, 7-14b). In the American Standard campaign (see figure 7-10), the color palette, lighting, theme, and type arrangements all contribute to correspondence among the ads. Although there is some variety in the template, the entire campaign has a unified look. While all the objects and images change in the campaign for Plasmon (see figure 7-22), the template and theme remain constant. (See also Chapter 9, on the ad campaign.) Even within a series of ads, one can establish unity with variety.

In music, continuity and discontinuity, in varying degrees, are used as a basic structuring dimension. The same holds for design. Variety is necessary to break continuity and create visual interest. You always want a visual surprise. Steven Brower, the creative director of *Print* magazine, says editorial design is about creating unity and discord to surprise the reader. Some level of discontinuity makes the entire piece more perceivable.

Unity must be maintained in television commercials, Web films, and Web sites as well. The Web site for the Polynesian Cultural Center establishes unity from screen to screen by keeping certain elements in the same position on the screen, which gives the user a good sense of "geography" (figures 7-15a, 7-15b). Variety is also crucial in TV spots and on the Web. We spend more time watching something unfold on television or moving through Web pages. Shifting things, whether it's the sound or the lighting or the cuts, while maintaining an underlying template or look can make things less boring.

7-14a, 7-14b
"Koskie"
"Guzman"
Agency: Hunt Adkins/Minneapolis
Creative Director/Copywriter: Doug Adkins
Associate Creative Director/Art Director: Steve Mitchell
Client: Minnesota Twins

The visual surprises—a log as a bat, winged shoes—work cooperatively with the lines to communicate the ad concept of getting to know the Twins.

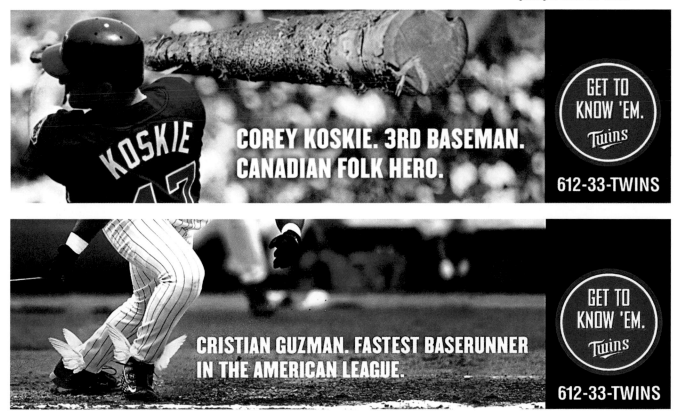

 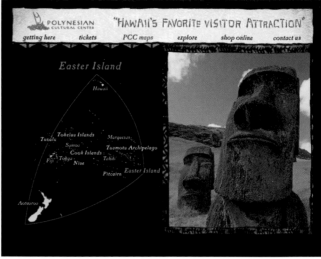

7-15a, 7-15b
Web site

Agency: Richter 7/Salt Lake City
Creative Director: T. C. Christensen
Designers: Mike Dunford, Ryan Anderson
Copywriter: Dave Newbold
Client: Polynesian Cultural Center

Creating visual correspondence among the pages, unity throughout the entire work, and rhythm and flow from page to page is crucial. Providing a sense of location for the visitor is equally important.

Rhythm

Whether you call it the "beat" or the "pulse," every design has rhythm. There should be an underlying tempo and meter that sets a pace and consequently a feeling. Elements can be arranged so that they are perceived at a rapid rate, at a slow rate, or at a rate that varies.

> *Rhythm* is a pattern that is created by repeating or varying elements, with consideration given to the space between them, and by establishing a sense of movement from one element to another. The key to establishing rhythm in design is to understand the difference between repetition and variation. Repetition occurs when you repeat visual elements with some or total consistency. Variation can be established by changing any number of elements, such as the color, size, shape, spacing, position, and visual weight of the elements in a design.[1]

Types of Compositions

In years past there were formulas for print ad compositions, as the legendary art director and designer George Lois points out in his book *What's the Big Idea?*

> Advertising has no rules—what it always needs more than "rules" is unconstipated thinking. The most significant advertising innovation in this century has been the Creative Revolution of the late 1950s and 1960s, when words and graphics finally merged. Until then, young artists entered the world equipped with nothing more than fatuous rules on the five or six ways to do a layout.[2]

The conventional thinking about layouts before the creative revolution (and, to the consternation of many, after) was:

- A large illustration or photograph above a headline, which was above a block of body copy, with the logo in the lower right-hand corner; *or*

- A headline above a large illustration or photograph, which was above a block of body copy, with the logo in the lower right-hand corner; *or*

- A big headline above a small illustration or photograph, which was above a block of body copy, with the logo in the lower right-hand corner.

Another legendary agency head, David Ogilvy, who felt strongly about particular compositions, listed rules for layout or composition in his book *Ogilvy on Advertising*.

7-16
"Condiment/Spaghetti Sauce"
Agency: DeVito/Verdi/New York
Creative Director: Sal DeVito
Art Director: Susanne Macarelli
Copywriter: Erhan Erdem
Client: eCampus.com

In this campaign, we see the same images labeled differently to make a point about why one needs eCampus.com.

There are as many ways to design a print ad or Web site as there are ways to design anything. What you need to do is take into account how well and fast the advertising message is communicated by applying principles of balance, visual hierarchy, unity, and rhythm. In an ad for eCampus.com, our eyes easily move from top to bottom along a line of movement based on a diagonal (figure 7-16). In a composition for the Atlanta Ballet, the line or headline is composed of two signs, Poison Control and Puncture Wounds, embedded in a very large photograph, which is an integrated way of fusing copy with the visual in composition (figure 7-17).

Since the creative revolution, advertising has come to look less and less like the visual sales pitches of the industry's early days. Advertising that doesn't look like advertising is meant to attract ad-weary viewers. Many art directors go for a posterlike quality, as in the dramatic "Goodbye Cal" ad for the Babe Ruth Museum (figure 7-18) or a film-noir-styled ad for Specialized (figure 7-19). The look of an ad can be borrowed from other formats—labels, logos, packaging, book jackets (figure 7-20), children's books (see figure 8-8), or signage (figure 7-21).

7-17
"Hospital"

Agency: Sawyer Riley Compton/Atlanta
Web site: www.brandstorytellers.com
Creative Director: Bart Cleveland
Associate Creative Director: Al Jackson
Art Director: Kevin Thoem
Copywriter: Ari Weiss
Photographer: Dave Kiesgen
Client: Atlanta Ballet
© 2001

The signs in a hospital setting are a modern way of explaining how Romeo and Juliet meet their untimely deaths.

ATLANTA BALLET'S
Romeo & Juliet
October 4-15. For tickets call 404-817-8700

7-18
"Goodbye Cal"

Agency: Arnika/Richmond
Creative Director/ Art Director: Michael Ashley
Copywriters: Dinesh Kapoor, Michael Ashley, Matt Fischvogt
Client: Babe Ruth Museum and Birthplace, Baltimore
© 2003 Arnika LLC

"This poster was conceived, created, sold, and delivered in forty-eight hours. The nonprofit museum wanted a presence at Cal Ripken's final home game at Camden Yards in Baltimore. The Babe Ruth Museum needed to promote a fascinating Cal Ripken exhibit to the baseball fans of Baltimore. We came up with the concept, found a photographer and printer to donate services, did massive retouching, and located a radio station to set up remotes to promote the posters and the museum. We distributed forty thousand posters at the game. The next week, the posters began popping up in droves on eBay as collector's items. The final cost to the museum for all of this work and publicity: $0."

7-19
"Killer Frames/Chair"
Agency: Butler, Shine & Stern/Sausalito
Creative Team: Patrick Plutchow, Ryan Ebner
Client: Specialized
© 2003 Butler, Shine & Stern

The dramatic film noir quality of this ad is arresting.

7-20
"Textbooks. Easy. Fast. Cheap"
Agency: DeVito/Verdi/New York
Creative Director: Sal DeVito
Art Directors: Anthony DeCarolis, Manny Santos, Abi Aron, Aaron Eisman
Copywriter: Pierre Lipton
Client: eCampus.com

What a natural solution to position the ad message on a faux textbook cover!

7-21
Pointe Orlando/Bath and Body Sign
Agency: PUSH Advertising/Orlando
Creative Director: John Ludwig
Art Director: Mark Unger
Client: Pointe Orlando/Bath and Body Works

Playing off a health department sign that reminds employees to wash their hands, this ad takes the reminder much further, to a point about what the brand offers.

Illusion

An illusion engages us by toying with our perception of space and reality. For example, you can create the illusion of movement on a two-dimensional surface—think of centripetal-like designs, think of cartoons that imitate motion, think of patterns that suggest movement. In print ads, the rhythmic structure of a composition can create movement up and down or across a surface. Other illusion effects involve space, sound, scent, and visual texture.

When you depict a three-dimensional space on a two-dimensional surface, you have to make certain decisions about the type of space, spatial relationships, and illusion you want to communicate. Distance from the work, point of view, and format are all important decisions in the composing process.

What Is Real?

An illusion can be so compelling that it forces us to touch the surface to make sure the objects are not real. Although three-dimensional solids cannot exist on a two-dimensional surface, you can create an illusion of their existence, as in D'Adda, Lorenzini, Vigorelli, BBDO's engaging campaign for Plasmon (figures 7-22a, 7-22b).

"The illusion of sound in a still and silent medium engages another sense, thereby capturing our attention. With illusion, art imitates life in a most interesting way."[3] A master designer, Herb Lubalin, once conjured the illusion of the sound of a cough in a print ad (figure 7-23). You can even conjure a scent, like the smell of cigar smoke, by creating atmospheric illusion. Creating the illusion or impression of texture with line, value, and/or color is called *visual texture*. It appeals to our sense of touch. Visual textures can be created with direct marks, indirect marks, or computer software. When you employ the illusion of sound, scent, or visual texture you're engaging more than just the viewer's sense of sight. Television and the Web include sound and actual motion; however, they too can conjure the illusion of scent.

Positioning the main lines of copy on the walls enhances the illusion of three-dimensional space in Heimat's brilliant compositions for the Hornbach brand (figures 7-24a, 7-24b). These ads break with convention by emphasizing the illusion of space by placing planes at angles (the walls) and by changing the point of view from which we enter the spatial illusion. In "Legends" we enter from the right-hand side, feeling as though our vantage point is higher than the man with the hammer. In "Sex," the visual point of entry seems to be right of center, where the drill "blocks" our way, yet heightens the spatial illusion.

7-22a, 7-22b
"Salmon"
"Apple"

Agency: D'Adda, Lorenzini, Vigorelli, BBDO/Milan and Rome
Creative Director: Stefano Campora
Art Director: Sara Portello
Copywriter: Andrea Rosagni
Photographer: Carlo Facchini
Client: PLASMON
© May 2000

Trompe l'oeil images, pictures that fool the eye, of notebooks and products engage the viewer's attention.

7-23
"Break Up Cough"
1956
Designer: Herb Lubalin
Courtesy of the Herb Lubalin Study Center of Design and Typography at the Cooper Union School of Art, New York

Lubalin was a master at communicating meaning through inventive typography.

7-24a, 7-24b
"Legends"
"Sex"
Agency: Heimat/Berlin
Client: Hornbach

Mixing sexual prowess with home improvement, these highly memorable ads create a visual style and brand spirit for the Hornbach home improvement superstores.

Notes

1. Robin Landa, *Graphic Design Solutions,* 2nd ed. (Albany: Thomson Learning, 2001), pp. 26–27.

2. George Lois with Bill Pitts, *What's the Big Idea? How to Win with Outrageous Ideas That Sell* (New York: Penguin Books, 1991), p. 13.

3. Robin Landa, *Thinking Creatively,* 2nd ed. (Cincinnati: HOW Books, 2002), p. 48.

8

The Design of Advertising and Expressive Typography

The Design of Advertising

"The question for every art director is not so much whether you can draw better or design better or even arrange elements better, but can your art persuade better? No other kind of art requires this cause-and-effect connection," writes John Lyons. [1]

Your idea may call forth a visual in your mind. Or your idea may be based on a juxtaposition or merge of visuals. At times, a really bang-up idea embodies the design execution. Or the idea and the design may have come to you at once.

Design possibilities are open-ended. Here are essential criteria to consider.

Audience and Appropriateness

Here's the cardinal rule: *know your audience*. Know what they'll tolerate. Know what they won't tolerate. Know what they find distasteful. Know their limits. Understand what they think is cool and not cool. Understand their humor, culture, frame of reference. Respect them. Don't underestimate your audience; *do* understand them. This advice applies to the design as well as the ad message. The success of ads by KesselsKramer for the Brinker Hotel proves how well they understood the prospective clientele of the Brinker (figure 8-1).

For example, if you're designing for a young audience, then the typography can be a small point size, whereas if you're designing for a mature audience, let's say seniors, a small point size might be unreadable and create frustration on the part of the reader. Similarly, thickly layered images and type, where type and imagery are obscured, may be more appropriate for younger audiences who have grown up on MTV and the design styles of skateboard magazines. Overtly sexual images or suggestiveness may attract some and offend others. An ad primarily or solely based on visual communication, rather than verbal copy, may be appropriate for an international audience, since verbal nuance may be lost across cultures.

Understand your client's brand or cause as well. Know what's appropriate for the audience as well as the brand and product or service category. Often, a brand platform or strategy has been created by the lead agency. Both the ad idea and execution should be appropriate for the brand, audience, and context.

8-1
"Now More Rooms Without a Window"
Agency: KesselsKramer/Amsterdam
Art Director: Erik Kessels
Copywriters: Johan Kramer, Tyler Whisnand
Illustration/Typography: Anthony Burrill
Client: Hans Brinker Budget Hotel

"The idea for the Hans Brinker was to make its weaknesses into strengths and celebrate in hotel language the fact that it is not one of the nicest hotels in the world."

Avoid stylistic incongruities. For example, let's say a product is native to Ecuador and its uniqueness is partially based on its origin. If an ad for this product is visually reminiscent of the Middle East, then the product's uniqueness may be lost.

It Shouldn't Look Like Advertising

When an ad looks like a million other ads we've all seen, it's a sure bet fewer people will care to pay attention to it. Unless you're shopping for a particular type of product or service—for example, a stereo system or a vehicle—you're not likely to be interested in what anyone is trying to sell you. With that in the forefront of your mind, it behooves you and your client to offer the public an ad that doesn't look typical or common.

Several things immediately announce to the viewer that what he or she is looking at is a print ad:

- The product as the main visual
- The logo
- A formulaic layout utilized by many others
- Copy that sounds like a sales pitch

Using the product as the main visual usually puts the potential consumer on alert. If you see an ad where a big box of Kleenex tissues is the dominant visual component, you immediately know that you are looking at an ad. Conversely, if you see an ad where the most dominant visual element is a striking metaphor for something soft or strong, then you might be more likely to look at it. In the following clever ads for Wrigley's Extra sugar-free gum, we don't see the brand until we get to the sign-off (figures 8-2a, 8-2b). When asked what makes a great ad, Kevin Roberts, CEO worldwide of the ideas company Saatchi & Saatchi, suggests: "Simplicity, relevance and an immediate emotional connection to the consumer's heart, through a stunning visual, humour, music or drama."[2]

8-2a, 8-2b
"When You Can't Brush"
Agency: DDB/Sydney
Art Director: David O'Sullivan
Copywriter: Michael Lee
Photographer: Julian Wolkenstein
Client: The Wrigley Company
© DDB Sydney/The Wrigley Company

Instead of seeing the product in the main visual, we are treated to amusing ways of reporting that it's not possible to brush.

As Roberts notes, an ad must make a strong emotional connection and be relevant to the viewer's life and needs. Using the product as the main visual is not a likely way to make an emotional connection or demonstrate relevance.

Certainly, there are always exceptions in which prominently displayed products work well, such as ads by Crispin Porter + Bogusky where the products—helmets—are used to create other visuals, such as the fire in "Passion" and a butterfly in "Beauty" (figures 8-3a, 8-3b). Not only are the ads graphically beautiful, but they cite the benefits of Giro helmets. Similarly, the products in the Sony ads at right become other things—footprints and musical notes (figures 8-4a, 8-4b). Although a postal stamp is used in an ad for PTT, the scale change and whimsy completely separate this ad from those that utilize the product in a pedestrian manner (figure 8-5). The product is paired with a very cheeky line in an outdoor board for Pork Farms (figure 8-6; see also the case study in Chapter 2). George Lois used the vodka bottle to great advantage in his classic ads for Wolfschmidt vodka (see figures 1-10a, 1-10b).

8-3a, 8-3b
"Passion"
"Beauty"
Agency: Crispin Porter + Bogusky/Miami
Creative Director: Alex Bogusky
Art Director: Tony Calcao
Copywriter: Rob Strasberg
Photographer: Mark Laita
Client: Giro

Giro helmets are stunningly arranged to create other striking forms.

8-4a, 8-4b
"Footprints"
"Notes"
Agency: FNL Communications/North Sydney
Creative Directors: Julian Horton, Mike Miller, Graham Nunn
Art Directors: Mike Miller, Luke Duggan
Copywriters: Julian Horton, Nathan Lennon
Photographers: Ian Butterworth. Andreas Bommert
Retoucher: Electric Art. Andreas Bommert
Client: Sony Australia

In "Footprints," the shape of the Walkman says "Listen while walking" in a way that no words could manage. In "Notes," the product as musical notes seamlessly merges Sony with music.

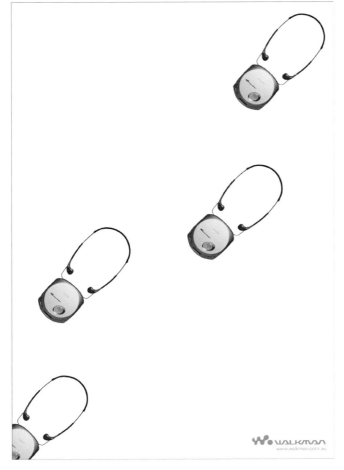

8-5

Agency: KesselsKramer/Amsterdam
Art Director: Erik Kessels
Copywriter: Johan Kramer
Client: PTT

These ads use scale in a novel way and play with reality. What's the real image, and what's the image on the stamp?

FELICITEREN DOE JE VOORTAAN MET 1 VAN DE 10 FELICITATIE-ZEGELS!
 POST

8-6
"Quiche My Ass"

Agency: Mustoes/London
Creative Directors: John Merriman, Chris Herring
Art Director: Mick Brigdale
Copywriter: Kevin Baldwin
Client: Pork Farms Bowyers (Northern Foods)

"This humor tapped into the humor of the time (1998) and was reflected in a series of posters with cheeky headlines poking fun at other foods, as well as challenging consumers as to how well packed their lunchboxes were."

Size of Logo/No Logo

As Paula Scher, a partner in Pentagram, writes in her book *Make It Bigger,* clients often want the logo bigger. Thinking that the logo, pictured bigger and more prominently featured, will sell much of anything is misguided. Though many logos have great graphic impact and carry the spirit of the brand, when they are dominantly placed in an ad they most often scream out to the viewer, "I'm an ad!" In her promotional poster for the Public Theater, Scher ingeniously incorporated the logo into the design concept (figure 8-7).

8-7
"Top Dog Underdog"
Studio: Pentagram/New York
Creative Director/Partner: Paula Scher
Client: The Public Theater

Scher is renowned for her typographic treatments and her ability to fully integrate type with image to communicate poetically.

In almost all contexts, the logo is the mark of the brand; it denotes which product, service, social cause, organization, or charity is under consideration. The context of a logo's use—on a package, shopping bag, T-shirt, print ad, Web site—often determines its impact and provides information. On a package, a logo is far more integral to the brand message than it is, say, in a print ad.

In print ads, logos are usually seen in the sign-off, grouped with the claim and product shot. On television, the logo is usually seen in the last two or three seconds of the ad. Some art directors use the logo as the main visual, rather than placing it in the sign-off. Ads where the main visual includes a photograph or illustration of the product in which the logo is clearly visible do not need to include the logo or product in the sign-off. If a person in an ad, for example, is depicted holding a cup of coffee with the brand's logo on the cup, that fulfills the requirement of showing the logo. The less prominent the logo, the more likely it is that the viewer's ad alarm will not be triggered.

Layout

Advertising art directors, more than ever before, are experimenting with layouts. The days of the formula where the main line resided at the top of the page with a squared-up halftone image under it and the sign-off in the bottom right-hand corner are waning. That type of formulaic thinking leaves little room for originality of brand spirit or for experimentation. Besides, viewers have seen that type of layout millions of times.

8-8

"Franchise Fred"

Agency: Crispin Porter +
Bogusky/Miami
Creative Director: Alex Bogusky
Art Director: Paul Keister
Copywriter: Bob Cianfrone
Illustrator: Doug Jones
Client: Telluride

Taking a format from another form of printed matter, this ad playfully explains the advantages of Telluride.

One day, Franchise Fred came to town. "I want to build my one zillionth Clone-A-Burger right here," he grinned. So all the people held a meeting. Mr. Snowboarder was there. Mrs. Hiker, Mr. Skier and Ms. Ski Instructor were there too. "No, no," they told Franchise Fred. "Your idea is not so good. We have come here to laugh and play and ride and ski all the livelong day. Your eyesore will ruin our happy mountain town." Franchise Fred made a big fuss. Finally, everyone said, "Well, there is some land above treeline." Then they took him way up there and left him. Maybe Franchise Fred made it home. But with 311 inches of annual snowfall, no one will really know for sure until the spring thaw. Telluride. A land where people come to play. The end.

Crispin Porter + Bogusky's ad for Telluride breaks away from any formula, utilizing the look and writing of children's books to make the point that Telluride is a place to play (figure 8-8). In another interesting concept, M&C Saatchi/Singapore utilizes the look of traditional Chinese paintings to convey the "off-road" idea (figures 8-9a, 8-9b). (See Chapter 7 for more atypical-looking compositions.)

If you examine ads according to the criteria below, you will learn which layouts break through and capture the viewer's interest. Look through any magazine and label each ad you see as either "typical ad appearance" or "atypical ad appearance."

What falls under the "typical ad appearance" category?

- Looks like a visual sales pitch
- Product is obvious
- Not visually unified
- Little graphic impact
- Not memorable
- No visual surprise
- Boring—you've seen lots of design executions (and ideas) like it before

8-9a, 8-9b
"River"
"Peak"
Agency: M&C Saatchi/Singapore
Creative Director: Shane Gibson
Art Director: Eddie Wong
Copywriters: Nicolas Leong, Paul Tan
Illustrator: Heng-Chia Oi Yong
Retoucher: Sally Liu, Procolor
Client: Performance Motors BMW

These ads promoted the X5, which is an off-road car. The Mandarin headline reflects the position of the car, and the tagline says "Ultimate driving machine."

What falls under the "atypical ad appearance" category?

• Visually surprising

• Visually engaging

• Something that stopped you

• Something that made you remember the ad message

• Seductive

• Fresh

• Motivating

• Worthy of being hung on your wall

The "atypical ad appearance" characteristics seem like a tall order. However, you'd be surprised—it's simply a matter of thinking that you're designing a unique idea rather than a typical sales pitch, as demonstrated in the attention-grabbing, inventive ads by Rethink, Canada, below (figures 8-10, 8-11). Try to think of a creative ad design as a winning solution both for your client and for art.

Almost invariably, beginning advertising students design their first print ads to look like 95 percent of all the ads they've ever seen. Why? They want to make the ad "look like advertising." Unfortunately, what they're doing is imitating the 95 percent of ads that are commonplace, rather than focusing on the 5 percent that break through and move us.

8-10
"Sandblasted"
Agency: Rethink Advertising/Vancouver
Art Director: Mark Hesse
Copywriter: Rob Tarry
Photographer: Robert Kenney
Client: Bootlegger

8-11
"Face"
Agency: Rethink Advertising/Vancouver
Art Director: Martin Kann
Copywriter: Heather Vincent
Studio Artist/Typographer: Genevieve Smith
Photographers: Gregory Crow, Tony Hurley
Client: Caboodles

An iron merged with sandpaper explains the fashion look.

By simply rearranging the features on the model's face, the ad makes us completely understand the point of the product.

Copy as Sales Pitch

For people reared on ads with little or no copy, copy-heavy ads are a red flag. Similarly, ads where the copy sounds like "a word from our sponsor" make the viewer wary. When copy sounds conversational, then the reader feels you're striking up a conversation, rather than pounding her over the head with a sales pitch. Speaking to the serious guitarist, the copy in ads for Gibson guitars by Carmichael Lynch is effective and doesn't have a commercial tone (figures 8-12a, 8-12b). (See Chapter 10, on copy, for more information.)

8-12a, 8-12b
"Emotional Baggage"
"No Distortion"
Agency: Carmichael Lynch/Minneapolis
Creative Director: Brian Kroening
Art Director: Randy Hughes
Copywriter: Glen Wachowiak
Photographer: Shawn Michienzi
Client: Gibson Guitar Corp.
© 2000 and 2001 Gibson Guitar Corp.

Mood is created by the photography and copy, which speak to the artist within and convey the benefit of playing a Gibson.

Text and Subtext

In an advertisement, what is represented is the denotation; connotation is how it is represented. *Denotation* refers to the literal meaning of a visual or typography—the explicit meaning. *Connotation* refers to the emotional or psychological associations that are connected to or related to a certain visual or typography by virtue of how it is presented—the implicit meaning. The denotative and connotative meanings of a visual or typography coexist, communicating text and subtext jointly.

Size and Media

Murray Badner once said, "It pays to advertise, but advertise where it pays." When you are working professionally, client and budget will dictate media, ad placement, and size. While you're a student, it's valuable to learn to design in formats of various shapes and sizes:

- a single magazine page
- a half-page
- a spread (two facing pages)
- consecutive ads
- ad-stickered bananas or apples (guerilla advertising)
- ambient design (near or at point of purchase)
- pavement
- go-cards
- signs on shopping carts
- outdoor boards

What works for a particular medium, such as a poster, may not work for another, such as an interactive kiosk or an ad coupon.

Design Pointers to Follow (and Sometimes Ignore)

Big visual, small type.

Big type, small visual.

Break lines of type to follow natural patterns of speech.

Don't break the line into two parts unless you have a darned good reason, as breaking the line slows down communication.

Don't make it look like advertising—avoid a visual sales pitch.

Resist the usual (credited to Ray Rubicam, of Young & Rubicam).

Balance the composition.

Create a visual hierarchy.

Avoid visual clutter.

Create visual interest.

Visually entertain.

An ad by Loeffler Ketchum Mountjoy (see figure 5-19) illustrates the compositional strategy of a large visual complemented by small typography, which immediately creates a visual hierarchy.

The Seamless Concert: Type and Image

In advertising, type and visuals operate in a unique way. They completely depend upon one another to communicate an advertising message. A synergistic relationship is created between words and visuals in the ads below by R & R Partners (figures 8-13a, 8-13b).

Advertising has moved into the world of subtle, rich graphic design. The formula of a clean bold sans-serif line at the top of the page, neatly stacked with an aesthetically pleasing photograph underneath and copy below, is in the ad design graveyard, or should be. The range of possible design solutions is enormous, from visceral illustrations, hand-scrawled text, and eclectic imagery to minimalist graphics—anything goes that serves the ad concept. The range extends from neominimalism to what is being called a "new maximalism."[3]

Certainly, software imaging and photo-editing programs shape many solutions. However, there has also been a return to handmade marks, drawn or hand-lettered type, silk-screened images, strange materials, and bizarre, organic, or unrefined typography. And

8-13a, 8-13b
"Bulldozer"
"Clown"

Agency: R & R Partners/Las Vegas
Creative Director: Ron Lopez
Copywriter: Gage Clegg
Art Directors: Jean Austin, Becca Morton
Photographer: Gary Jensen
Client: Laughlin Shoot Out
© 2001

Historical type and borders used along with vibrant colors put the "cowboy" theme in the context of a contemporary event.

there's plenty of wit and whimsy, too, as in Young & Laramore's ad for an art school that combines hand-drawn elements (both visuals and lettering) with digital type (figure 8-14). When photo-editing is used well, the results can be stunning, as in Armando Testa's ads for Allegri (figures 8-15a, 8-15b).

When print was king, typography was the factor that could make or break designs. For print and traditional advertising, type must still be carefully considered and superbly designed (even if it's hand-scribbled). On the Internet, the environment is fundamentally different, and type is taking a backseat to the "experience" of the design (for now), though certainly clarity and legibility—which can define a good user experience—are critical for new media.

Whether you're working with a new carrier of content or a traditional one, type and image should work in seamless concert. Specifically, the type and image should:

- Communicate a message together
- Give off the same feeling or work ironically or confront each other
- Have a similar look or style
- Have an authentic voice
- Speak loudly or softly
- Play well together, like a duet, so that they feel related and thoughtfully integrated
- Evoke memories

Imagery can be substituted for type, as in PUSH's elegant ad for Living Quarters (figure 8-16).

8-14

"Standing"

Agency: Young & Laramore/Indianapolis
Creative Director: Charlie Hopper
Associate Creative Director/Senior
Writer: David Nehamkin
Art Director: Anne Taylor
Client: The Atelier Art School
© 2000 Young & Laramore

With humor, this interesting execution combines a drawing with handwriting, stamped type, mailing label typography, and newspaper ad typography.

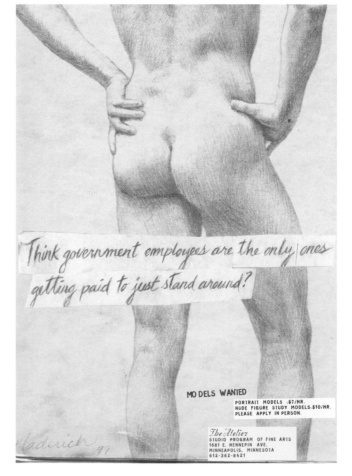

For **H₂O** lovers.

allegri

For **H₂O** lovers.

allegri

8-15a, 8-15b
"H₂O Lovers"
Agency: Armando Testa/Milan
Creative Directors: Maurizio Sala, Michele Mariani
Art Director: Paola Balestreri
Copywriter: Sonia Cosentino
Photographer: Brigitte Niedermair
Client: Dismi 92 S.p.A.—Allegri
© 2001

One can't help but look at these atypical fashion images, where fall clothing is displayed with panache. Playing off surrealism, the ad grabs the viewer's attention and differentiates the brand with intelligence and sophistication.

en ance.

LIVING
QUARTERS

8-16
"Enhance"
Agency: PUSH Advertising/Orlando
Creative Director: John Ludwig
Art Director: Ron Boucher
Photographer: Doug Scaletta
Client: Living Quarters

Furniture is used to replace a letter form. In this way, the denotation of the word is transferred onto the furniture.

AS LONG AS THERE ARE OLD LADIES WHO STINK AT CROSSING STREETS, WE'LL BE HERE.

CUB SCOUT ENROLLMENT IS HERE. WWW.JOINCUBS.COM

8-17a, 8-17b, 8-17c
"Crime Reports"
"College Scholarships"
"Crossing Streets"
Agency: Carmichael Lynch/Minneapolis
Art Director/Illustrator: James Clunie
Copywriter: Tim Cawley
Client: Cub Scouts

Elemental yet whimsically graphic images, which would carry well from a distance, are used to represent the Cub Scouts.

The line for "Crime Reports" reads: "Very few crime reports start with 'the suspect, a former Cub Scout, was last seen . . .'." The line for "College Scholarships" reads: "Funny how all the college scholarships seem to go to kids with 'interests.'"

Creating, Selecting, and Working with Images

You can create an image in every conceivable way, from taking a photograph to making a silk screen, from drawing on paper with a rosebud dipped in coffee to drawing in a software program. The nature of the image should depend upon what you're trying to communicate, upon your idea.

The main visual can be positioned anywhere, depending upon your idea and design solution.

The main visual can be:	Images can be:
An illustration	Created
A graphic illustration	Found and used as is
A photograph	Found and manipulated
A photomontage	Montaged
A combination	Photo-edited

Certainly, the type of media where your ad will appear may dictate which image would work best. A full-color hand-painted illustration may not scan well for a black-and-white newspaper. A found image that is very small will be grainy when blown up to the size of an outdoor board, perhaps too grainy to even be aided by photo-editing. Before designing, know the context—the media placement.

Access to stock photography has made some students and professionals too comfortable, selecting only from available images rather than creating images themselves or hiring photographers or illustrators. Don't be seduced. For student work, if you do use stock, then make it your own by *substantially* altering it—that means really change 70 percent of it in some way—for your portfolio.

Making images from scratch—with hand tools, a camera, or software—is the best way to go. It's all yours! The image can be the hero of the piece, and you know you created it. Whether you take your own photos with a great camera or an inexpensive one, whether you draw skillfully or sketch, the visual is yours. The range of possibilities for creating imagery is enormous. Carmichael Lynch's ads for the Boy Scouts use pictograms combined with witty lines (figures 8-17a, 8-17b, 8-17c).

Typography

Type can be the hero of an ad or moving image, as in "Z," an ad for a fencing school by DeVito/Verdi (figure 8-18), and "Visual Music," created for a hearing-impaired audience by Brokaw Motion (figures 8-19), which is based on song lyrics. "It's the kinetic hierarchy of typography relating to the song as it is sung. The typography is the primary performer on-screen, while images and color are edited in the background to flow with the musical dynamics of the song."

The typography for a campaign for ink!, an independent local coffee shop, was created from signs around the neighborhood (figures 8-20a, 8-20b). The resulting composites of typography and the color palette create a very strong visual look for the brand.

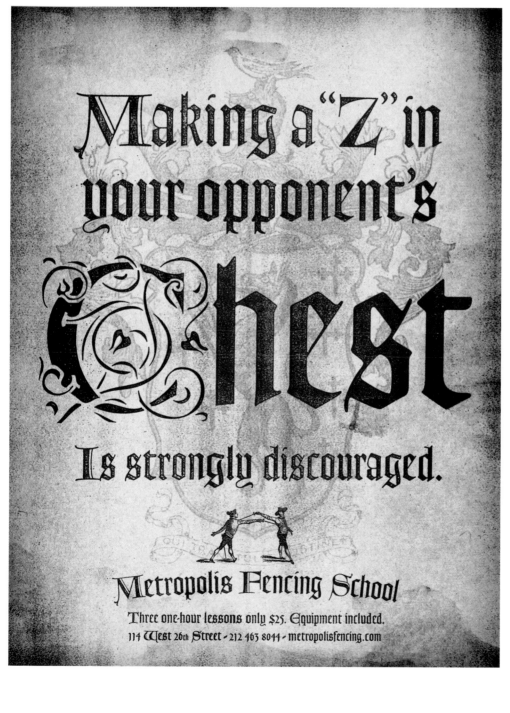

8-18
"Z"
Agency: DeVito/Verdi/New York
Creative Director: Sal DeVito
Art Director: Jim Wood
Copywriter: Peter Lipton
Client: Metropolis Fencing School

Historically appropriate type incisively carries the message of this fencing school.

1

2

3

4

8-19
"Visual Music"
Studio: Brokaw Motion
Art Director/Designer: Gregg Brokaw
Designer: Gregg Brokaw
© 2002

"This personal project was an experiment to help the deaf visually 'hear' a song, and I believe it succeeded, judging from the deaf community's warm reception."

8-20a, 8-20b
ink!
Agency: Cultivator Advertising & Design/Boulder
Creative Directors: Tim Abare, Chris Beatty
Art Director: Marco Pipere
Copywriter: Tim Abare
Photographers: Scott Coe, Marco Pipere, Matt Neren

The Cultivator philosophy is "To create work that is surprising, relevant and propels our clients forward."

Expressive Typography

Type can also be a quiet complement to a dominant visual. Any thoughtful typographic treatment has a voice. It can be:

- Decoratively ironic
- Something that plays with our perceptions
- Fastidiously crafted and kerned
- Grungy
- Hand-scrawled
- Hand-lettered
- Out of control (to create an effect)
- A sweet confection
- Mean-spirited
- Loud or noisy
- Quiet or low-key
- Demure
- Gallant
- Heroic
- Frightening (and I'm *not* referring to novelty fonts that mimic dripping blood)
- Vigilantly integrated with image
- Something that conjures up forms
- Merged with imagery
- Curiously shaded with meaning

Verbal/Visual Relationship

If you think of the relationship between the verbal message (the type or copy) and the visual message as that of an old-time comedy team, where one is the straight person and one is the funny person, then you can begin to understand this: if you have an unusual verbal message (one that is humorous, odd, curious, zany, or shocking), then the visual should be straightforward, as in Sawyer Riley Compton's campaign for the Ritz-Carlton (figures 8-21a, 8-21b). If you have an unusual visual, then the verbal message (the line of copy) should be straightforward (see figure 8-11). The "comedy team" formula is well regarded by many.

Visually Driven Versus Copy-Driven

An ad that relies on the visual to communicate most of the ad message is visually driven (see, for example, figure 8-10). Instead of using a line of copy to explain just how thrillingly scary amusement park rides are, pictograms are positioned at a specific site on the rides (figures 8-22a, 8-22b); these novel ads communicate through visuals alone.

An ad that relies on the copy to communicate most or all of the ad message is copy-driven (see, for example, figure 8-18). Most ads prior to the creative revolution of the 1960s were copy-driven; the visual was secondary or simply supported the ad message. The most imaginative work during the creative revolution was synergistic—the copy and visual worked together to communicate the ad message (see, for example, figure 3-3). In the late 1990s and now in the twenty-first century, ads tend to be visually driven, especially when they are aimed at a youthful or international market. Youthful audiences reared on music videos tend to respond to visuals more than text. When aiming at an international audience, it's a safe bet that a visual will translate across cultures better than language.

The font you choose should:

Help express the idea

Be appropriate for the "voice" of the ad

Be readable or at least legible (depending upon the message, product, audience)

Work with the branding campaign (may have to)

Rewards meant for the afterlife can be collected here *early.*

8-21a, 8-21b
"Hereafter"
"Three Wars"

Agency: Sawyer Riley Compton/Atlanta
Creative Director: Bart Cleveland
Art Director: Laura Hauseman
Copywriters: Sanders Hearne, Brett Compton
Photographer: Tibor Nemeth
Client: The Ritz-Carlton
(www.ritz-carlton.com)
© 2003

Large photographs of incredibly tempting tropical scenes coupled with witty lines make us ache for a vacation at the Ritz-Carlton.

Its hard to believe only three world wars have been fought over this island.

8-22a, 8-22b
"Coaster"
"Corkscrew"

Agency: Rethink Advertising/Vancouver
Art Director: Ian Grais
Copywriter: Ian Grais
Photographer: Hans Sipma
Client: Playland

The blue bathroom sign pictograms are easily seen against the black-and-white photographs. These ads are essentially saying: "These rides are so scary that you'll . . ."

8-23a, 8-23b
"Belt Buckle"
"Chances Are"

Agency: Austin Kelley Advertising/Atlanta
Creative Directors: Mark Robinson, Jim Spruell
Art Directors: Dave Galligos, Steve Andrews
Copywriter: T. J. Aseltyne
Photographer: Tommy Crow
Client: Barn Fly
© 1998

Shirt patterns coupled with witty lines explain the nature of the brand and target audience.

The Rest of the Page

Often, students will take great care in selecting or creating an image and designing with type, only to leave the background as they found it—white.

Part of designing with type and image is designing the entire format. Is white the appropriate background color? Would another flat color work? A modulated color? A texture? A pattern? Another image? A big letter? Close-ups of shirt patterns are gainfully used in ads by Austin Kelley Advertising (figures 8-23a, 8-23b). Think about the page as a whole. Think holistic design.

Pointers for Designing with Type

Here are some pointers from professional designers with varying numbers of years in the profession. You'll notice that some advice overlaps; I left it in so that you get the idea that some thinking is universal and well worth heeding.

Stefan Sagmeister, Sagmeister Inc., New York

1. Make it huge, or make it tiny.

2. Have the content determine the form.

3. Have the content fight the form.

4. Build the type and photograph it.

5. Use Helvetica only.

Carlos Segura, Segura Inc., Chicago

1. Use the appropriate font for the job, not the best one installed in your computer (do your homework). Typography is the single most important element that contributes to the "body

language" and "tone" of a piece of work. (Having a favorite font can be dangerous because you tend to use it often.)

2. Be size-appropriate. Small type on a billboard does not work. Put your work in context.

3. Explore. A lot. Even after you think you've got it. Start again. You'd be surprised at what comes up. Even better, have several people look at the same problem. The solutions will astound you.

4. Seek opinions. This is hard, I know, but it does help.

5. Ignore number 4. (Only if you know what you are doing.)

Deborah M. Rivera, Alexander & Richardson, New Jersey

1. Type does not need to be big to be noticed or meaningful.

2. Do your font research!

3. Fonts can aid you in your message, as they are capable of expressing a mood, voice, or tone.

4. Try this when experimenting with a font: all lowercase, all uppercase, and both upper- and lowercase.

Michael Sickinger, Firmenich, New Jersey

1. Always make sure your type conveys the same feeling as the piece it's going into; every font has an attitude.

2. Type, by itself, can be the design.

3. Try hand-drawn type.

4. If your headline has a serif, your text copy generally shouldn't, and vice versa.

5. When animating type, words flying by quickly or blinking can give off a very powerful effect.

6. Cropped details of letterforms can produce interesting shapes that can serve as an image.

7. Incorporating images into ascenders and descenders can sometimes work well for logos and headlines.

8. Using pictographic images in place of letters can be provocative (for example, the logo for the *Sopranos* TV series, where the letter *r* is replaced by a gun).

Denise M. Anderson, DMA, New Jersey

1. Make choices appropriate to project objectives (client, market, period, etc.).

2. Keep the selection interesting (for example, if choosing Didot, which is a serif font, choose a second font that has a slightly different serif, so that it stands out).

3. When choosing headline type, review each letter you will need, to see if those letters are interesting. The font may have the sexiest *s* you have ever seen, but if it is not in your headline, it will be of no use to you.

4. Make sure text fonts are easy to read.

5. Use the various weights and styles of a font for variation, rather than choosing combinations of two or three fonts. Too many fonts may make a piece look like it was designed by an inexperienced designer.

Steven Brower, *Print* magazine, New York

1. Never, ever, ever stretch type. It distorts the letter forms, creating thin verticals and thick horizontals, among other ghastly things. There are hundreds of condensed faces available to suit your needs.

2. Use a maximum of two faces per piece, usually a serif face and a sans serif face. You need to get written permission to use three.

3. Do not use text type as display type.

4. Do not use display type as text type.

5. Never, ever, ever, ever, ever stretch type.

Robynne Raye, Modern Dog Design, Seattle

When I asked Robynne Raye for her rules, she replied: "So here's the thing; I don't really have rules. I just try to make type look good; it's a very subjective thing nowadays. Okay, hmmm, I'll try. This really is hard.

"Personally, I'm really attracted to customized type when it fits. So when in doubt, just do it yourself. For example, don't be tempted to use a hip '60s font for a poster based on a '60s play. Those designers back then would've done it by hand (or at least customized it in the computer if they had one!), so don't be afraid to give it a shot. It almost always looks better, even with very little effort. Trust me, it's true.

"Don't ever stretch type unless you have a really good reason. (Like for a book cover—'I want this to look super ugly because the writer sucks!') Actually, there are a few moments when stretched type does work—for example, when trying to create a home-grown look for a "Have you seen my lost cat?" poster. But in most cases, it just looks bad.

"Keep type away from the edge of the paper and/or screen. For some strange, universal reason, every entry-level designer takes type right up to the edge. Type looks and reads better when it has a little space around the letter form. Of course, it almost goes without saying: when you're going after an uncomfortable feeling, take it right up to the edge.

"When in doubt, use Akzidenz-Grotesk (all caps) if you can get away with it.

"All rules are made to be broken."

Notes

1. John Lyons, *Guts* (New York: AMACOM, 1989), p. 45.

2. http://www.saatchikevin.com/livingit/q&aindex.html.

3. Andrea Codrington, ed., *365: AIGA Year in Design 22* (New York: American Institute of Graphic Arts, 2002), p. 114.

INTERVIEW Erik Kessels

The design of your print work is so varied and interesting. How many of the design decisions were intentional?

The execution of these ads comes directly after thinking of a good idea. It should never be the other way around. An idea comes nine out of ten times from a very intuitive feeling. Sometimes it even happens that the idea is discovered while a client is explaining his or her problem. After that, there is, of course, some time to work on it, but the idea you had in the first meeting won't get any better; it only moves into an execution process that fits well with the idea. A bad idea cannot get better with excellent execution, while a good idea leads to a logical execution.

How do you generate so many different design ideas?

This is the nice thing about working in a creative industry. It means finding new territory for a new client every time. I like to work as broadly as possible. The different design ideas come with the different clients. Each client, each brand, each product, and each project I work on comes from a different place, so it makes sense that their design comes from a different place. This way we make sure that we always have a diverse set of clients and projects and that clients come to us because of this diversity. If we did everything with one formula, then we would run out of clients very quickly. The style we have is to have endless styles, and this keeps our minds open all the time.

How important is it for an ad's design to communicate on an emotional level with the consumer?

If an ad doesn't communicate on an emotional level, it is almost definite that it is worthless. An ad with no emotion is like a message from a cement block: no feelings, no ideas, nothing to say. Choosing the right emotion for your message is very important; don't keep it out for fear of being too emotional.

You believe that "the consumer is your brand." How do you get to millions of individuals with a print ad? Television ad?

There is never a guarantee that one ad of any kind will reach millions of individuals or say the right kind of thing to everyone. But at least there should be a dialogue started that is

Cofounder of
KesselsKramer

8-24a, 8-24b
"Now More Rooms Without a Window"
"Check In. Check Out"

Agency: KesselsKramer/Amsterdam
Art Director: Erik Kessels
Copywriters: Johan Kramer, Tyler Whisnand
Illustration/Typography: Anthony Burrill
Photographers: Anushka Blommers, Niels Schumm
Client: Hans Brinker Budget Hotel

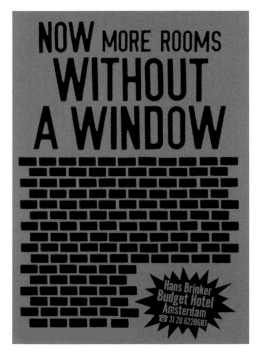

With tongue-in-cheek humor, these ads are quintessential KesselsKramer work.

8-25a, 8-25b
"Do Create"

Agency: KesselsKramer/Amsterdam
Product Design: KesselsKramer, Droog Design
Photographer: Bianca Pilet
Client: do

"Droog Design approached KesselsKramer and proposed to have several designers come up with products for do. They were to be presented at the Milan Fair in 2000. The products are meant to force users to put their personal mark on them. They were shown together with large photographs showing the context and the users after they had done their duty."

more dimensional than the piece of paper a consumer holds or the flat box a consumer watches. Mass communication usually feels just like that: mass. And this is what millions of individuals probably don't like.

You've said, "Use your communication to make people think or to promote social change." What can advertising creatives do to help the world? What is their social responsibility?
Advertising is a business. Businesses are more and more involved in how the world works. Businesses work with governments to decide laws, foreign policy, market behavior, the free market. Social change for the good needs to start in the business world as well as in the public and not-for-profit areas. Advertising is communication through the world's media. As the people who work in this area, it is often our responsibility to use this media to raise issues, discuss the unpopular, and open people's minds to what is happening in the world besides just selling a new car. Why waste the fantastic opportunity of communicating in a memorable way on just selling everyday products when the product can also be aid, action, or mutual responsibility?

In 1998 KesselsKramer developed its own brand, do. What is this brand about?
Do is a brand that doesn't do it all for the consumer. It asks a bit of the consumer in terms of co-creation, development, and action. By definition, do is a brand that depends on what you as an individual do. It means taking on the relationship and function of the brand instead of leaving it all to some group of people in an office somewhere who think they know exactly what you want. In this way, do is much different and has the chance to be an inspiration, to change thinking, and to put some surprise in life.

How do you convince a client to buy a radical ad idea?
We normally work with clients who are willing to work with us on these ideas and come to us specifically for these kinds of concepts. New concepts are always startling to people if they haven't been involved in the process. We work directly with clients and have no layers buffering the people who come up with the ideas. This direct way of working produces the best results. It can also surprise us sometimes. This is good.

How can a brand have a "conversation" with a consumer?
Just the same way as a person. A person has many different sides to them. A person has emotions. A person can inform other people by shouting, laughing, crying, or writing a compelling letter. With this in mind, a brand, which is the creation of a person, can behave the same way as a person and hold a conversation.

What are your "structures" about? Are they an integral part of your creative brief?
Each assignment requires a different set of criteria. Each need is a bit different. We work very intuitively and naturally to find the right structure. Sometimes it is one person who creates a brand book, or it's everyone in our company spending an hour on a question. We like to keep things flexible, and the only structure we have is a clear understanding of what the problem is that needs to be solved. Once we know that, then the possible solutions become clearer.

How would you define creative?
I would define it as always looking for a new way to say and do things that is both meaningful to yourself, your audience, and your client.

Can advertising inspire? Enlighten?
Advertising always has the chance to tell somebody something new or ask them to think differently. This is not always inspiring or enlightening, but there is always hope.

9

Flexibility:
The Ad Campaign
and Creativity

Designing Print Campaigns

Once you have your strategy formulated and have conceived advertising concepts or ideas, then it's time to design. When designing a campaign—more than one ad based on the same strategy and an elastic idea—there are many factors to keep in mind.

Campaigns demonstrate your ability to stretch a theme and formulate several related ideas. Within a campaign, some variation in your design/art direction demonstrates your ability to run with an idea and design direction.

There must be a *central thought,* an underlying idea or related ideas, or a theme carried throughout the campaign. That central thought is communicated visually through the design of the campaign. Here's the gist: find a way to make the benefit of your brand or social cause relevant to the audience's lives, and express it in an atypical visual/verbal design.

Establish a visual look or framework to carry throughout the campaign. Unity is paramount; certainly you can establish unity with variety, and this may be preferable.

A look or framework is established by:

Layout/placement

Typography: style, alignment, and fonts

Tone/expression: you design it, the audience feels it

Color

Style

Choice of photography, illustration, collage, or any visual vehicle utilized

Use of space, angles, straight lines, flat space versus illusion of three-dimensional space

Form and Content

Not only must the ads in a campaign be related by an overall intention—concepts, look, tone, and copy—but the relationship of form and content in the campaign should be appropriate and meaningful. Form and content together should express the overall campaign theme as well as the individual ad idea.

The copy and manner of the wording must be consistent. The tone of the copy should either be consistent with the choice of font and visual, or in contrast to it, depending upon the desired communication.

Finally, a campaign must have visual impact, which can mean a visual surprise, visual interest, visual drama, a visual jolt, or a breakthrough look.

Triplets Versus Cousins

If you study campaigns, you'll notice that there often seems to be an underlying template—a compositional structure or format—that is utilized for individual ads in a campaign. The visual changes, the line changes, but the compositional template stays the same. Other elements that are maintained might include the color palette, style of images, work from the same photographer or illustrator, or font family. I call that type of campaign "triplets": each composition is identical to the others. That's the way most campaigns are designed.

In Mullen's campaign for L. L. Bean, the template is constant: the photograph, line, and catalog are all positioned in the same place in each individual ad (figures 9-1a, 9-1b). The specific "feel" of each ad is different due to the mood and subject of the photographs. Each photograph depicts different types of people—families, individuals, groups—enjoying the outdoors. The mood and idea of the campaign appeal to people who think of the outdoors as a friendly, relaxing place, not as a site of extreme conditions or arduous activities.

In order to get people to realize the value of reading the local paper, Forsman & Bodenfors/Gothenburg's campaign "Local Knowledge" points out things you would have known or could know by reading the morning paper (figures 9-2a, 9-2b, 9-2c). In each outdoor poster, the type alignment (centered) is the same, the arrows act as pointers to local particulars, the claim and logo are located in the same position, and all are black and white.

9-1a, 9-1b
"Street Address"
"Recess"

Agency: Mullen/Wenham, MA
Chief Creative Officer: Edward Boches
Creative Directors: Jim Garaventi, Greg Bokor
Art Director: Greg Bokor
Copywriter: Jim Garaventi
Photographer: William Huber
Client: L. L. Bean
© Mullen

Mullen wanted to capture the outdoors that most people want to spend time in—a less extreme, more friendly outdoors—to make consumers feel that L. L. Bean is for them.

9-2a, 9-2b, 9-2c
"Local Knowledge"
Agency: Forsman & Bodenfors/Gothenburg
Art Directors: Staffan Forsman, Staffan
Håkanson
Copywriter: Björn Engström
Photographer: Henrik Bonevier
Client: Göteborgs-Posten

By actually pointing to local things,
this campaign cleverly
communicates the idea that the
things happening in your local
community are covered in the
morning paper.

Forcing us to do a double take, BMP DDB's campaign creatively urges us not to forget to put Lurpak butter on our food (figures 9-3a, 9-3b, 9-3c). Each ad in the campaign has a plate of food centered on the page against a blue background with the sign-off at bottom right; the template is identical.

Then there are what I call "cousins," that is, a campaign where there is variation in the composition, color palette, and type of imagery, yet the campaign still holds together and manages to maintain a look. The variation doesn't interfere with the unity of the entire campaign and the way it addresses the viewer. By varying the image—some close-ups and some cropped torsos—there is some variety in the uncommon D'Adda, Lorenzini, Vigorelli, BBDO campaign for Francesco Biasia handbags (figures 9-4a, 9-4b, 9-4c). What remains constant is the use of Polaroid images to depict the handbags, the position of the copy and logo, the lighting of the photos, the attitude, and the use of silhouetted images.

Variation occurs in an inspired campaign for Joe's Upholstery—the background landscapes are all different, and the furniture appears at different points in the compositions (figures 9-5a, 9-5b, 9-5c).

Many clients and creatives believe that repetition is crucial and so tend to prefer "triplet" campaigns, whether in print, on TV, or digital; triplets make sure that the viewer immediately recognizes the brand message. This approach holds that the more we see the ad, the more likely we'll get and remember the message. Others think that once a viewer has seen one ad in a series, they'll be bored if the next ad in the campaign looks almost exactly the same, and will ignore it. One could make a case either way. I teach the idea of maintaining a unified campaign look while having enough variety to engage the viewer each and every time he or she sees an ad in the series, and to ensure that the ad and brand don't have to reintroduce themselves. Edward Boches, chief creative officer at Mullen, offers this advice: "A campaign can be unified in any number of ways. Layout, color, tone of voice, personality. Usually, the smaller the budget or the less familiar the brand, the more disciplined you need to be in making everything come from the same place. For larger clients, say a Nextel, you can take more liberties."

Your campaign idea should be elastic enough to accommodate several ads, and your design solution should be expandable; it may be necessary to create many ads for one campaign based on a central thought.

9-3a, 9-3b, 9-3c
"Peas"
"Crumpet"
"Sweetcorn"
Agency: BMP DDB/London
Photographer: David Gill
Agent: Siobhan Squire
Client: Arla Foods—Lurpak

Using yellow sticky notes to look like butter, this campaign "reminds" us to use Lurpak on all types of food.

9-4a, 9-4b, 9-4c
"Polaroid"
Agency: D'Adda, Lorenzini, Vigorelli, BBDO/Milan and Rome
Creative Director: Stefano Campora
Art Director: Gianpiertro Vigorelli
Copywriter: Vicky Gitto
Photographer: Ilan Rubin
Client: Francesco Biasia
© July 2002

Polaroid images of handbags as an earring, a halter top, and a bra confirm the bag as an important part of the fashion statement, just like any other part of one's ensemble. Photographer Ilan Rubin puts a creative spin on contemporary images.

9-5a, 9-5b, 9-5c
"Desert"
"Flowers"
"Sunset'

Agency: Arnika/Richmond
Creative Director: Michael Ashley
Art Directors: Michael Ashley, Diana Tung
Copywriter: Michael Ashley
Client: Joe's Upholstery, Virginia Beach
© 2003 Arnika LLC

Combining line drawings of furniture with full-color photos to suggest the various fabrics and feelings yields a very interesting visual execution.

Advice from Paul Renner

Says Paul Renner, associate creative director on ESPN, Wieden + Kennedy, New York: "By the time you get done reading this sentence, someone just flipped the page of a magazine and your ad just went bye-bye. (You'd be lucky to get someone's attention that long!)

"Which brings me to your question: 'What are the essential components of a print campaign?' I will spell it out: s-t-o-p s-o-m-e-b-o-d-y. We live in a society that moves a million miles a minute. People have heard it all and seen everything . . . or have they?

"A good print campaign is only as good as the idea that holds it together. A central thought, carried throughout the campaign, will make people s-t-o-p and feel something.

"Make them (a) gaze out a window to ponder something you just brought to their attention, (b) call someone they love because you (that's right, you) reminded them what is important in their lives, (c) squirt orange juice out of their (collective) noses because you made them laugh when they weren't expecting it (my personal favorite), and (d) *angry* (I would suggest this only if you are doing a PSA—it doesn't go over well with automobile campaigns).

"Make people feel something. If you do that, they will remember you. And they may even buy the blender you are trying to sell them.

"Obviously you know how important I think an idea is to the campaign. Finding the voice for your client is even more crucial. Who is this company? What is this company? What does it stand for? Does it scream, 'Over here'? Or does it ask politely to look their way? Once you tap into that, the campaign has legs to stand on. Suddenly, there is a rock you can go back and touch each and every time.

"Now that you know where you are coming from tonally, and you have come up with the 'great idea,' you can match that with graphic elements. Your palette, so to speak. The typeface you pick and which point size you use. Use of color, or not. Where to put the logo, or no logo. (Remember, we are talking to people who have seen everything, so why not?) Illustration? Long copy? No copy? Just a photo? What style of photography is right for the idea and the brand?

"I find one of the biggest decisions you make as an art director is picking the photographer (if your solution requires a photo). Usually, a photo sets up a visual tone for your campaign. The reader turns the page, and *bang!* Then he reads (if you're lucky). It's the first thing he sees. There are so many different photography styles, and each one says something very different. A campaign can be held together by style of photography alone.

"Carrying a look throughout the campaign is a smart thing to do. There are no rules to creating that look. But by doing so, your ads don't have to reintroduce themselves each and every time they're seen. The reader might see one or two, and then the third and fourth ones that a reader sees keep strengthening the idea. That doesn't mean the same joke three or four times.

"A great print campaign, if done well, may prompt some readers to rip out your ad and hang it in their cube . . . yikes! Check your kerning!"

Creativity

Problem Solving

Whether you are creating a solution for print or TV or new media, you are solving a problem. As my colleague Professor Martin Holloway points out in my book *Thinking Creatively*: "It is important to keep in mind that in graphic design, problem-solving and creativity occur simultaneously. If graphic design does not solve a problem, then it is simply self-indulgence— a kind of pointless talking to one's self."[1] Not only do you need to think critically about formulating an idea, you must think critically about the strategy. It's always better to think in terms of your brand, making your campaign theme specific to your brand or cause. Here's a little test: Could another brand, product, service, or cause easily fit your campaign idea? If you could easily replace your brand, then your theme or idea is probably too generic.

Creative Approaches

A creative approach in advertising must be appropriate for the product or service and communicate and enhance the client's message—form follows function. For example, the creative visual surprises that constitute Bartle Bogle Hegarty Asia Pacific's campaign for Levi's explain the nature of the product—"The classic men's 501 now re-cut for women" (figures 9-6a, 9-6b, 9-6c, 9-7). Says the agency, "The jeans are a female version of the timeless 501 men's jeans, and the idea is based on the even more timeless connection between a man and a woman.

"The poses were constructed in such a way as to form one intertwined being out of two people. The models swapped around until a natural connection was apparent and different poses were experimented with on the shoot day to achieve the best possible combinations.

"The campaign was shot in a London studio by the prolific Nadav Kander. A veteran commercial and art photographer, Nadav was selected because the creative team felt that he could best capture the intimate and seamless connection the idea required. He was well up to the task."

It is vital to note that no other industry, other than Hollywood's film industry and television programming, demands constant creative solutions the way advertising does. Learning to think creatively is learning a way of thinking.

What Makes a Campaign Work?

Viewers will notice it.

Each individual ad will grab the viewer's attention.

It is distinctive to your brand.

The idea makes sense for your brand or cause.

It endears your brand or cause to the public.

It is consistent with the brand voice.

Your idea and/or theme is elastic—you can create many ads based on the original theme.

It could run forever (almost).

It will work across media.

Other art directors wish they had thought of it!

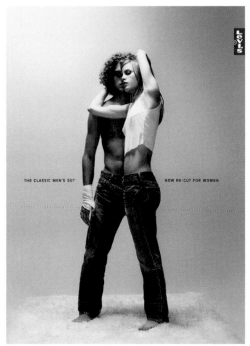

© Levi Strauss/Photo by Nadav Kander

© Levi Strauss/Photo by Nadav Kander

9-6a, 9-6b, 9-6c
"Standing"
"Hugging"
"Lying"
Agency: BBH Asia Pacific/Tokyo
Creative Director: Steve Elrick
Art Directors: Marthinus Strydom, Alex Lim
Thye Aun
Copywriters: Marthinus Strydom, Alex Lim
Thye Aun
Photographer: Nadav Kander
D.I.: Metro Imaging, Anthony Crossfield
Client: Levi Strauss Japan K.K.
© Levi Strauss/Photo by Nadav Kander
September 2002 - March 2003 in Japan only

This campaign has found its way onto almost every printable surface, ranging from magazine ads and billboards to painted buses and free postcards.

© Levi Strauss/Photo by Nadav Kander

9-7
CD for Levi's
Agency: BBH Asia Pacific/Tokyo
Creative Director: Steve Elrick
Art Directors: Marthinus Strydom, Alex Lim
Thye Aun
Copywriters: Marthinus Strydom, Alex Lim
Thye Aun
Photographer: Nadav Kander
D.I.: Metro Imaging, Anthony Crossfield
Client: Levi Strauss Japan K. K.
© Levi Strauss/Photo by Nadav Kander
September 2002 - March 2003 in Japan only

A compilation CD features a collaboration of male and female artists.

© Levi Strauss/Photo by Nadav Kander

When designer Luba Lukova spoke at Kean University about her work, she said that her creative ideation phase includes experimenting with creative approaches, such as merging two different things into one new thing (figure 9-8). Merges are used in a campaign for *La Cucina Italiana* to cleverly illustrate the idea of "the magazine with the kitchen in the offices" (figures 9-9a, 9-9b, 9-9c).

Outdoor posters cleverly refer to an object or edifice to point out the advantage of using the classified ads (figures 9-10a, 9-10b). All the posters utilize full photographs with type over the photographs in a flush left alignment.

9-8
"Lukova at MICA"
Announcement Poster

Studio: Luba Lukova Studio
Designer: Luba Lukova
Client: MICA
© Luba Lukova

Replacing the scales of the fish with a dried-up riverbed merges ideas of water, life, and death.

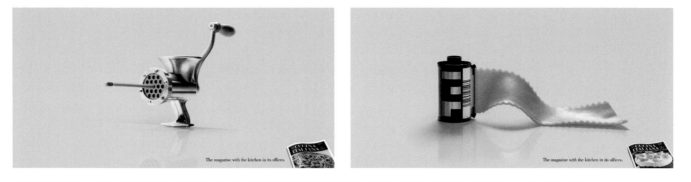

The magazine with the kitchen in its offices.

The magazine with the kitchen in its offices.

9-9a, 9-9b, 9-9c
"Mincer"
"Film"
"Typewriter"

Agency: D'Adda, Lorenzini, Vigorelli, BBDO/Milan and Rome
Creative Director: Stefano Campora
Art Directors: Pier Giuseppe Gonni, Vincenzo Gasbarro
Copywriters: Nicola Lampugnani, Federico Ghiso
Photographer: Fulvio Bonavia
Client: La Cucina Italiana
© October 2002, © July 2002

Merging office and film supplies with kitchen appliances acts to differentiate this magazine's content.

9-10a, 9-10b
"Classified Ads"

Agency: Forsman & Bodenfors/Gothenburg
Art Directors: Staffan Forsman, Staffan Håkanson
Copywriters: Hjalmar Delehag, Björn Engström
Photographers: Henrik Ottosson, Lennart Sjöberg
Client: Göteborgs-Posten

Humorously, this campaign employs positioning and nearby buildings and trees to communicate the message—what you might need, you'll find in the classifieds.

Using visual analogies, a series of provocative ads for Club RTL, a theme television station, utilize cropped images and close-ups of objects and clever wordplay (figures 9-11a, 9-11b, 9-11c). These ads are cousins; there is some variety in the compositional template, including the position of the objects as well as the position of the line and logo.

Visual Surprises

One can design an aesthetically pleasing piece that communicates, and one's client might be perfectly happy. However, many art directors dream of transcending that level, of taking the great creative leap, of creating a visual surprise or an extremely expressive visual. It's all about getting the viewer's attention in the first place and then informing or selling.

Using visuals that surprise, ads for Polk ChoiceMail definitely grab the viewer's attention (figures 9-12a, 9-12b). Both ads use beautifully lighted photographs, with the copy, in the format of a warning, at the bottom. In both ads, the viewers are close to the objects; in one, we seem to be right in front of the fence.

With a touch of surrealism, an Allegri fashion campaign grabs our attention and keeps our interest (figures 9-13a, 9-13b).

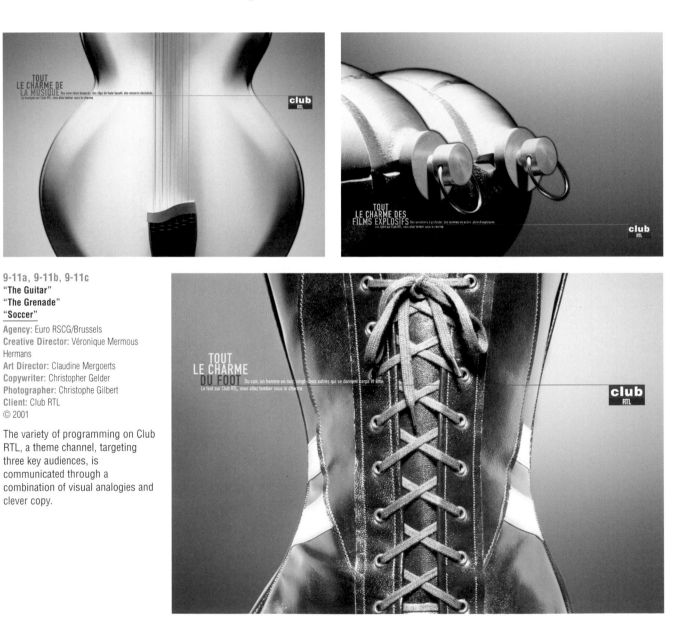

9-11a, 9-11b, 9-11c
"The Guitar"
"The Grenade"
"Soccer"

Agency: Euro RSCG/Brussels
Creative Director: Véronique Mermous Hermans
Art Director: Claudine Mergoerts
Copywriter: Christopher Gelder
Photographer: Christophe Gilbert
Client: Club RTL
© 2001

The variety of programming on Club RTL, a theme channel, targeting three key audiences, is communicated through a combination of visual analogies and clever copy.

9-12a, 9-12b
"Caution"

Agency: Sukle/Denver
Creative Director/Art Director: Mike Sukle
Photographer: Todd Droy
Digital Art: Alan Jones
Client: Polk ChoiceMail

The surest way to be noticed is with an attention-grabbing visual.

9-13a, 9-13b
"Wind Please"

Agency: Armando Testa/Milan
Creative Directors: Maurizio Sala, Michele Mariani
Art Director: Paola Balestreri
Copywriter: Sonia Cosentino
Photographer: Marino Parisotto
Client: Dismi 92 S.p.A.—Allegri
© 2002

This fashion campaign breaks out of the "image" category with extremely imaginative visuals.

Expressive Visuals

If you think of an ad as an opportunity to create a visual idea that is as expressive as possible while still communicating, then probably you're on track toward creating visual impact and getting people's attention.

The communication should not be obscure, and it certainly should not be buried, as it is with some print and TV spots that are so vague that they do not communicate. Creativity should serve the ad message. Creativity is there to make a brand or cause interesting, more compelling, and relevant.

Peperami's feisty characters distinctly point out the spicy nature of the food product and give lots of personality to the brand (figures 9-14a, 9-14b, 9-14c). The font is completely appropriate for the peppery character voice, and the template changes to add variety to the campaign look. Using a baseball as the background for a campaign for the Ty Cobb Museum not only is appropriate for the client and message but creates an atypical look sure to attract the viewer (figures 9-15a, 9-15b, 9-15c).

9-14a, 9-14b, 9-14c
"Leg Man"
"Stomach Acid"
"Animal"

Agency: Lowe/London
Creative Director: Charles Inge
Art Director: Matt Allen
Copywriter: Liam Butler
Photographer: Paul Bevitt
Typographer: Lynne McIntosh
Client: Peperami

Feisty Peperami characters communicate the nature of the food brand.

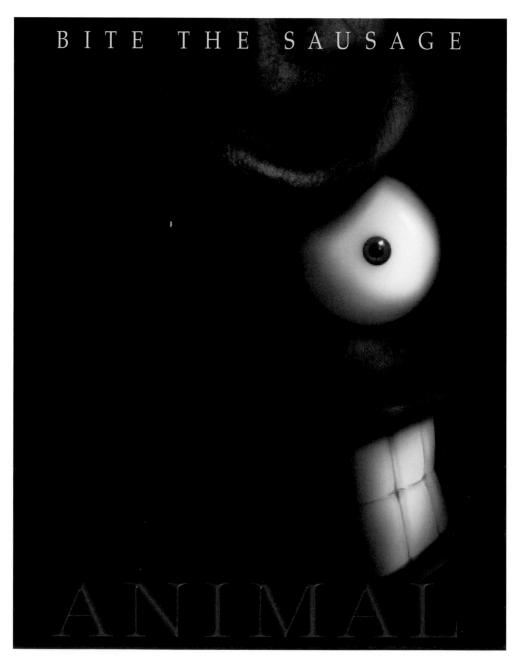

9-15a, 9-15b, 9-15c
"Patton"
"Depression"
"Coffin Maker"
Agency: Sawyer Riley Compton/Atlanta
Web site: www.brandstorytellers.com
Creative Director: Bart Cleveland
Associate Creative Director: Al Jackson
Art Director: Rick Bryson
Copywriter: Brett Compton
Digital Photography: Vertis
Atlanta/Imagination Brewery
Client: Ty Cobb Museum
© 2002

If it makes sense for your idea, then a design solution might be based on:

Juxtaposition

Texture

An odd point of view

Combining photographs with drawings

Abstraction

Color combined with black and white

Odd scale

Montage

Handmade elements and/or handwriting

Bizarre visuals

An illusion of three-dimensional space, scent, motion, texture

Odd comparisons

9-16a, 9-16b, 9-16c
"Corporate Radio"
"Arrogant"
"Sell Out"
Agency: Matthews|Evans|Albertazzi/San Diego
Art Director/Photographer: Dana Neibert
Copywriter: John Risser
Client: The Casbah
© Matthews|Evans|Albertazzi 2002

Juxtaposing cropped images that appear to be near the viewer with the faraway image of the Casbah creates a dynamic contrast. Placing the sharp-witted copy on the cropped images as if it were a natural part of them makes the ad idea fluid.

"Corporate Radio" tagline reads: "Bands so new and fresh, corporate radio hasn't had a chance to ignore them yet."

"Arrogant" tagline reads: "Where crass, arrogant, multi-millionaire musicians played when they were only crass and arrogant."

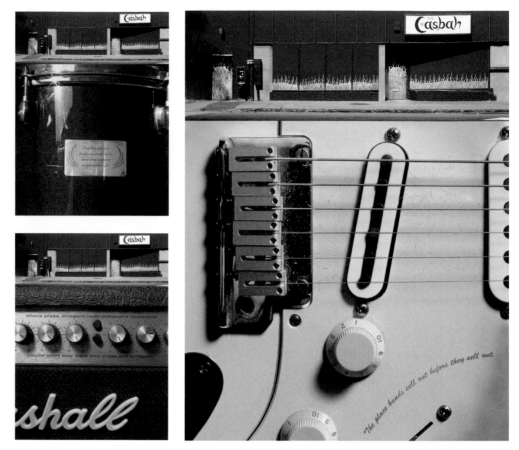

Juxtaposing close-ups of an amplifier, guitar, and drum with a photo of the Casbah, the ads above have great visual interest (figures 9-16a, 9-16b, 9-16c). See Chapter 4 for more on visual metaphors and analogies.

To communicate the importance of water conservation, Sukle uses the deletion strategy—visualizing what the world would be like without water (figures 9-17a, 9-17b, 9-17c). Replacing water with ketchup, motor oil, and milk grabs our attention and makes a convincing point at the same time.

Ping When They Pong

Think of it this way: if everyone in a room is wearing a blue denim shirt except for one person who is wearing a green satin shirt, who would stand out from the crowd? If 99 percent of TV ads are in color, then why not think of utilizing black-and-white or duotone film? They're ponging, so you ping. Take the least traveled path.

There are fads in most design arenas—trendy color palettes, trendy fonts, two people everyone is casting for voice-overs, typographic arrangements that are prevalent. At times the introduction of new technology creates a trend. Thus, if everyone seems to be using photo-editing software to create visuals, create yours by hand. If every art director is relying on photography, use illustration or an interesting hybrid. Without a doubt, your ping has to be appropriate for your audience and brand as well as work for your idea.

Make It Your Own

Find inspiration from other arenas, such as art history, interior design, architecture, ephemera, primitive signage, wrapping-paper patterns, eighteenth-century prints, previous

9-17a, 9-17b, 9-17c
"Nothing Replaces Water"
Agency: Sukle/Denver
Creative Director: Mike Sukle
Art Director: Norm Shearer
Photographer: Joseph Hancock
Client: Denver Water

Certainly, the quality and focus of the photography contribute to the power of the message.

When you want to feed your creativity, try:

Combining things

Rearranging things

Using metaphors

Mixing metaphors

Turning things upside down, inside out

Replacing things

9-18a, 9-18b, 9-18c
"Cork"
"Hardware Store"
"Really Good Cheese"
Agency: Mullen/Wenham, MA
Chief Creative Officer: Edward Boches
Creative Directors: Jim Garaventi, Greg Bokor
Art Director: Dylan Lee
Copywriter: Monica Taylor
Photographers: Ray Meeks, Stock
Client: Swiss Army Brands
© Mullen

This campaign plays off the brand's reliability, precision quality, and famous red color.

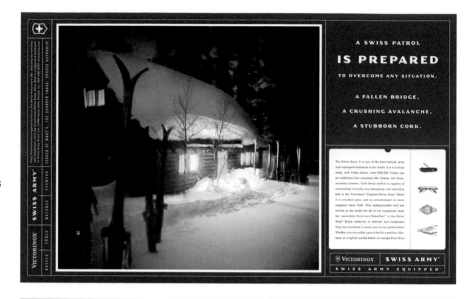

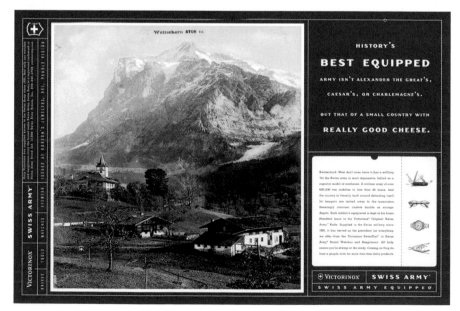

eras, industrial design, fashion design, floral arrangements, sushi arrangements, crafts, and countless others. Make it your own. Add range to your design repertoire. This means putting your own twist on it, not stealing.

How can an Aztec temple inspire a look for an interactive ad? Can celadon-glazed stoneware of the Koryo dynasty inspire a visual for a print ad? There is an enormous difference between copying another art director and finding inspiration in another discipline or source. Borrowing typographic ideas from old orange crates or cigar boxes, utilizing Navajo patterns, or incorporating pieces of old maps is about getting inspired.

Be open to inspiration from alternative sources.

Style of an Ad

Style is a visual look based on the particular characteristics that contribute to the overall appearance. Type choice, color palette, texture, pattern, compositional modes, types of visuals, graphic elements, and imagery all contribute to a look. A style may be current, retro, historical, personal, particular to an era, flamboyant, classic, and so on. Any style should add to a design solution's freshness in look and feel as well as be appropriate to the idea and brand or cause.

There are designers and art directors whose styles are immediately recognizable, and regardless of which brand they are designing for, they impose their style on it. If a brand is well served by your personal design style (which may mean that the brand gets noticed, is harmonious with the brand's essence, differentiates the brand from the competition, and makes it memorable), that's fine.

That said, just because a brand has a look and feel, that shouldn't prevent you from experimenting with various design styles, as long as the style you choose works with the brand personality or essence. Some companies have standards manuals that state ways in which their logo can be used; this often establishes a point of departure for what you can do. Always, there should be a consistent brand message across all design and advertising solutions.

Designing to the Brand Image

To ensure that the ad has the same values—same intentions, emotional range, level of craftsmanship, spirit—as the brand, your design should feel like the product and have the same mystique. The uses of color, type, style, and compositional ideas in your ad designs may all have to relate to the brand campaign look. Consistency with slight variation is the key.

A good campaign should brand the product, service, or cause. Also, it should fit into the entire branding strategy and *not* be generic (able to fit any other brand). The history and heritage of the Swiss Army knife are communicated through the brand's color, red, and the concept of being prepared and equipped (figures 9-18a, 9-18b, 9-18c). The ads are designed with compartments, to link to the design of the knife's different utility areas. This template also allowed for ease of displaying not one but two logos. The idea of being equipped provided a flexible brand strategy platform that pulls from the Swiss Army knife's heritage and history, yet is relevant to today's consumers.[2] This campaign demonstrates just how specific one can be to a brand's spirit; this is the complete opposite of a generic campaign idea.

Notes

1. Robin Landa, *Thinking Creatively*, 2nd ed. (Cincinnati: HOW Books, 2002), p. 139.

2. Lisa Hickey, *Design Secrets: Advertising*. (Gloucester, MA: Rockport Publishers, 2002), p. 62.

chapter 10

Copy

Advertising giant David Ogilvy once said, "If you're trying to persuade people to do something, or buy something, it seems to me you should use their language, the language they use every day, the language in which they think. We try to write in the vernacular."[1] Some of the greatest advertising lines have two things in common: they don't sound like a sales pitch, and they ring true. Some have even found their way into the common lexicon.

Just do it (Nike)

Hey, you never know (New York Lottery)

Got milk? (California Milk Processor Board)

Give a damn (National Urban League)

Where's the beef? (Wendy's)

What happens here, stays here (Las Vegas Convention and Visitors Authority)

Besides sounding like something you'd say to your friend during a conversation, these lines do something that is vital to good copy and successful advertising: they embody a solid idea and campaign strategy. And successful copy doesn't sound like advertising.

What Comes First—the Line or the Visual?

When creating an ad, which comes first—the line or the visual? It depends. Here are a few scenarios:

• A creative team knocks ideas back and forth and settles on a couple of ideas, and then the team's members go their separate ways—the writer writes and the art director designs, both working on the ideas they generated together.

• One member of the team thinks of a line or visual, and they go from there. At times, the writer can generate a visual idea. An art director can parent a line.

• Based on an idea generated by the team, the visual and line are born concurrently.

It can happen in any number of ways. Some people think in words; ad great George Lois recommends writing first. Others think in images. Still others are switch hitters. It really doesn't matter which comes first, as long as both line and visual work synergistically and are based on a solid idea. In any case, at some point, the writer writes and/or crafts the line and body copy, and the art director designs. Since a creative team generates ideas in unison, each member of the team must bring other expert skills to the team effort. The writer must be a good writer, someone who knows her craft very well. The art director must be a good designer, someone who is highly trained in graphic and advertising design and is capable of finely tuned executions with impact.

Visual and Words: How Should They Work Together?

In both unconventional and conventional approaches, the key is that visual and words together communicate a whole message that is greater than the sum of the parts, as in a brazen ad by R + R Partners (figure 10-1).

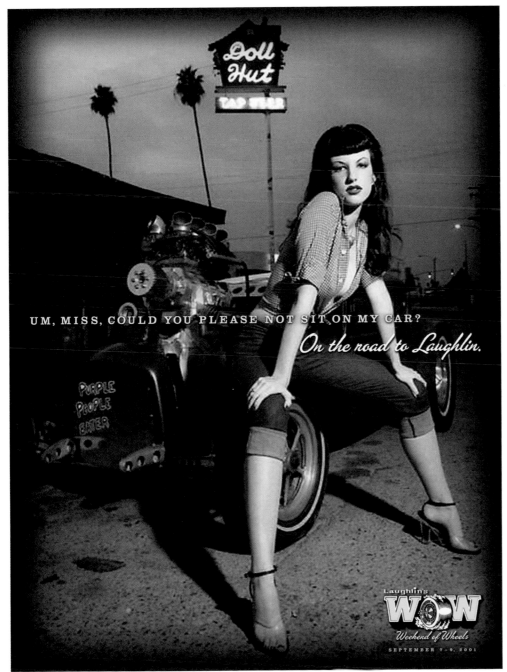

10-1
"Weekend of Wheels"
Agency: R & R Partners/Las Vegas
Creative Director: Ron Lopez
Copywriter: Gage Clegg
Art Director: Becca Morton
Photographer: David Perry
© 2001

The man speaking the line in this ad is so enamored of his "wheels" that he ignores the sexy woman. The color palette and retro clothes add to the appeal and personality of the brand

Most creative professionals would agree that when one—the line or visual—is the "star" or "hero" of an ad, then the other should take a supporting role. If both visual and words are competing for the consumer's attention, then it may cause confusion or a power overdose. The visual and words should work cooperatively, complementing each other, as in Rethink's hilarious outdoor board for Playland (figure 10-2). This doesn't mean that the line and visual have to be similar; it means one has to be the yin to the other's yang, to complete the other, the way the visuals and copy complement one another in the Martin Agency's campaign for the John F. Kennedy Library Foundation (figures 10-3a, 10-3b). "Bobby was JFK's best friend and vice versa. So our first goal is to educate people about this relationship. We explored the library's photo archive looking for photos that showed them working together. Then it was just a matter of finding the right words," said Joe Alexander, the Martin Agency's creative director.

10-2
"Enjoy"

Agency: Rethink Advertising/Vancouver
Art Director/ Copywriter: Ian Grais
Photographer: Hans Sipma
Client: Playland

The thrill of an extreme amusement park ride is communicated quickly, succinctly, and with great humor.

10-3a, 10-3b
"June 3, 1963, Russia Surrenders"
"Older Brothers"

Agency: The Martin Agency/Richmond
Creative Directors: Hal Tench, Joe Alexander, Cliff Sorah
Art Directors: Cliff Sorah, Tom Gibson
Copywriter: Joe Alexander
© John F. Kennedy Library Foundation

"While historically accurate, the campaign is also fun and speaks of family values in a manner with which we can all identify," said Tom McNaught, director of communications for the John F. Kennedy Library and Museum. "The campaign generated enormous public interest in Robert Kennedy and the significant role he played in his brother's administration."

Here are several modes with a complementary visual/verbal relationship:

- The words determine the visual form.
- The words fight the visual form, creating contrast or irony.
- The words are straightforward and the visual is unusual (that is, humorous, odd, curious, zany, shocking).
- The visual is straightforward and the words are unusual (that is, humorous, odd, curious, zany, shocking).

In the last two modes, the visual and copy have a kind of comedy team relationship. Either the copy or the visual is the straight man, and the other is the funny person. One can't help but look at the unexpected visuals in Sukle's campaign for Downtown Denver (figures 10-4a, 10-4b); the visuals are delightfully zany and the line is straight: "Take a break from the mountains." Conversely, Matthews/Evans/Albertazzi's ad for the San Diego Lawn Bowling Club has straight visuals coupled with amusing lines (figure 10-5), as does Mustocs' monumental-feeling outdoor board for the Epsom Derby (figure 10-6), where the line is unexpected and the visual is graphically exciting. About the latter ad, Mustoes' case study states: "We needed to find something that would reflect the prestige of the event, but also tapped in to its accessibility. . . . By focusing on the people that attend the event we could

Take a break from the mountains.

Downtown Denver. Denver Pavilions. Larimer Square. And a free shuttle in between. A few reasons why the 16th Street Mall is the most visited mile in Colorado. Want more? Check out The Urban Eye at downtowndenver.com.

Take a break from the mountains.

10-4a, 10-4b
"Bear in Music Store"
"Porcupine on Light Rail"
Agency: Sukle/Denver
Creative Director: Mike Sukle
Art Director: Norm Shearer
Photographer: Joseph Hancock
Client: Downtown Denver

Outrageous visuals are almost a sure bet to get a viewer's attention. When those visuals express an idea, then you've got a really great chance at persuading a viewer.

bring to life why the event had been so successful for such a long time—it was part of the fabric of British life and the British summer."

In any of these modes, the visual and line complete each other in communicating the whole ad message.

10-5
"Stop, Squat, and Roll"

Agency: Matthews|Evans|Albertazzi/San Diego
Art Director/Photographer: Dana Neibert
Copywriter: John Risser
Client: The San Diego Lawn Bowling Club
© Matthews|Evans|Albertazzi 2002

The historical-looking sepia-colored tone, type, and graphic elements and the interesting angles of photography are complemented by witty copy.

10-6
"Biggest Day Out"

Agency: Mustoes/London
Creative Director: John Merriman
Art Director: John Merriman
Copywriter: John Merriman
Illustrator: Matt Cook
Client: Epsom Derby

The copy following the line "was designed as an integral part of the ad, using a distinctive calligraphy-style font; it read as a who's who of people who would, could, and have attended the Derby. This wasn't a name-dropping list, but a list of the types of people who participate in this great day out—from dog food tasters to pole dancers, vicars to milkmen."

Visual or Words: Which Should Dominate?

Copy-driven? Or visually driven? Art directors, naturally, would testify to the power of visuals. Copywriters, certainly, would argue that words are powerful tools.

As noted in Chapter 8, visually driven ads are those in which the visual carries the weight of the ad message or in which there is no copy other than the sign-off; the visual captures the viewer's attention first. Copy-driven ads convey the advertising message primarily through the words, and there may be no visual other than the design of the typography and the logo or product shot in the sign-off; the copy captures the viewer's attention first. For example, a campaign by DeVito/Verdi for New York Metro is copy-driven (figures 10-7a, 10-7b); the wry copy carries the message. In a dramatic campaign for the Multiple Sclerosis Society, the ads are visually driven (figures 10-8a, 10-8b). Of course, in many of these ads, the copy and visual support one another—there is a synergistic relationship between them, and they work entirely cooperatively to convey the ad message.

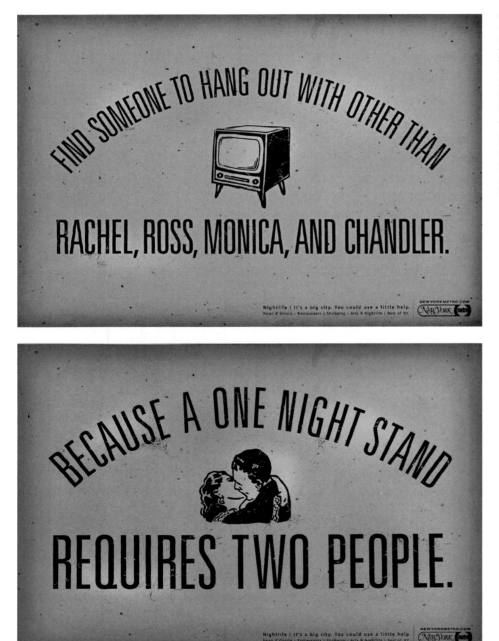

10-7a, 10-7b
"Rachel, Ross, Monica, and Chandler"
"Because a One-Night Stand Requires Two People"
Agency: DeVito/Verdi/New York
Creative Director: Sal DeVito
Art Directors: Anthony DeCarolis, Brad Emmett
Copywriters: Pierre Lipton, Erik Fahrenkopf
Client: New York Metro

The acidic wit of the copy is perfect for a New York audience that prides itself on sophisticated humor. This agency is known for its razor-sharp wit. The tagline in this campaign reads: "Nightlife. It's a big city. You could use a little help."

10-8a, 10-8b
"Paralysis"
"Incontinence"
Agency: Saatchi & Saatchi/London
Creative Director: Dave Droga
Client: Multiple Sclerosis Society

Using switches coupled with dramatic visuals, these PSAs explain how someone afflicted with MS never knows which part of her or his body will shut down, and urge us to donate toward finding a cure.

To best determine what is right for your brand or social cause and audience, you could ask a few questions:

Does this audience prefer to read or look at pictures?

Are the words interesting enough for people to read them?

Is the visual compelling enough to stop people, grab their attention?

If the ad will be used internationally, is it wiser to be more visual than verbal?

Is the convention of a headline plus a visual still viable? Are there other intelligent ways to think of the words as part of the ad message?

**YOU DON'T NEED DUMB LUCK.
MILDLY STUPID LUCK WILL DO.**

MYSTIC LAKE CASINO

How Many Words Are Too Many?

If a headline is interesting, I'll read it. In its all-copy ad for Mystic Lake, Hunt Adkins knows its audience well, and the humor makes the ad appealing (figure 10-9).

Being concise is critical. My mother used to call it "short and sweet." My colleague Alan Robbins advises students to delete what can be deleted while still retaining meaning.

Too short a headline may be a problem. Many novices try to communicate a message in one- or two-word headlines, which is an extremely difficult task. Sure, there are brilliant ad lines, such as "Got milk?" and "Happy hunting." However, those lines were penned by pre-eminent professionals. But, hey, try it; you never know.

Also, the length of the headline should be appropriate to the format. A large number of words on a billboard does not work, whereas a few choice words can be extremely effective (see the fun and surprising outdoor boards in figures 2-8 and 10-2). As designer Carlos Segura, of Segura Inc./Chicago, suggests, "Put your work in context."

Conventions

The classic advertising formula is a visual plus a line, and most advertising creatives still employ it. There are times when that convention doesn't make sense. Too, the postmodern approach seems to be more visually driven. Perhaps it has to do with reaching a larger, more heterogeneous audience; perhaps it's the natural outgrowth of a generation reared on visual media such as television, films, and music videos. All of us are under siege by information; perhaps visuals offer a welcome respite from the contemporary information overload.

For an international audience, relying on words rather than images can be problematic. Visuals tend to be more universally understood. At times, copy can translate poorly from one language to another, causing unforeseen problems; for example, when McGruff the Crime Dog asked readers to "take a bite out of crime" in Mexico, the line took on a negative connotation. Sometimes, visuals can cause problems when aimed at a universal audience. When Landor/San Francisco designed the BP logo, they made sure that the number of petals in the flower was considered a lucky number in all the countries constituting the BP market.

Conversely, when addressing a particular market segment, copy-driven ads—where the words carry the main message—can communicate very clearly (see figure 10-18).

10-9
Relaunch for Casino Under New Identity
Agency: Hunt Adkins/Minneapolis
Creative Director/Copywriter: Doug Adkins
Associate Creative Director/Art Director: Steve Mitchell
Client: Mystic Lake

Hunt Adkins differentiated Mystic Lake from other casinos with a jocular campaign. Doug Adkins says: "Humor is the best tool we have to get past people's well-earned cynicism for one brief moment, giving us an opportunity to share our message with them."

Writing Creatively

"The secret of all effective originality in advertising is not the creation of new and tricky words and pictures, but one of putting familiar words and pictures into new relationships," said Leo Burnett.

Writing creatively involves thinking critically and thinking freely and originally. It's not that what you write has to be absolutely new—it just has to sound fresh, not predictable. It also has to sound as though you're engaging in a natural conversation with the reader.

What's creative about "Give a damn," the National Urban League's former claim? It embodies an idea, it calls us to act in a meaningful way, it's emotional, and it's dramatic yet informal. The beauty of a line such as "Hey, you never know" is that it is both very true and natural to the vernacular.

What's creative about "Got milk?" Well, Jeff Goodby could have written "Do you have any milk?" or "Got any milk?" Both of these say "Got milk?" but neither says it memorably. The casualness of the line adds to the credibility. Exorcise predictability and cliché from a sales pitch and you'll be writing creatively.

In a print campaign for Porsche, the Carmichael Lynch agency "gets at the emotional thrill of being a Porsche owner and driver." In one ad, an analogy is made to the explosive energy a dog must feel when his leash breaks (figure 10-10).

10-10
"What a Dog Feels When the Leash Breaks"
Agency: Carmichael Lynch/Minneapolis
Client: Porche Cars North American, Inc. PORSCHE, BOXSTER and the Porsche Crest are registered trademarks and the distinctive shapes of PORSCHE automobiles are trade dress of Dr. Ing h.c. F. Porsche AG. Used with permission of Porsche Cars North America, Inc. Copyrighted by Porsche Cars North America, Inc.

Pointers for the Novice

When writing copy, here are some rules to live by:

Make sure the line embodies an idea.

Write naturally, in a conversational tone.

Know your brand; capture the brand's essence.

Avoid cliché.

Be logical, clear, and concise.

Make it relevant.

Don't talk down to the consumer.

Absolutely no racial, ethnic, religious, gender, or age stereotypes or slurs.

Say It in the Line—Don't Rely on the Body Copy

Most people don't bother to read body copy. People who are engaged by the line and visual may go on to the body copy. People who are seeking information, such as consumers searching for stereo equipment or someone looking for a phone number in a public service ad, will be interested enough to read the body copy. However, it's sensible not to rely on the body copy to transmit the principal message. The line plus visual should communicate the foremost message, and the body copy supports that message and adds to it. Often, it helps to write the body copy first; that process may generate a line.

It's Established in the Claim

It used to be called a slogan. Today we call it a claim, tagline, end line, or strap line. The tagline should embody the overarching strategy of an ad campaign, conveying the benefit or spirit of the brand or social cause.

When the client's strategy is strongly asserted in the claim, then the idea follows suit willingly and affirmatively. If for any reason the ad concept isn't fully communicated, the claim can clarify or round out the communication, advises Gregg Wasiak, creative director, The Concept Farm/New York.

Once you come up with the idea for the claim, the entire campaign should embody the same spirit and reason for being, as in Work's campaign for Crestar Bank (figure 10-11). Cabell Harris of Work says about the Crestar campaign concept: "Research and account planning revealed that rather than using the traditional 'warm and fuzzy' and overpromising appeals common to the industry, Crestar would be better served by direct, honest, and understated communications. No bank-speak. Instead, Crestar would relate to the consumers from their point of view rather than the bank's. The ads themselves demonstrate that we understand their concerns. The campaign centered around a decidedly unbanklike tagline: 'We're a bank. Banks need customers.'" Similarly, in a campaign for New York Metro, a three-part claim rounds out the meaning (see figure 10-7).

Some great examples where the claim establishes the spirit and strategy of the communication:

Think different (Apple)

Friends don't let friends drive drunk (U.S. Department of Transportation)

Don't leave home without it (American Express)

The "Do I Sound Like a Sales Pitch?" Test

Some lines, such as "Introducing the tingly tang of amazing CheesWhip Dip," just sound like a bad advertising sales pitch. Others, less badly written, such as "You'll love our new and improved cheese dip," still sound like a sales pitch.

Once you've written a line or body copy, it is highly advisable to try saying it aloud. Does it sound stiff? Or like an annoying salesperson trying to sell you something? It should sound like something you'd say in conversation with a friend.

The claim "You're a lot luckier than you think" for Mystic Lake Casino (figures 10-12a, 10-12b), by Hunt Adkins, sounds like a line I can relate to, and it's written in a conversational, natural tone.

DO YOU ENJOY DEALING WITH BANKS?

OR ARE YOU NORMAL?

Most people would rather clean the oven with a toothbrush than deal with some mess-up on their bank account. Sorry, we can't guarantee we'll never mess up. But if we do we can guarantee that we'll make it up to you with our package of cash guarantees. To find out more about them, call 1-800-CRESTAR, visit www.crestar.com or stop by your local branch.

CRESTAR
We're a bank. Banks need customers.

10-11
"Are You Normal?"
Agency: Work, Inc./Richmond
Creative Director: Carolyn Tye McGeorge
Art Director/Designer: Cabell Harris
Copywriter: Kathleen Lane
Client: Crestar Bank

The newspaper campaign used a combination of bold, proactive headlines, spot color, and short copy, and the ads developed were crisp and memorable. Mindful of the mandate to "execute overnight if needed," the agency used all type, thus reducing turnaround time (which would otherwise be extended if illustration or photography had been used).

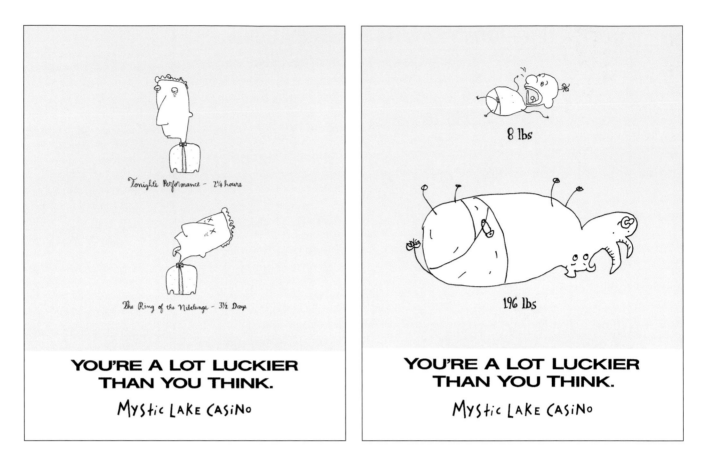

YOU'RE A LOT LUCKIER THAN YOU THINK.

Mystic Lake Casino

Tonight's Performance – 2¼ hours

The Ring of the Nibelungs – 3½ Days

8 lbs

196 lbs

YOU'RE A LOT LUCKIER THAN YOU THINK.

Mystic Lake Casino

10-12a, 10-12b
Agency: Hunt Adkins/Minneapolis
Creative Director/Copywriter: Doug Adkins
Associate Creative Director/Art Director: Steve Mitchell
Client: Mystic Lake Casino

These very amusing ads offer the tagline "You're a lot luckier than you think."

The "Do I Sound Like Something No One Would Ever Say to Anyone Else?" Test

"Taste the music." This was a line for a wine campaign, though I've forgotten which brand (not a good sign of the efficacy of the ad to begin with). I understand what the writer was trying to say about the wine. He was making an analogy. But it's too remote, too literary. I'd never say it to anyone, ever. I don't think I'd even write it in a literary format.

Intention and Idea Generation

"The key to coming up with a great ad is finding that one clear, concise, engaging idea. This holds true for all advertising mediums: print, radio, TV, outdoor, etc.," notes Eric Silver, executive creative director, BBDO Worldwide, New York.

Why would someone need a dictionary? "Upgrade your language" seems to be the simple yet compelling answer underlying Mullen's campaign for Houghton Mifflin (figures 10-13a, 10-13b, 10-13c).

To persuade someone to donate blood or give money to a charity, you've got to make a connection. You've got to touch him, touch his emotional core. The reader should be able to recognize some element of life, something relevant to his experience. The reader should be prompted to think: "Oh yeah, that's so true!" "That's me you're talking about." "You know me." An ad aimed at tourists visiting New York City has the tone that tourists expect and find endearing about forthright New Yorkers (figure 10-14).

Copy should be completely pertinent to the advertising proposition and entirely appropriate for the audience. Would you write an antidrug campaign directed at kids and one directed at parents the same way, with the same type of rhythm and language?

10-13a, 10-13b, 10-13c
"Ambulate"
"Aqueous"
"Circumvolve"

Agency: Mullen/Wenham, MA
Chief Creative Officer: Edward Boches
Creative Director: Jim Hagar
Art Director: Paul Laffy
Copywriter: Brian Hayes
Photographer: Dan Nourie
Digital Artist: Dave Nadeau
Client: Houghton Mifflin
© Mullen

By replacing common words with less-common synonyms, these ads urge us to seek out help from the dictionary.

10-14

**"Our magazine is a lot like
the average New Yorker . . ."**

Agency: DeVito/Verdi/New York
Creative Director: Sal DeVito
Art Directors: Abi Aron, Rob Carducci
Copywriters: Abi Aron, Rob Carducci
Client: Time Out New York

With a clever play on words, this
ad communicates the benefit of
the magazine.

10-15

Agency: Carmichael Lynch/Minneapolis
Creative Director: Jim Nelson
Art Director: James Clunie
Copywriter: Tom Camp
Photographer: Ron Crofoot
Client: EJ Sunglasses

The functional benefit of wearing sunglasses is demonstrated
by the cropped photograph of a face, focusing on the
expression in the eyes, coupled with irreverent copy.

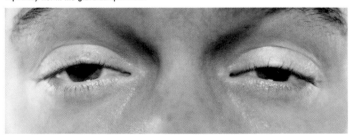

Whose Voice Is It?

In any ad, words take on a persona or identity. Is the copy in the ad telling you what to do or how to behave? Does the headline take on a maternal tone? Does it sound like a friend who is advising you?

Perhaps the headline is in the voice of the person pictured in the ad, as is the case in a wry ad for EJ Sunglasses (figure 10-15). Or does the voice represent the brand, as in a campaign for American Airlines aimed at the Latino market, where the tone is earnest and the words express an important subject (figures 10-16a, 10-16b)?

The words that come to us from ads are somewhat disembodied. It's in the context of the entire ad, the words plus the visual, that we can decipher who is speaking to us, and whether or not we want to listen. Copy also sets a tone or mood. It can sound formal, informal, corporate, scientific, friendly, acerbic, or just about anything else. Colle + McVoy's ad for the Minnesota Department of Tourism actually tells us who is speaking (figure 10-17). With what seems to be a glib memo of sorts, one's "coworkers" suggest a much-needed rest and some relaxing fun by exploring Minnesota.

Process

Tim Delaney of Leagas Delaney, who is renowned for his wickedly clever headlines and acerbic wit, advises, "I'm fairly relaxed about writing, so I just do it. I'm not afraid of it. I'm not thinking, 'Oh my God, I'll never crack this.' I learned this when I was young. . . . Early in my career someone told me that all you have to do when you get blocked is keep writing any old rubbish. And it'll come to you, eventually. But most people don't do that. They sit there wringing their hands, or they get up and walk away."[2]

The point is that thoughtful writing requires critical thinking. And one thought leads to another; as you write, you'll be thinking.

Write a lot. Try writing what might be considered the body copy first. Imbedded in the body copy may be your headline.

Writing should be viewed as an opportunity to play, and play hard. You have to love the process of writing. Try not to rush the process.

When you first start writing lines, just keep writing. Don't judge what you've written

YOU CAN CHOOSE
A CHAIR BY ITS COLOR.
BUT NOT PEOPLE.

We believe that assurance leads to innovation, and that fresh ideas happen more often when our employees can be themselves. To help with this vision, we have 14 Employee Resource Groups, from Latino to African-American. Our message is clear: we take individuality seriously. Because people deserve to be treated like people. For more information about Employee Resource Groups or job opportunities, visit us at aacareers.com.

AmericanAirlines

PENCILS ARE ALL
THE SAME.
PEOPLE ARE NOT.

AmericanAirlines

10-16a, 10-16b
"Office Supplies"
Agency: Zubi Advertising/Coral Gables
Senior Art Director: José Reyes
Senior Copywriter: Alberto Orso
Art Buyer: Jorge Chirino
Associate Creative Director: Héctor Fabio Fabio Prado
V.P. Creative Director: Emmie Vázquez
Client: American Airlines

"This campaign was designed to smash the mold of traditional diversity advertising. Rather than showing a rainbow of ethnicities, we chose to take a very simple, straightforward approach: people are not objects and should never be treated as such. The many and varied diversity programs already in place at American Airlines gave us the ammunition to take such a bold approach."

10-17
"Take Your Vacation Days, Please—Your Coworker"
Agency: Colle + McVoy/Minneapolis
Creative Director: John Jarvis
Art Director: Jon Montgomery
Copywriters: Eric Husband, Dave Keepper
Photographer: Layne Kennedy
Client: Minnesota Office of Tourism
© 2002

A convincing line coupled with a photograph suggesting a refreshing vacation communicates the message that many of us need time to explore states such as Minnesota.

until much later. If you're judgmental during the early stages, then you may block a better line. Usually, one line leads to another.

Write a good number of lines. Give yourself a good deal from which to choose. Edit later. Revising and editing are part and parcel of the art of writing.

Style

Many experts agree that the style of writing should emanate from the brand and serve the idea. Certainly, there are writers whose style is evident. However, early in your career, it may behoove you to allow your idea and the brand strategy to dictate the style. Most importantly, you need to concern yourself with thoughtful, intelligent writing. When your writing is intelligent and original, style may develop or kind of slip itself in there when you least expect it.

Feed Your Writing

Read, read, read.

Read great writers' works. Here are some suggested modern writers: Philip Roth, Alice Walker, John Updike, Saul Bellow, Amy Tan, Toni Morrison, Jane Smiley, V. S. Naipaul, Gao Xingjian, Günter Grass, Jhumpa Lahiri, Rachel Cusk, Oscar Hijuelos, Richard Russo, José Saramago, Nadine Gordimer, Dario Fo, Wislawa Szymborska, Seamus Heaney, Pär Lagerkvist, and Kenzaburo Oe.

Read a great daily newspaper, one that wins journalism awards. Read notable comedies.

Write, write, write.

Keep a journal.

Write letters to friends.

Write funny descriptions of things.

Write song lyrics about the ingredients in chicken soup.

Listen to what people say in conversation.

Read. Listen. Write.

Gregg Wasiak, creative director (and copywriter) of the Concept Farm, advises that the best copywriting exercise is writing radio spots. Writing for radio teaches timing and storytelling. There are no visuals to catch someone's attention—it's all about the words, rhythm, and pace.

Notes

1. Denis Higgins, *The Art of Writing Advertising: Conversations with Masters of the Craft* (Lincolnwood, IL: NTC Business Books, 1990), p. 93.

2. Warren Berger, "Lunch with Tim Delaney," *Creativity*, May 2001, p. 23.

INTERVIEW Valerie Graves

How did your studies in screenwriting, directing, and film production at New York University prepare you for a career in advertising?

Actually, I was ten years into my career in advertising before I took those courses. Frankly, they were a revelation. As a copywriter, I'd been struggling to communicate my vision to the directors whose job was to bring my ideas to the screen. Getting a real understanding of filmmaking—just a whole vocabulary of the art form—transformed me and the process of making commercials into much more of a true collaboration.

You have achieved what most people only dream of. What advice can you offer young creatives and aspiring creatives?

Believe in yourself and your talent. It may sound trite, but sometimes you'll be the only one who does. And, of course, prepare yourself with a good general education, because advertising uses everything you know.

What type of social responsibility do advertising agencies and their clients have to the community?

To understand and respect them.

What was it like to be on the national advertising team of the 1992 Clinton/Gore campaign?

It was fabulous. I couldn't stop pinching myself to make sure it was real. Bill Clinton is hands-down the smartest person I've ever met, and he is *cool*. I worked with superstar colleagues like Donnie Deutsch, David Angelo, and Linda Kaplan, who remains a friend to this day. The biggest differences between political advertising and my normal work were probably the development time (there isn't any; once the ad campaign is set, concepts are constantly being created, sometimes in hours), the constant focus group testing (usually two or three times a week), and the weight that focus groups carry in a political campaign. Several commercials that I did never aired because they were extremely effective with voters who were already in our camp. Political ads are about *winning* votes.

What is the importance of advertising agencies with specific market expertise?

We make the connections that general market agencies don't. By definition, if your job is to speak to everyone, you're not focused on any one group of people. Members of minority groups really respond to the personalized invitation that agencies like ours bring, because historically, "everyone" wasn't necessarily meant to include us. We bring an understanding of the core values and life experiences of our audiences that makes our messages resonate deeply, while at the same time remaining acceptable to the general audience. General market work is a notice on a public bulletin board; ours is an engraved invitation sent to the home.

What are your hopes for the future of advertising?

I hope we'll stay flexible and creative during a time of changes brought about by technology. If, in fact, the thirty-second spot is an endangered species, concepts like brand integration, a more organic way of having consumers encounter our clients' products, will become more important. Already I've had the opportunity to produce a film that included my client's product in a natural way—more than conventional product placement, but different from just a long-form commercial—and I look forward to the opportunity to do more innovative, exciting stuff like that.

Senior Vice President and Chief Creative Officer, UniWorld Group Inc.

Virtually eliminates the need
to have any game.

Ford *Thunderbird*

www.fordvehicles.com

10-18
Thunderbird Print Launch
Agency: UniWorld Group, Inc./New York
Creative Director: Valerie Graves
Client: Ford Motor Company
© 2002 Ford Motor Company

A photograph taken at a dynamic angle is complemented by a clever line targeting the audience.

What common thread runs through successful advertising? Creative advertising?
I'd say true insight into why and how a consumer uses a product is the key to successful advertising. For me, originality and flawless execution in the presentation of that insight are great creative.

How do you respond to a client who does not understand your idea?
These days, I make a real effort to see the idea from that person's point of view—to try and understand *why* the person isn't getting it. Because really, what else can you do? Convince the client that he or she is stupid? You never win a fight with a client, even if it seems you did. Besides, maybe there's a real problem of clarity, something that can be fixed. I should add that this is easier to do when you're the chief creative officer, not the copywriter or art director who gave birth to the idea.

Can advertising help us discover our humanity?
Probably, but I'd be happy if it just *reminded* us of our humanity,

How do the ads your agency creates reflect our lives? Understand us?
Because our work is targeted, it reflects aspects of entire cultures. From heritage to humor to music to heroes, we bring what we know to help our clients connect.

What's your personal advertising philosophy?
Tell the truth about the product and the consumer, and make sure they both have on their Sunday clothes while you're doing it.

What has your professional experience been like as a woman in a male-dominated ad world?
Half the time I was a black female in a white-male-dominated world, which was okay as long as I didn't try to do anything especially female or black. The other half of the time I've spent in a black agency, dealing with white clients, where the challenge is to show them what *is* especially black about what I do. That said, it's a fun job.

Your creativity, drive, and achievements inspire others. What fuels your creativity?
The fear of not being creative enough is what drives me. I believe there are infinite creative ideas in the universe, and I just want some of them to constantly manifest through me. I usually am inspired by pure art. Poets, artists, musicians, filmmakers, etc. They are the ones doing the real high-wire act—the best of them aren't copying anybody. Maya Angelou is a personal hero; she did some really crazy things on the path to becoming the artist she is. She taught me not to be afraid to make a fool of myself, because you never know what may come of that foolishness.

What do you look for when hiring young creatives?
Talent. If they have that, they can learn the rest. If they don't have it, nothing else matters.

You're at the top of your game. You've won prestigious awards and gotten accolades galore. What do you still wish to accomplish?
I want to create a piece of art that will outlive me. By the way, I hope I'm *not* at the top of my game yet.

INTERVIEW Guido Heffels

**Creative Director, Copy,
Heimat/Berlin**

Your creative work is an inspiration to the global advertising community. What inspires your ideas?
In Germany I have never spent an evening with advertising people that ever inspired me in any way. Ideas result from the opposite: personal experiences, events in one's life, fragments of a conversation you heard on the underground, a good record, a good film, a good magazine feature, or simply just a weekend in bed. Inspiration happens when you live.

What advice would you offer to people aspiring to be art directors or copywriters?
Beg to differ!

What are the hallmarks of a good campaign?
A simple unique strategic platform, a simple creative thought, a simple, untrendy, memorable execution, no compromises. Four of a kind always wins. First the viewer's attention, then the awards.

Should ads in a campaign look the same (exact compositional template) or can they look substantially different from one another?
A good campaign is always more than just a series of advertisements, no matter what they're like. A campaign is a clever, convincing underlying idea that can have many forms of expression.

If I always have the feeling that the same company is talking to me, then at the end of the day it doesn't matter what the promotional tools look like.

This, of course, clearly contradicts everything the corporate design agencies spell out to us on a daily basis, and clients are also difficult to convince of this.

In the final analysis, though, it is the logical consequence of a perfect corporate identity, a unique way of seeing yourself that needs no visual standardization. Perhaps, rather, a playing field on which you can move around freely.

If you consider yourself an auteur in this collective medium, how do you protect your vision through the assembly line process?
In a nutshell: you mustn't leave the assembly line process to itself to begin with. You have to become a part of the process and be prepared for every new station. That means think like a consultant, think like a client, think like a chief executive. But never, ever think and argue like a creative. Because a creative pursues different (more egoistic/artistic) objectives to everybody else (effectiveness/profit). So, as a creative, I have to develop my argumentation based on the objectives of others. When it comes down to it, the other stations of the assembly line process don't care about the creativity. So I mustn't come to them with this argument to begin with. This is the only way you can safely get brilliant ideas to the finish line. And you must not and should not leave this up to anyone else. So: go along to client meetings too, listen, react, present arguments. Anyone who has developed a good campaign and then allows it to go through the channels uncontrolled should not be surprised if it gets improved to death or even killed off altogether.

If the object is to sell the product, does that ever suffer by someone trying to utilize the medium for his own artistic needs?
A good creative always has a strong ego that needs its form of expression. If you can manage to combine your own ego with the meaning or purpose of advertising (i.e., selling products/images), great advertisements will result.
If you get in your own way, it shows in your work-"Aha, that's a Guido Heffels ad, not an Adidas advertisement at all." Pity. Pass Go again and don't collect $200.

In order to get a viewer's attention, do you have to defy convention?

There is always somebody who makes up rules: an ad must work in so-and-so-many seconds, a poster headline shouldn't be longer than five words. Funnily, it is precisely those things that move the world that throw these kinds of rules out the window.

These days the man on the street is so clever and informed about advertising that you can usually only still reach him by charmingly ignoring his communicative expectations: posters with headlines that are way too long, advertisements you only understand after a quarter of an hour, but which are so interesting you gladly take the time to read them. New and fresh always means unconventional at the same time. [See figures 7-24a, 7-24b.]

Should an ad offer a benefit?

Should a client pay for an advertisement that has nothing to say? A benefit need not necessarily be a lower price or a product benefit, though. But at the end of the day, there must be something in it for the viewer of an ad. Maybe it is a smile on his lips with which you bring a product to mind. That 's a lot already.

How should a campaign fit into the strategic plan for a brand or public service announcement?

The longer I have worked in this business, the more I have learned to believe in strategy. Thus a campaign must always be part of the strategy-it must have a function, an answer to the question "Why this way and no other way?" A strategic plan is always much bigger and more comprehensive than a campaign. There are positioning models, purely marketing concerns, trade support, etc. At some point every campaign must fulfill a subgoal within the master plan, otherwise it is worthless and therefore meaningless. [See figures 6-23a, 6-23b, 11-9.]

There is a trend toward "no-copy" ads. What do you think about ads that completely depend upon the visual to communicate?

We are currently experiencing the end of this no-copy trend. The symbol doublets1 are adding up, the platitudes have been done to death. The age of art direction and the written word is dawning again.

What is the future of advertising?

Advertising or even communication has always adapted itself to the development of the media over the millennia, from word-of-mouth advertising through the first posters and printed books to radio/television and finally now the Internet. So the question of the future of advertising will at the same time always be a question about the future of the media. The medium is and will be the message.

I think that events and sponsoring in particular will play a greater role in the future. Especially if the decline of the global social systems continues as it has. There will be Sony Streets and McDonald Universities. In fact, there already is an AOL Arena in Hamburg.

Why have you chosen advertising for artistic expression?

The work in advertising is a wonderful, constantly changing mixture of discipline and creativity. I never know exactly what I will be working on in a month. That keeps you young and alert. Also, with every new client you can always learn and experience something new. Things you would probably never have found out about otherwise. The production of special glass, DIY shops, news editing offices, possibilities for preventing skin cancer, making newspapers, etc., etc. Not bad, don't you think?

11

Beyond Print Media: Television Commercials, Interactive Media, and Guerilla Advertising

Television

"Entertainment sells," according to Cliff Freeman & Partners/New York. And that's probably enough to understand broadcast advertising.

People watch television programs mostly to be entertained. Entertaining programming attracts sponsors. And advertising sponsors means revenue.

And Now a Word from Our Sponsors . . .

There you are sitting on your living room sofa, and the program you've been waiting for all week is periodically interrupted by commercial messages. Although a few critics say that the commercials are better than the programs, television commercials still interrupt television programming.

Many people are annoyed by those interruptions. Others just zap around for two minutes until their program comes back on. Many head for the refrigerator. Some stare blankly. A television commercial has to do several things to get people to watch and to keep them from zapping or making a quick phone call or retrieving a snack or taking out the trash or checking their e-mail or . . .

In order to attract consumers, television commercials have to:

- Entertain

- Be seductive

- Be believable

- Communicate a clear message

- Look and feel fresh (not have the look, tone, and feel of a pedestrian television commercial)

- Get people's attention before they zap or leave the room

- Work in the context of television programming during the commercial break

And, without question, a television commercial has to:

- Endear the brand to the consumer

- Create a desire to act on behalf of a social cause or charity (for PSAs)

- Create awareness of a social cause (for PSAs)

- Persuade the consumer to buy into the brand

- Reinforce the brand image, lending to a cohesive portrait of the brand

- Call the consumer to action—to buy, to call, to donate

- Be a somewhat friendly visitor, conscious of being viewed in people's homes

And a television spot has to do all these things in thirty seconds. Or even fifteen seconds. At the very most, sixty seconds.

A television commercial, also called a TV spot, is a promotion for a brand. A PSA communicates a message on behalf of a nonprofit organization for a social cause. The "Lamp" TV spot for Ikea by Crispin Porter + Bogusky is creative *and* clearly positions the brand (figure 11-1). The concept in this ad mocks sentimental feelings about "disposable" furniture. We watch someone throw out an old, unstylish lamp along with the garbage. As the person sits comfortably in her apartment, the lamp sits on the curbside on a miserable rainy night. Through camera angles, lighting, and music, we are set up to feel sorry for this lamp. Then a man walks into the camera's view and with a Swedish accent says to us, "Many of you feel badly for this lamp. That is because you are crazy. It has no feelings and the new one is much better." This agency's ability to develop creative ideas renders brands more interesting.

What TV Can Do

Let's start with what the medium of television has to offer:

- Motion

- Time: Fifteen-, thirty-, or sixty-second formats

- Sound: music, voice, sound effects

- Special visual effects

- Narrative

In print, you have two or three seconds to capture someone's attention. If you lose the consumer in the first second, you've lost 'em. Period. With television, you may lose someone's attention in the first two or three seconds and then recapture his attention in the next five seconds, if he's still on the sofa. People drift in and out when watching television.

On television, you can tell a story with the aid of voice, music, and motion. In a TV spot by Mullen for a special television program, *Evolution*, the music is a key factor in the advertising concept (figure 11-2). We watch and listen to a series of men—alone and doing everyday activities, such as clipping toenails and lifting weights—sing, in their own amateur

11-1
"Lamp" TV spot
Agency: Crispin Porter + Bogusky/Miami
Creative Director: Alex Bogusky
Associate Creative Director: Paul Keister
Art Directors: Mark Taylor, Steve Mapp
Copywriter: Ari Merkin
Producer: Rupert Samuel
Director: Spike Jonze
Production Company: Morton Jankel Zander
Client: IKEA

Wry wit is the earmark of this unusual campaign, letting people know that they shouldn't feel sorry for their disposable furniture.

11-2

"Evolution—Let's Get It On" TV spot

Agency: Mullen/Wenham, MA
Chief Creative Officer: Edward Boches
Creative Director/Art Director: Greg Boker
Creative Director/Copywriter: Jim Garaventi
Director of Broadcast/Producer: Alyson Singer
Client: WGBH
© Mullen

With an unlikely cast singing pop lyrics that don't quite match their image, this TV spot draws us in.

why bother with men, when cloning is a more efficient form of reproduction?

voices, "Let's Get It On" (a song written by Marvin Gaye and Ed Townsend). This hilarious slice of life comes alive with the aid of music—a no-can-do in print. Television is perfectly suited to storytelling. However, any story told in fifteen, thirty, or sixty seconds has to be compressed. You don't have the luxury of time that filmmakers enjoy. In television commercials, if you don't account for every second—if every second isn't interesting and engaging—then you may lose the viewer entirely.

And the spot must be focused toward communicating a message. Certainly, a commercial can be highly entertaining or bizarre, but a commercial message must be communicated. It is not art for art's sake. On one hand, you definitely *don't* want a TV commercial that is all sales pitch. On the other, you don't want to bury the sell so deeply that no one knows what the commercial is selling. The "When I Grow Up" TV spot for Monster.com, by Mullen, clearly communicates the benefit of the brand (figure 11-3). Taped in black and white, which adds to the sense of irony, we hear children say what they want to be when they grow up; they make such startling statements as: "I want to be a yes-man." "I want to be forced into early retirement." "I want to be underappreciated." The penultimate frame reads: "What do you want to do?" When we see the last frame of the TV spot, which reads "There's a better job out there," we realize that many people don't have the job they had hoped for, but that Monster.com can help them find that job. About his agency's work for Monster.com, Edward Boches, chief creative officer, comments: "All creative solutions come from the same two places: the section of the brain responsible for inspiration, and the section

11-3
"When I Grow Up" TV spot
Agency: Mullen/Wenham, MA
Chief Creative Officer: Edward Boches
Art Director: Monica Taylor
Copywriter: Dylan Lee
Director: Bryan Buckley
Agency Producer: Sarah R. Monaco
Client: Monster.com
© Mullen

Though humorous, these spots are poignant enough, in terms of people's aspirations, to make us realize the importance of using the Monster.com service.

in charge of discipline. Monster followed a logical path that went like this: 'Should we talk about what we are or what we believe in? If we believe in something, what should it be?' How about your inalienable right to a fulfilling career? That's the logical part. Then comes: 'How do we say it?' How about the promise of a great job by starting with the misery of a bad one? After that it's inspiration and the wisdom not to settle for a bad idea and to recognize a great one when it comes along."

Structuring a Commercial

Sorry, there are no formulas. Or rather there are formulas, but they can be trite and predictable. And that's why I won't offer any. As Eric Silver, executive vice president and group executive creative director, BBDO Worldwide/New York, says, "We owe it to ourselves to throw out the formulas. And have as much fun as we can in a very stressful business. In the end, our clients will thank us for it."

There also are conventions, which come and go. From the early days of television until today, formulas have changed, with each decade ushering in new trends.

The *structure* or *form* of a commercial refers to the selection and arrangement of the components. There are as many structures for television commercials as there are for film, prose, poetry, or music. The structure should flow out of the brand strategy, the creative brief, the idea, the tone you want to set, the feeling, and the audience to whom you want to communicate, as does a TV spot for the MINI by Crispin Porter + Bogusky (figure 11-4), where we

11-4
"This Is America" TV spot
Agency: Crispin Porter + Bogusky/Miami
Creative Director: Alex Bogusky
Associate Creative Director: Andrew Keller
Art Director: Amee Shah
Copywriter: Scott Linnen
Producers: David Rolfe, Rupert Samuel
Director: Baker Smith
Production Company: Harvest
Client: MINI
©2004 The MINI name and logo are registered trademarks of the MINI division, BMW of North America, LLC.

With a very funny twist at the end, this little road trip captures our interest.

see a young man thoroughly enjoying his music and "motoring" in his MINI. A British police officer pulls him over for driving on the wrong side of the road, whereupon the young man reacts: "This is America, man." Suddenly we realize the MINI is now available in America.

Of course, you can think of a commercial as being like storytelling, containing characters, goals, conflicts, scenes, and a plot line. When telling a story, one must consider the element of time. How do we experience the time? In what sequence do events occur? Basically, a story moves in either a linear pattern (in chronological sequence, from A to B to C to D) or a nonlinear pattern (not in chronological sequence).

On creating linear structures, Professor Alan Robbins of Kean University advises: "To me, all stories—whether they are novels, commercials, comics, films—follow the same structure: beginning, middle, and end.

"The beginning is the snare, the catch, the lure, the setup. Some image or description that grabs the reader or viewer's attention and sets up a question, a dilemma, a mystery that calls out for an answer.

"The middle is the explication or unfolding of events, actions, intentions that are consequences of the beginning.

"The end is the resolution of or answer to the beginning setup.

"What changes regarding the different formats is the medium of communication (images, words, sounds, etc.) and the length of exposition. The setup in a commercial can take only a few seconds; in a novel, many pages. That's why most story projects begin with a story outline. We use index cards to do this, although screenwriting software now sets these up automatically.

"I would suggest to anyone working on a story format to begin with an outline that answers the questions posed by this structure. (1) Beginning: what's the first thing that happens that will be intriguing, fascinating or captivating to a complete stranger? (2) Middle: what is the sequence of events that follows that will keep the viewer's attention step by step? (3) End: what is the last thing that happens and how does it resolve or answer the situation set up in the beginning?"

There are advertising professionals who advocate starting the commercial with a big splash, a captivating beginning. That way, you're capturing someone's attention right off. Others disagree. Yet others advise ending with a twist—building the story one way, only to surprise the viewer at the end.

"We must get the attention of the consumer *by any means necessary.* . . . To not do so is a disservice to the client," says Eric Silver, a creator of must-watch television commercials

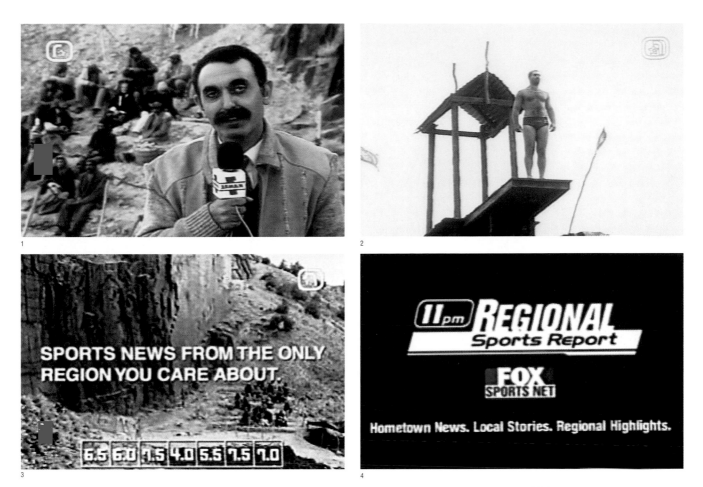

that are unpredictable and timely. Some ad critics call the trend "oddvertising," and some call it "mockumentaries." Silver's ads often feature outrageous antics and a break with formulaic thinking. A campaign for Fox Regional Sports depicts bizarre sports from various areas around the globe; the "Turkey/Cliff Diving" spot (figure 11-5) shows the sport of diving from a high board into earth rather than water. The message is "Watch only the sports that are relevant to you." The appeal is humorous exaggeration that makes an excellent point about watching regional sports on Fox.

There are many ways to structure a commercial, where a complete gem of a story can unfold in less than a minute (you need at least a few seconds at the end for the logo and claim). Of course, the structure should grow from the idea. Here are things to consider:

Whose point of view is the story being told from?

Is the idea plot-driven? Is it character-driven?

Is there a single protagonist? Are there multiple protagonists?

Are you offering a logical reading of the story line?

Is comic timing key?

Is it deconstructionist? Is it self-conscious as an ad?

If a particular structure or pattern seems to be prevalent or trendy, don't use it. Ping when they pong. Take my mother's advice; she said, "Look at what everyone else is doing and then do something different." If you use a prevalent pattern or structure, your TV spot will just blend in. Viewers notice patterns; they may not be conscious of it, but their brains recognize them. Harwich-Hook's commercial for Stena Line breaks away from the typical ferry

11-5
"Turkey/Cliff Diving"

Agency: Cliff Freeman & Partners/New York
Creative Director: Eric Silver
Art Directors: Rossana Bardales, Taras Wayner
Copywriter: Dan Morales
Director: Traktor
Producer: Clair Grupp
Client: Fox Regional Sports

Giving us a darned good reason to watch Fox Regional Sports, these ads appeal to a cheeky sense of humor. With outrageous antics, this spot absolutely captures one's attention.

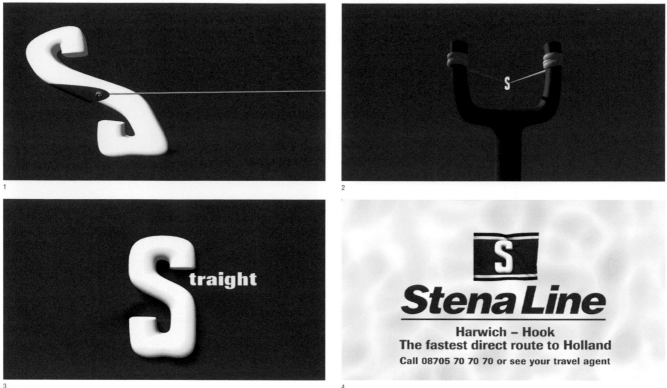

1

2

3

4

11-6
"Straight"

Agency: Mustoes/London
Creative Directors: Andy Amadeo, Mick Mahoney
Art Director: Lee Hanson
Copywriter: Mark Prime
Production Company: Moving House
Director: Paul Smith
Client: Stena Line (Harwich-Hook of Holland)

This TV spot is a good lesson in learning to zig when the competition zags, in order to differentiate your client's brand or cause.

line formula with an animated spot (figure 11-6). To differentiate Stena, Mustoes took "the *S* from the Stena logo. We made this the centerpiece of every execution, creating a look that both stood out from the classified clutter and was instantly recognizable as Stena. To maximize brand impact further, the 'S look' was also stretched into all aspects of Stena Line's communication and corporate identity, ranging from Internet banners and Web site home pages through to brochure design, mail shots, on-board promotions, and promotional merchandise."

The main points to remember are:

• Get attention.

• Keep attention.

• Be ethical.

• Be relevant.

• Serve as a call to action.

First, your television spot has to capture the viewer's attention. Second, you have to keep the viewer's attention. Third, your advertising message, in both text and subtext, must be ethical and respectful. Fourth, your message and delivery needs to be relevant to the audience. Fifth, you've got to call the viewer to action.

Other important points to keep in mind when structuring a commercial are:

• Be clear.

• Be fresh.

• Be appropriate.

• Communicate clearly.

• Make the message and delivery relevant to the consumer.

Storyboard

A *storyboard* is a series of drawings, sketches, or photographs of key shots of a planned television commercial, accompanied by text, used to visually explain an idea. It acts like a diagram of the commercial before it goes into production. Here is a storyboard for Fox Sports (figure 11-7) that combines photography and drawings to delineate the story line, which is about two urban youths, Jerome and Alan, who are both basketball fans and professional basketball player wannabes.

A storyboard serves several purposes. It helps the creative team visualize their idea. The creative team uses their storyboard to sell their idea to their creative director, and the agency

11-7
"Utah Jazz" storyboard
Agency: Cliff Freeman & Partners/New York
Creative Director: Eric Silver
Art Director: Reed Collins
Copywriter: Eric Silver
Director: Kuntz and Maguire
Producer: Kevin Diller
Client: Fox Sports

This hilariously irreverent spot points out the benefits of watching a regional sports broadcast.

Utah Jazz :30
(Urban Stoop)

uses it to sell the idea to the client. After the client approves the idea, the storyboard is used to explain the idea to the director. Seeing an idea in pictures, almost like a cartoon strip, helps everyone better understand how the idea will play out on television.

Relevance

There are a number of things that appeal to most people. The Mullen agency's philosophy relates to this ideal platform: "A television spot can tell you what to do. It can tell you why you should believe. But the best have the power to make you feel, to connect with you emotionally, to tap into shared beliefs."

People need to relate to what an ad is saying, whether the ad is for a brand or is a PSA. Getting to people may mean that your characters feel and act "real" (they talk and behave the way real people do in conversation and don't sound contrived) or that you've included details from observations of life that contribute greatly to the authenticity of the message. In its spot for Oxygen, Mullen aims to hit a nerve with a primarily female television audience (figure 11-8) and succeeds, communicating the idea that Oxygen, both on TV and online, is pro-women and about women. Ironically, this TV spot utilizes a standard beauty pageant question: "What one thing would you do to make the world a better place?" Various contestants answer, and parts of their answers add up to an assertive statement about women.

11-8
"Pageant" TV spot
Agency: Mullen/Wenham, MA
Chief Creative Officer: Edward Boches
Creative Director/Copywriter: Tim Roper
Art Director: Toygar Bazarkaya
Agency Producer: Sarah Monaco
Client: Oxygen
© Mullen

Satirizing beauty pageants, this spot aims to appeal to the female target audience.

It's a Matter of Style

Tone can be set with music, visual style, elements of a film or television genre, or, ideally, a combination thereof. A genre film is a type that is widely utilized and shares basic common characteristics, subjects, settings, and events. Certain genres and styles can invoke particular moods. As with all forms of visual communication, form and content should be synergistic; that is, the form of your idea should enhance your message.

Genres

Action

Comedy

Drama

Family

Film noir

Gangster

Horror

Musical

Mystery or suspense

Road movie

Romantic comedy

Science fiction

Urban comedy

War

Western

Styles

Abstract

Art film

Black comedy

Blockbuster movie

Cinéma-vérité

Documentary

Expressionistic

Farce

Jump-cut visual style

Magic realism

Mixing old and new styles

"Mockumentary"

Music video

New wave

Parody

Realism

Social realism

Surrealism

Directions, Moods, and Tones

Borrowing from other forms of communication (for example, comic books, how-to manuals)

Contemporary

Dark and gritty

Emotional storytelling

Ethereal

Futuristic

Handheld camera

Hard-edged slice of life

High-tech feeling

Homemade

Ironic

Low-tech feeling

Moody

Nostalgic

Pastoral

Primitive

Period piece

Real-time

Retro

Sexual

Slapstick

Vignettes

Schützen Sie Ihre Kinder.
Schützen Sie sich selbst.

11-9
"Mutter" TV spot
Agency: Heimat/Berlin
Creative Director: Guido Heffels
Client: Arbeitsgemeinschaft Dermatologische Pravention

This PSA forcefully grabs our attention with surprise and drama, making its important message about skin cancer prevention memorable.

On Creativity and the Future of TV Commercials

"You can't sell a man who isn't listening," said Bill Bernbach. It's true. You want to capture and keep people's attention, and the only way to do it is to be interesting. An ad, whether it is print or television, has to be creative enough to carry us through several viewings. The same print ad will appear in several magazines during the course of a month or several months. Television commercials, with a few exceptions, air more than once during a period of time. It is important to structure the ad so that it is interesting when viewed multiple times, as in the PSA created by Heimat about skin cancer prevention, which is as captivating as any great film (figure 11-9). We see a mother looking at photographs of her baby daughter enjoying good times at the beach in the sun. We read: "They will thank you for all you have done." Then the doorbell rings, and the mother warmly greets her daughter, who is now grown. Abruptly and dramatically, the daughter falls toward the camera, apparently dead from skin cancer. We are told: "It takes twenty years for sun exposure to turn into skin cancer. Protect your children. Protect yourself."

At first, the spot "I Have" (figure 11-10) looks like a slice of life; we see a woman preparing to cook, only to find empty Pork Farms pork pie wrappers. She asks her husband and son: "Who's been eating pork pies?" And sheepishly, both reply, "I have." All three are surprised when someone outside their window answers, "I have." Cut to the street, and everyone says "I have." Once on the street, the film speeds up with music and percussion sound effects to add a comical quality to what started out with a very different mood. The spot ends with: "Pork Farms. The nation's secret love." (See the Mustoes case study in Chapter 2 for more information.)

1

2

3

11-10
"I Have" TV spot
Agency: Mustoes/London
Art Director: Ros Sinclair
Copywriter: Sean Thompson
Director: Jeff Stark, Stark Films
Client: Pork Farms Bowyers (Northern Foods)

This spot is a very clever and entertaining way to say that pork pies are a delicious and filling snack that everyone enjoys.

1

2

3

4

11-11
Campaign for Freedom: "Church"

Agency: DeVito/Verdi/New York
Creative Director: Sal DeVito
Client: The Ad Council

"The Ad Council solicited agencies from across the country, and we are proud to have been one of four selected in the initial introduction of the Campaign for Freedom. This advertising recognizes that it is every American's responsibility to protect our country's freedom and not take it for granted."

In a spot that is part of the PSA "Campaign for Freedom," we see people who have to practice their faith in hiding, in a basement (figure 11-11). A frame reads: "What if America weren't America?" The tagline is "Freedom. Appreciate it. Cherish it. Protect it." It is a poignant reminder of the freedom Americans enjoy.

Today, we confront prime-time broadcast network shows in which advertisers' products or services are worked into variety or news segments, both live and taped, instead of traditional commercials. Even in the face of this newer breed of ad, John Butler, of Butler, Shine & Stern, advises: "Television advertising isn't going anywhere. The form may change somewhat along the way—possibly longer form, or embedded more seamlessly into programming. In the end, whether or not it's a TiVo or some other form of new technology that's put into a consumer's hand that gives them the power to skip over our spots, in the end, they are either going to want to see what we create, or not. I think if something is relevant enough and gets enough people talking, those TiVo folks will seek it out. So maybe the technology will actually make advertising agencies and clients create things that are more relevant and more interesting than ever before."

Interactive Media

New media or old media, the question remains: "What's in it for me?" Consumers want a benefit. People come to the Internet for a variety of reasons—for gathering information, for shopping, for entertainment, for chatting, or just for browsing. If I am visiting an advertising Web site and it's interesting, I might take a look around. If it's easy to navigate, I might stay awhile. If it's entertaining or interesting, I might come back, and the brand may even be able to build a relationship with me. Since the Internet is relatively new, people expect to be entertained in novel and compelling ways, and they don't want to waste their time.

What's the Same? What's Different?

Pretty much the same design principles and advertising precepts that apply to the traditional media of print, direct mail, and television also apply to interactive advertising. What distinguishes interactive advertising is the online communication between consumer and advertiser. Online communication can be transformed into a relationship between the consumer and the brand or social cause. Along with direct marketing (advertising mailed directly to the consumer), interactive advertising (also called digital marketing) has the greatest potential for intimacy, for establishing a dialogue between brand and consumer, and for information gathering. Print and TV leave the consumer more passive, delivering a monologue.[1] When asked what the Web can do that traditional advertising media can't, Hillman Curtis, chief creative officer and founder of hillmancurtis inc., replied:

"Offer an experience that users can choose to experience and to repeat—one that is shaped by their feedback, that is constantly being updated, that's exciting and demands that traditional advertisers start rethinking their campaigns. It's not about thirty seconds or sixty seconds or one page in a magazine—it's about brands becoming elastic and responsive and at the same time remaining consistent."

Print and television are both mature media. The Internet is in its infancy and will evolve both technologically and creatively. Thus, as of yet, we don't know the Internet's full potential. (We still don't know advertising's future or next frontier either.) What we do know about the Internet is that the success of an ad design depends upon a team's knowledge of traditional design principles, nonlinear function, content, functionality, how to engage visitors, how to add value to the visitor's experience, ease of navigation, and anticipation of visitors' behavior.

Traditional advertising moves in a linear fashion; the Internet does not. Visitors can move around a Web site at their own discretion—and, certainly, exit at their own discretion. People don't necessarily have to enter at a site's home page or exit at "the end." Thus, the site designer must offer the consumer a valuable experience at every turn. The technical part of an interactive advertising team must know what can be done and how to do it. Like television consumer advertising at its best, interactive advertising must be entertaining.

An example of an intriguing and entertaining online concept and refined execution are BMWfilms (figure 11-12). The BMWfilms are a series of short online-only films, supported by other media and directed by venerable film directors, in which the central character of the films uses his expert driving skills in a BMW. About these Internet films, Jim McDowell, executive marketing director, BMW North America, said, "With the films, we attempted to do something completely different. We thought that perhaps the answer wasn't in advertising to our prospects but in entertaining our prospects. People absorb entertainment differently than advertising. Out of that thinking, Fallon suggested the idea of Web films. . . . We felt these films should appeal to our core prospects; they'll know the world-famous directors and see a name brand (the director's name) on their computer screen. And because it's based on the Internet, it's available anywhere you are at any time."

McDowell continues: "Many directors were intrigued with the prospect of doing something directly on the Internet. They had been thinking about such a project but needed a source of funding, with few creative restrictions. John Frankenheimer signed on early, thus paving the way for others. Now, quite a few directors are very interested.

"If you ask all of these directors, they won't call these films commercials. They're not viewing them as thirty-second TV spots, but view them as really short movies. . . . What's really nice is that, in the future, when someone does a retrospective of John Frankenheimer films, our BMWfilms will be on the list!"

11-12
"The Hire" poster and
BMW Interactive Films

Agency: Fallon Worldwide/Minneapolis
Client: BMW
© 2004 BMW of North America, LLC, used
with permission. The BMW name and logo are
registered trademarks

"You get your impression of brands from so many different sources. In the films, people have seen many aspects of what the actor—that is, the BMW—can do. Think of Clive Owens, the driver and central character in the films, as the cowboy and the BMW as his trusty horse. One thinks of what the car did in each film—one notices the BMW's power of braking, steering, acceleration, agility, and balance in the movies, all done without special effects," notes Jim McDowell, executive marketing director, BMW North America. The BMWfilms series brought together leading film directors, leading Web technologies, and a luxury automobile brand for a groundbreaking project.

Part of an ingenious marketing campaign introducing the MINI into America, including a wide array of unconventional advertising, these Internet films are vehicles intended to drive visitors to the MINI Web site. In "Clown" (figure 11-13), we see at the side of the road a clown whose little decorated car has broken down. To the clown's delight, a fellow driving a MINI stops to give the clown a lift. The clown—being a clown—happily squirts the driver with the magic flower in his lapel, twice. Unhappily, the driver keeps on motoring. The clown continues clowning around, mimicking the driver driving. Losing his patience with the clown, the driver speeds up, demonstrating how quick and agile the MINI is. Finally, the driver pulls over to throw the clown out of his car. The final frames read. "It's small. But it's no clown car." Using a silent-film technique, as well as black-and-white film that looks distressed (to imitate the quality of silent films), adds to the slapstick humor, and we get the message that the MINI is "no clown car."

In "Bulldog," another Internet film, a bulldog encounters a MINI in a motel parking lot (figure 11-14). The film's director sets up wonderful shots of the bulldog and the MINI face-to-face. After staring intently at the MINI for a good while, the bulldog looks perplexed.

11-13

"Clown" Internet film (:60)

Agency: Crispin Porter + Bogusky/Miami
Creative Director: Alex Bogusky
Associate Creative Director/Art Director: Andrew Keller
Associate Creative Director /Copywriter: Bill Wright
Producers: David Rolfe, Rupert Samuel
Director: Baker Smith
Production Company: Harvest
Client: MINI
©2004 The MINI name and logo are registered trademarks of the MINI division, BMW of North America, LLC.

The agency's solution was to make the MINI fun—making "Let's motor" an enduring and fun concept. Reminiscent of silent film comedies, this Internet film engages the viewer with great humor and style.

11-14

"Bulldog" Internet film (:45)

Agency: Crispin Porter + Bogusky/Miami
Creative Director: Alex Bogusky
Associate Creative Director/Art Director: Andrew Keller
Associate Creative Director /Copywriter: Bill Wright
Producers: David Rolfe, Rupert Samuel
Director: Baker Smith
Production Company: Harvest
Client: MINI
©2004 The MINI name and logo are registered trademarks of the MINI division, BMW of North America, LLC.

This "let's get acquainted" Web commercial, in which a bulldog is intimately intrigued by a MINI, endears the brand to the consumer with a bit of humility and fun.

Exploring, the bulldog walks around the side of the car. Then we read: "Let's get acquainted." How does a dog get acquainted? We see the bulldog sniff the MINI's tailpipe. Finally we read, "Let's motor."

Internet films and "webisodes" (Internet spots intended to resemble films) are potentially great marketing tools. I say "potentially" since the success of the film depends upon many factors, including the creative team behind the film, the marketing director, and the support media used to promote it. Here's why Internet films can be very useful tools in an advertising campaign:

• They have entertainment value.

• The brand is the star of the film.

• A visitor seeks out the film, unlike conventional mass media advertising, which is forced onto the audience; because the visitor seeks out the film, she will be far more receptive to the advertising message.

• People tend to tell friends to go see an Internet film via viral marketing—e-mails spreading the positive buzz.

• Buzz may be generated in the press (free publicity) depending upon who directed the film and the creative level of the film.

Important Points

What are the essential considerations for interactive advertising? Says Kevyn Smith, creative director, Peel Interactive Media/Seattle, "I think that the biggest consideration for interactive advertising is time. You need to hook the user right away. With technology today being so infused into our everyday lives, people's attention span is a lot shorter than it used to be. The average user viewing any interactive advertising, whether it's on the Web, a kiosk, or a hand-held device, needs to be hooked right away, or you have lost them. People's time is important, and they need to have immediate satisfaction right away to want to explore more.

"With a lot of our pieces, we try to hook the user right away, by presenting them with a cinematic intro to the piece and an overview that sucks them in right away—well, hopefully. At the same time, we give them access to the navigation right away and an option to skip the intro so that people looking for info can get at it right away, as in our Web site for Amnesty International" (figure 11-15).

"I think that another consideration is doing something within interactive advertising that cannot be done in traditional advertising. Find a way to supplement it and be an extension of what already is going on. So for instance, with a product you are trying to market, or a service, use interactivity to sell that product, or advertise it in a different way, than what is normally done offline. Get the user to interact with the brand in a way that they can't through print and TV," Smith concludes.

When I asked Jon Maltby, creative director, Blast Radius, to imagine the Jon Maltby interactive advertising workshop, here's what he said would be important: "I prefer to call it digital marketing; it is beyond advertising.

"One important consideration is deciding what it is going to take to cover it digitally. If it begs banners, then we create banners. If it begs wireless, use a PDA. If it begs digital marketing, then we do that.

"Understand why you're doing something. Without a problem to solve, there's no point in working toward a solution.

"Understand your audience, what the user needs, and everything should map back to that.

"The execution is the key to making it a delightful experience.

"Understand the real business needs for a digital application to exist.

"When creating for an online environment, if a user or a person can experience what you've created anywhere else, then it's a waste of time. A movie online that you can't see anywhere else in the world, then go for it. Ask, 'Is this done anywhere else in our consumers' life?'"

B.U.C.

When designing interactive advertising, it's essential to keep the following mantra in mind: B.U.C., which stands for *beneficial, usable,* and *captivating*.

From the visitor's point of view:

• Is this interactive advertisement beneficial to me?

• Is it usable? (Can I find what I need? Is it frustration-free? Can I get around easily?)

• Does it captivate my attention? Is it visually interesting? Would I want to come back?

Hillman Curtis advises: "My process is best illustrated in my book, *MTIV* (blatant product pitch), but the process is actually seven steps; listen, unite, find the theme, concept, eat the audience, filter, and justify. Without rewriting the book, let me just say that the theme of my process is inclusivity. That is, to break down the walls that may exist between you and your client, and together you tell the story of the brand/person/place/thing. That does involve uncovering the theme that powers the story, and then it's helpful to find inspiration that shares that thematic undercurrent and use it as a starting point or a map for your own designs."

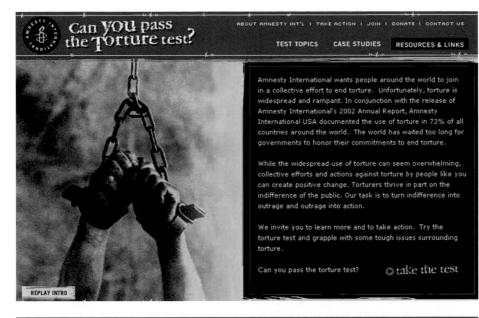

11-15
"Can You Pass The Torture Test?"

Web site: www.amnestyusa.org/stoptorture/
Agency: Peel Interactive Media/Seattle
AI USA Project Lead: Kevin Reid
Studio Director: Tania Aleo
Creative Director/Flash Designer: Kevyn Smith
Interactive Director/Flash Designer: Dan Riley
Executive Producer: Cathryn Buchanan
Sound Designer/Composer: John McCaig
Site Design/Development: Peel Interactive Media
Client: Amnesty International USA
© 2002

Using fonts and a color palette to communicate the severity of the message in a very organized framework, this site conveys a strong feeling about the content and makes navigation easy.

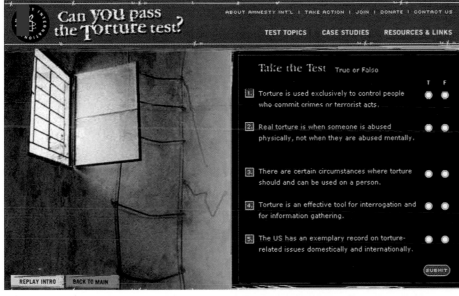

Other Interactive Advertising Media

We live in a networked society. CD-ROMs, kiosks and other electronic exhibit systems, interactive posters, intranets, extranets, digital marketing, text messages on mobile phones, rich media banners, and software interfaces for mobile devices and networked appliances are becoming almost as commonplace as traditional media. With all these vehicles for communication, we can inform, entertain, and educate as never before. Anywhere someone turns—to his wristwatch, to his handheld computer, to a kiosk in a mall or pharmacy—he can get information or be engaged.

"I think that the biggest role of any new media in interactive advertising is finding a way to push information to the consumer faster, quicker, and in a more interesting manner," says Kevyn Smith. "At the same time, perhaps being able to get an emotional response back from the consumer and have them interact with the product or service in some way. This will right away establish an emotional connection between consumer and product, and the longer and more intimate the interaction is, the stronger the sell. Forms of new media such as wireless devices, touch-screen kiosks, CD ROMS, and DVDs are, I believe, used to sell products in a different way, and present information differently to different user types. Advertisers can reach people on the go through wireless devices; people in stores can be reached with in-store kiosks; and you can use CDs and other portable media for promoting products or services in one simple format."

The Future

In the next generation of advertising we may become part of the ads which are customized for us, and us alone. Next-generation advertising will make us stars of our own commercials, with customized digital advertising aimed directly at individual consumers. That type of hook in advertising may make people very happy. If executed well, people may no longer crave to see celebrities hawk brands; they'll be happy to replace the celebrities with themselves.

Perhaps the future will hold more information-based advertising, via the Internet, in an editorial style. More and more people are using "word-of-mouse" Web sites to find information about brands, where brands' reputations are delineated and critiqued.

Once a consumer initiates a dialogue with a brand, responds to questions, offers data, she will receive incentives or rewards. The incentives may be as traditional as coupons or free products or entertainment. Brands, at this point, will have to do two things: respect their customers' privacy and offer them more value. The Web is a very young medium and is evolving every year.

For students of advertising, Taxi created an informative and typographically oriented Web site (figure 11-16). Of course, the best way to get people to interact is to be interesting, intriguing, easy to understand and use, and engaging, which takes us back to the core of traditional advertising precepts, considered in combination with newer ones concerning navigation and consumer behavior in relation to visiting a Web site. These factors are taken into account in Taxi's design of the Web site.

It's important to remember that many campaigns today are integrated, which means they include more than one medium. For the Detroit Pistons, Olson + Company designed an extensive campaign including a fan site, thank-you posters, season ticket renewal mailer, outdoor boards, and metal posters (figures 11-17a, 11-17b, 11-17c, 11-17d, 11-17e, 11-17f, 11-17g). Their concept plays off the idea that Pistons fans are ardent. The visual style of the thank-you posters suggests a grassroots and homemade feeling. According to Olson + Company,

A winning combination of great typography, good graphic design, and skillful information architecture retains viewers and allows them to move deeper into the site.

IDENTITY CRISIS.

NOT YOU, WE MEAN THE CAN. BUT, WHILE WE'RE ON THE SUBJECT OF YOU, YOUR MERE PRESENCE HERE SUGGESTS YOU MAY BE ONE OF THOSE CURIOUS TYPES WHO CAN'T HELP STICKING THEIR NOSE IN EVERYWHERE. GOOD. DESPITE ANY SUPPOSED HARM TO CATS, WE SAY CURIOUSITY IS A WONDERFUL THING AND WE HAVE A FEELING YOU MIGHT JUST FIND THIS SITE VERY INTERESTING. CLICK ON THE SILVER TIN TO ENTER AND WE'LL STOP BEING SO MYSTERIOUS.

< ENTER >

☐ BIG IMPACT   ☐ BRIGHT MINDS   ☐ BIG FUTURE

THIS IS A SITE ABOUT, DRUM ROLL PLEASE, CAREERS IN ADVERTISING. YOU MAY THINK BEING AN ADVERTISING PROFESSIONAL INVOLVES HELPING YOURSELF TO A 3 MARTINI LUNCH BUT IT'S REALLY ABOUT HELPING THIS CAN. WE TAKE THIS NAKED CAN AND WE GIVE IT STYLISH CLOTHES. WE ISSUE THIS CAN BOTH A NAME AND A PERSONALITY. THIS CAN COMES TO US AS 12 CENTS WORTH OF RAW MATERIALS AND WE TURN IT INTO A BUCK. IN SHORT, WE ADD VALUE. VALUE TO THE CAN, VALUE TO THE CAN'S CREATORS AND EVEN VALUE TO THE PEOPLE WHO CONSUME THE CAN AND THROW IT AWAY. THIS SITE WILL GIVE YOU A FLAVOUR FOR THIS BUSINESS WE LOVE AND, MORE IMPORTANTLY, HELP YOU DETERMINE WHETHER YOU MIGHT COME TO LOVE IT. THE FIRST SIP COMES FROM CLICKING ON ANY OF THE HEADINGS ABOVE.

☐ BIG IMPACT   ☐ BRIGHT MINDS   ☐ BIG FUTURE

BIG IMPACT.

GET A BETTER UNDERSTANDING OF WHAT ADVERTISING AGENCIES DO FOR THEIR CLIENTS BY REVIEWING THESE THREE CASE STUDIES
CAUSE   CULTURE   COMMERCE

the concept behind the work is that Detroit is, flat-out, the hardest working team in the NBA. The visual style of the thank you posters reflects the gritty, blue-collar work ethic of the city and its team. The outdoor boards were planned to run in sequence. As Olson + Company puts it: "For one week, the oversized Afro of All-Star Pistons' player Ben Wallace was the talk of

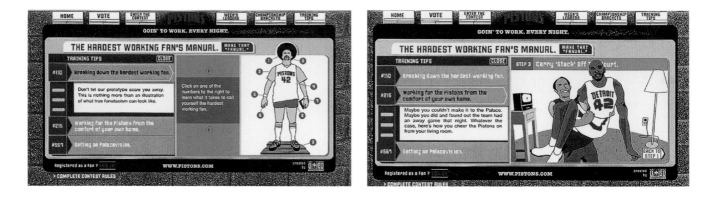

Detroit. The payoff board featured the ticket offer: put $100 down and sit closer to Ben's 'fro than ever before." Another board featured "a pair of oversized sneakers. A week later," reports the company, "we revealed that the giant feet were those of Jerry Stackhouse, no longer with the Pistons, and presented the offer of better seats."

11-17a, 11-17b, 11-17c, 11-17d,
11-17e, 11-17f, 11-17g
"Goin' to work. Every night." Hardest-Working Fan Site
"Get Closer" Outdoor Boards
Thank-You Posters
Season Ticket Renewal Mailer
"Punch In for the Playoffs" Metal Posters

Agency: Olson + Company/Minneapolis
Creative Director: John Olson
Art Directors: Cindy Olson, Mike Caguin
Copywriters: Tom Fugleberg, Derek Bitter
Client: Detroit Pistons
© 2002

"Piston fans don't go to the game. They go to work."

Interactive advertising is still open-ended. Every day there's a new format online for getting to an audience. Hillman Curtis' work includes a great range of online motion and site design (figures 11-18, 11-19). About the most important considerations in interactive advertising, Curtis says, "There's really only one rule, and that is that every pixel be a positive and accurate reflection of the brand. That means that the way a site loads is just as important as what it loads . . . that the way motion is used is just as important as what element or text is moving, and that the way a site is usable is just as important as the content you're navigating towards."

11-18
Adobe Dreamscape
Agency: hillmancurtis, inc.
Creative Director: Hillman Curtis
Designers: Ian Kovalik, Matt Horn
Producer: Homera J. Chaudhry
Animation: Ian Kovalik, Matt Horn
Music: Matt Horn, hillmancurtis, inc.
Client: Adobe Systems Incorporated
© Adobe Systems Incorporated, 2001

This promotional piece combines flat shapes with photography to create an unusual look.

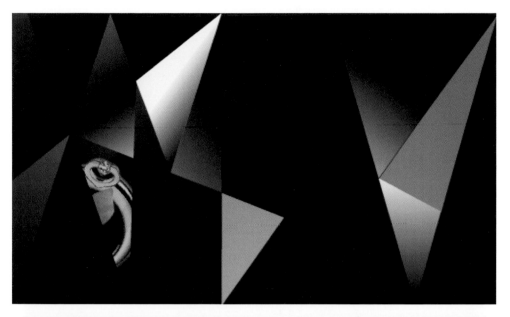

11-19
Motion Graphics
<u>**Advertisement for Cartier.com**</u>

Agency: hillmancurtis, inc.
Creative Director: Hillman Curtis
Designers: Hillman Curtis, Ian Kovalik, Matt
Horn (hillmancurtis, inc.); Linda Bergmark
(Avence)
Producers: Homera J. Chaudhry (hillmancurtis,
inc.), Randall Koral (Avence)
Programmer: Gabe Garner
© Cartier, 2001

Using motion and placing the jewelry
in unusual settings makes this piece
stand out.

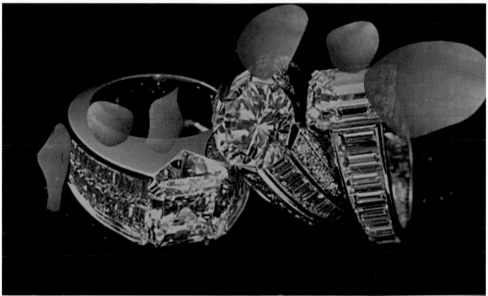

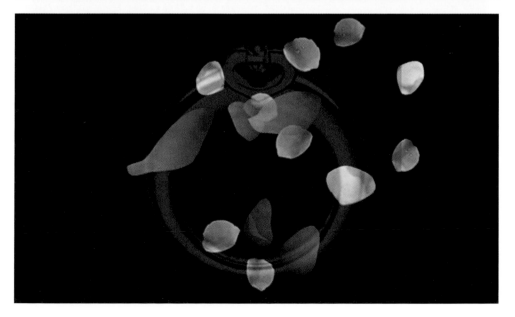

Guerilla Advertising: Unconventional Methods and Media

Guerilla advertising (also called unconventional advertising, stealth marketing, nontraditional marketing, or, when conducted on the Internet, viral marketing) is advertising that "ambushes" the viewer. It appears or is placed in unpaid media in the public environment—places and surfaces where advertising doesn't belong, such as the sidewalk or on wooden construction site walls. For the most part, unconventional advertising is used to grab the attention of a cynical public, to break through to the viewer in unexpected places and ways. Advertisers with small budgets find unconventional media appealing, as the cost of advertising on television or in large-circulation magazines may be prohibitive.

What Is an Ad?

Most people's response to the question "What is an ad?" would be "A television commercial, an outdoor board, or a print ad in a magazine." The definition of advertising has been greatly expanded to include an endless number of inventive (and perhaps interruptive) ways that brands, as well as social causes, are brought to the public's attention. Would you consider a product placement in a film an advertisement? How about a hanger with a message on it? Playing off the hanger as a tool that people use to retrieve keys locked inside their cars, Rethink distributed over two thousand BCAA hangers to dry cleaners, using this novel approach to convey the benefit of belonging to the BCAA road assistance program (figure 11-20). Guerilla marketing can be anything from living and breathing actors doing stunts—a kind of walking ad (see figure 11-23)—to inventive stampings on sidewalks.

For the MINI, Miami-based agency Crispin Porter + Bogusky created a wide range of fun, unconventional experiences, including manuals sent to owners before delivery of the car, MINIs attached to the top of SUVs, Internet films, and wild postings (figures 11-21a, 11-21b, 11-21c). Wild postings, which are also called snipes, can be put up on scaffolding, wooden construction site walls, or any vertical surface that isn't considered "owned" advertising space. Agencies hire a group of individuals who put up posters all over a designated area (during the wee hours).

11-20
"Hanger"
Agency: Rethink Advertising/Vancouver
Art Directors: Ian Grais, Martin Kann
Copywriter: Heather Vincent
Client: BCAA

Unconventional ads can have enormous impact because they catch the audience unaware.

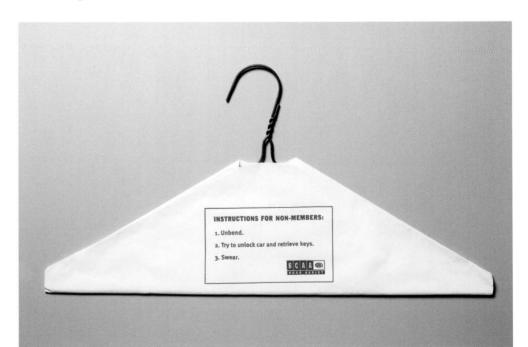

11-21a, 11-21b, 11-21c
Wild Posting: "Match"
Wild Posting: "Conga"
Wild Posting: "Boxing Glove"

Agency: Crispin Porter + Bogusky/Miami
Creative Director: Alex Bogusky
Art Director: Amee Shah
Copywriters: Scott Linnen, Andy Carrigan
Photographer: Mark Laita
Client: MINI
© 2004 The MINI name and logo are
registered trademarks of the MINI division,
BMW of North America, LLC.

By using comparisons that are unusual for a car brand, this campaign distinguishes MINI as the car that is novel, and it stays with the brand strategy of the fun of motoring.

11-22a, 11-22b
"K9to5 Print"
Agency: KBPWest/San Francisco
Creative Director: Jeff Musser
Art Director: Joe Hosp
Copywriter: Darren Crew
Print Producer: Erica Kozocas
© KBPWest

This guerilla campaign cleverly ambushed viewers into thinking they were reading missing-pet posters.

To get under people's ad radar, KBPWest created ads designed to look like missing-pet posters. Mostly, the guerilla ads went up on telephone poles (figures 11-22a, 11-22b).

Online or Viral

Online guerilla or viral marketing is online advertising that people pass on to share with friends and colleagues, either because they think it's entertaining or because they are offered an incentive.

Ambient

Ambient media advertising is placed near or at the point of purchase, thereby targeting consumers at the time when they are most likely to buy or contribute.

11-23
"Wien in Mode"
Studio: Sagmeister Inc./New York
Concept and Design: Stefan Sagmeister
Client: Museum of Modern Art, Vienna

What Guerilla Advertising Does Best

Guerilla advertising has enormous potential. It can make people notice—that is, it can break through to consumers in ways that traditional ads don't or can't, as did "Wien in Mode" by Sagmeister Inc. for the Museum of Modern Art in Vienna (figure 11-23). Sagmeister comments: "'Wien in Mode' is a fashion show held yearly in the Museum of Modern Art in Vienna. The concept was to dress up the regular Viennese advertising kiosks with actual fabric. The public relations company responsible for booking the kiosk space for the posters messed up, and eight weeks before the show we found ourselves with no outdoor advertising space.

"We simply built our own kiosks out of aluminum, polyester, and fabric, put them on wheels, and hired students to 'drive' them around the pedestrian zones."

Guerilla advertising can:

- Enhance and support the efficacy of traditional media advertising campaigns
- Earn press coverage and free publicity and buzz
- Be cost-effective—you can create a good amount of unconventional ads for the cost of one television spot
- Get to people when they're not expecting advertising
- Get to target audiences more efficiently
- Be interactive

Part of the benefit of unconventional advertising is the free publicity that it generates. This promotion was featured in most newspapers and made the evening news.

11-24a, 11-24b, 11-24c
Paperboy Recruitment Campaign
Agency: Forsman & Bodenfors/Gothenburg
Art Directors: Staffan Forsman, Staffan Håkanson
Copywriters: Björn Engström, Martin Ringqvist
Photographer: Henrik Ottosson
Client: Göteborgs-Posten

Want to work as a paperboy? This unconventional campaign allows you to try the job on for size.

For example, in its "paper-boy recruitment campaign," Forsman & Bodenfors/Gothenburg uses an unconventional approach, employing humor and trial runs (figures 11-24a, 11-24b, 11-24c). The poster at right, which is part of a campaign for ABC Canada Literacy Foundation, asks the viewer to interact by pressing a button (figures 11-25a, 11-25b, 11-25c); the campaign is integrated with traditional print ads.

Context

In what context do you view an ad? The environment within which an ad exists or takes place affects the way in which the viewer perceives and digests the ad, and ultimately what she takes away from the advertising experience.

For example, most viewers understand that commercial television is paid for by advertisers. We expect television programming to be interrupted by television commercials, and we respond to them in a variety of ways: by watching them with attention, by zoning out, or by zapping them, among others. Similarly, we expect to see store signs, brand names on shopping bags, outdoor boards, and magazine and newspaper advertisements. We're getting used to seeing ads in bathroom stalls, on top of and inside taxicabs, and on coffee sleeves. We expect marketing at nightlife events, graffiti media campaigns, take-out box advertising, marketing on retail bags and the bottoms of pizza boxes, snipe media campaigns, street team promotions, promotions in the sand at the beach, messages popping up at us on the Internet, ads on the sidewalk—almost anywhere at any time. How an ad gets to us can aid in endearing a brand or cause to us—or it can result in pushing us away, having an undesired negative effect.

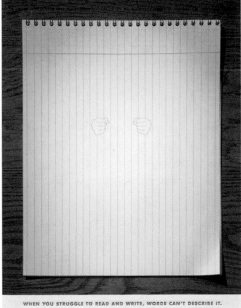

11-25a, 11-25b, 11-25c
"Blank Sheet"
"Jail"
"Maze"

Agency: Taxi/Toronto
Client: ABC Canada Literacy Foundation

Using lines on a ruled piece of paper, these ads make an emotional connection with the viewer. The interactive outdoor poster makes a very dramatic point by both the invitation to press and the message sent.

WHEN YOU STRUGGLE TO READ AND WRITE, WORDS CAN'T DESCRIBE IT.

Incredibly, 5 million Canadians have serious problems with reading, writing and math. You can help. To learn more, visit www.abc-canada.org or call 1-800-303-1004. ABC

WHEN YOU STRUGGLE TO READ AND WRITE, WORDS CAN'T DESCRIBE IT.

Incredibly, 5 million Canadians have serious problems with reading, writing and math. You can help. To learn more, visit www.abc-canada.org or call 1-800-303-1004. ABC

Usually, it's the smaller brands or brands with lower budgets that turn to guerilla advertising. Since much of guerilla advertising involves the unauthorized use of unpaid media space, such as public property, well-established brands, for the most part, shy away from it.

When you view a television commercial, you are most likely at leisure in your home, sitting on your sofa. When you're leafing through a magazine, you may be at your kitchen table or relaxing on a chaise lounge. Perhaps during these moments of leisure, you are more receptive to the advertiser's messages. Or perhaps, since you expect to see the ads, you're on your guard and your advertising radar is working.

When an ad takes you by surprise, when it ambushes you in a public space or in the airport, perhaps you're not receptive because you've just been accosted, or maybe you're more receptive since your ad guard is down. Guerilla advertising is effective when it is entertaining; it is offensive when it accosts or seriously intrudes. As advertising creeps more and more into our environment, we must be judicious about its placement and its effect on popular culture and on people. Respecting people is critical.

In the early days of advertising, first radio programs and then television programs were sponsored by American brands such as Texaco, Colgate, and Gillette. Today there is a movement back toward sponsorship, also called "branded entertainment." Certainly, this works for big brands, such as Coca-Cola and American Express. For example, Meow Mix brand cat food has its own cable television program, created by Kirschenbaum Bond & Partners/New York. Other brands partially sponsor television programs by prominently featuring their brands on the sets.

The practice of product placement, embedded advertising in television shows, has dramatically increased, as advertisers worry that viewers are not watching television commercials. Some advertising pundits predict that product placement may end the supremacy of the television commercial spot. This practice is under fire by advocacy groups such as Commerical Alert, which call product placement "an affront to basic honesty."

Is someone more likely to drink a brand of wine because James Bond drank it in a film or because that person viewed a print ad for the brand? Would someone zap a television commercial but seek out an Internet film? Would someone throw out a direct mail promotion but pass along an online marketing piece to obtain a freebie? It all depends upon the audience!

Notes

1. Jan Leth, "The Nature of Online Advertising: It's Dialogue, Not Monologue," *Print* 54, no. 6 (2000), p. 108

Select Bibliography

Aitchison, Jim. *Cutting Edge Advertising* (Singapore: Prentice Hall, 1999).

———. *Cutting Edge Commercials* (Singapore: Prentice Hall, 2001).

Barthel, Diane. *Putting On Appearances: Gender and Advertising* (Philadelphia: Temple University Press, 1988).

Berger, Warren. *Advertising Today* (New York: Phaidon Press, 2001).

———. "Lunch with Tim DeLaney." *Creativity*, May 2001.

———. "Lunch with Sal DeVito." *Creativity*, October 2001.

Bond, Jonathan, and Richard Kirschenbaum. *Under the Radar: Talking to Today's Cynical Consumer* (New York: John Wiley & Sons, 1998).

Codrington, Andrea, ed. *365: AIGA Year in Design 22.* (New York: HarperCollins International, 2002).

Curtis, Hillman. *MTIV : Process, Inspiration and Practice for the New Media Design* (New York: New Riders Publishing, 2002).

DeVito, Sal. "La vida DeVito." *One: A Magazine* 6, no. 2, Fall 2002.

Goodrum, Charles, and Helen Dalrymple. *Advertising in America* (New York: Abrams, 1990).

Gordon Lewis, Herschell, and Carol Nelson. *Advertising Age Handbook of Advertising* (Lincolnwood, IL: NTC Business Books, 1999).

Heller, Steven, and Elinor Pettit. *Graphic Design Time Line* (New York: Allworth Press, 2000).

Hickey, Lisa. *Design Secrets: Advertising* (Gloucester, MA: Rockport Publishers, Inc., 2002).

Higgins, Dennis. *The Art of Writing Advertising: Conversations with Masters of the Craft* (Lincolnwood, IL: NTC Business Books, 1990).

Ives, Nat. "Advertising." *New York Times,* December 29, 2003.

Landa, Robin. *Graphic Design Solutions,* 2nd ed. (Albany: Thomson Learning, 2001).

———. *Thinking Creatively* (Cincinnati: HOW Books, 1998).

Lehrer, Jeremy. "Ad Infinitum." *Print* 54, no. 5 (September/October 2000 LIV:V)

Leth, Jan. "The Nature of Online Advertising: It's Dialogue, Not Monologue." *Print* 54, no. 6, 2000.

Levenson, Bob. *Bill Bernbach's Book: A History of the Advertising That Changed the History of Advertising* (New York: Villard Books, 1987).

Lois, George. *What's the Big Idea?* (New York: Plume, 1991).

———. *Sellebrity* (New York: Phaidon Press, 2003).

Lois, George, and Bill Pitts. *The Art of Advertising: George Lois on Mass Communication* (New York: Harry N. Abrams, Inc., 1977).

Lyons, John. *Guts* (New York: AMACOM, 1989).

Maas, Jane. *Adventures of an Advertising Woman* (New York: Fawcett Crest, 1986).

McDonough, John, and Karen Egolf, eds. *The Advertising Age Encyclopedia of Advertising,* 3 vols. (New York: Fitzroy Dearborn, 2003).

Merri Meyer, Jackie, ed. *Mad Ave: Award Winning Advertising of the 20th Century* (New York: Universe, 2000).

Muller, Marion. *Dorfsman and CBS* (New York: American Showcase, 1987).

Myerson, Jeremy, and Graham Vickers. *Rewind: Forty Years of Design and Advertising* (London: Phaidon Press, 2002).

O'Leary, Noreen. "The 30-Second Spot Is Dead Long Live the 30-Second Spot." *Adweek,* November 17, 2003.

O'Toole, John. *The Trouble with Advertising: A View from the Inside,* 2nd ed. (New York: Times Books, 1985).

Phillips, William H. *Film: An Introduction,* 2nd ed. (Boston: Bedford St. Martin's, 2002).

Rosen, Jonathan. "Writers on Writing: A Retreat from the World Can Be a Perilous Journey." *New York Times,* May 7, 2001.

Rothenberg, Randall. "The Advertising Century." http://www.adage.com/century/rothenberg.html.

———. *Where the Suckers Moon: The Life and Death of an Advertising Campaign* (New York: Vintage Books, 1994).

Sullivan, Luke. *Hey, Whipple, Squeeze This: A Guide to Creating Great Ads* (New York: John Wiley & Sons, 1998).

Taylor, Catharine P. "What Really Mattered in 2003." *Adweek,* December 22, 2003.

Twitchell, James B. *Twenty Ads That Shook the World: The Century's Most Groundbreaking Ads and How It Changed Us All* (New York: Three Rivers Press, 2001).

Vanderbilt, Tom. "The Fifteen Most Influential, Important, Innocuous, Inane, and Interesting Ad Icons of the Last 500 Years (in No Particular Order)." *Print* 54, no. 6, 2000.

Wells Lawrence, Mary. *A Big Life in Advertising* (New York: Alfred A. Knopf, 2002).

Special Issues of Periodicals

One: A Magazine 6, no. 3, Winter 2003. Theme: Guerilla Advertising.

Print 54, no. 6, 2000. Theme: Advertising Design and the New Economy: A Special Report.

Online Sources

www.adweek.com/adweek/creative/best_spots_01/02.jsp

www.adcouncil.org

www.adage.com/century

www.iloveny.com

www.lurzuersarchive.com

www.mullen.com

www.smokeybear.com

www.saatchikevin.com/livingit/q&aindex.html

www.admuseum.org

www.admuseum.org/museum/timeline/timeline.htm

Video

Sell and Spin: A History of Advertising (A&E Home Video, 1999).

Index